OXY

by Otto Snow

Thoth Press
P.O. Box 6081
Spring Hill, Fl 34611

Made and printed in the United States of America

ISBN:0-9663128-2-1
LCCN: 2001118636

Poppy photograph from Grant Heilman Photography, Inc.
Cover by Otto Snow

Table of Contents

The Opium Poppy and Other Poppies by Charles C. Fulton (1944)

Opium Poppy Cultivation and Heroin Processing in Southeast Asia

List of Illustrations

List of Maps

This book is dedicated to János Kabay.

"...work is not a struggle for survival,
as people believe it to be,
but a life fulfilling sacred duty,
which is enriched by knowledge," János Kabay

Acknowledgement

I want to thank the following agencies and organizations for their information used in this book: United Nations Office for Drug Control and Crime Prevention; National Drug Intelligence Center; Drug Enforcement Administration, Intelligence Division, Strategic Intelligence Section; U.S. Department of Agriculture, Agricultural Research Service; U.S. Patent Office; Department of Health and Human Services, Substance Abuse and Mental Health Services Administration; National Library of Medicine; British Patent Office; German Patent Office; Published International Literature On Traumatic Stress (PILOTS Database); U.S Census Bureau; St. Petersburg Times; all the research scientists and reporters that made this book possible.

I also want to thank Rick Doblin, Ph.D. and the staff at MAPS (Multidisciplinary Association for Psychedelic Studies) for their dedication and perserverance in the development of medications to help those with PTSD.

READER'S NOTICE

This book is for information purposes only. No person is allowed to produce controlled substances without proper permits and authorization. To take/give substances for human consumption whether legal or illegal without a very thorough knowledge of the substance and the health (mental as well as physical) condition/s of the individual is destined to produce catastrophic results and legal ramifications.

Publisher and author take no responsibility for inaccuracies, omissions, or typographical errors. References are included for those seeking greater detail/descriptions.

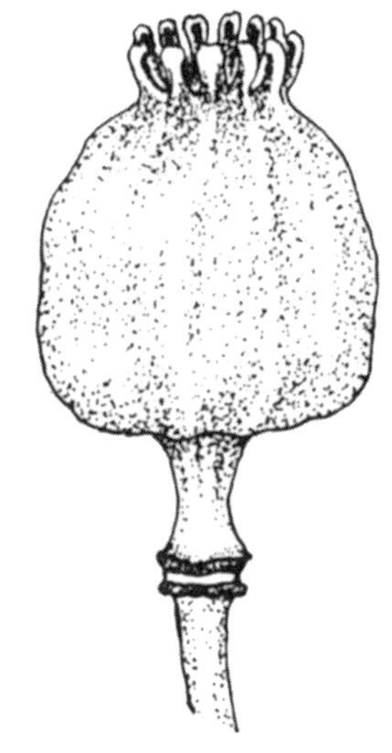

Papaver somniferum
Seed Capsule

Source of graphic: Seeds and Fruits of North American Papaveraceae; Technical Bulletin No. 1517; by Charles R. Gunn and Margaret J. Seldin; published by Agricultural Research Service, United States Department of Agriculture; published July 1976.

OXY

Oxy stands for oxycodone, a narcotic agonist used to treat moderate to high level pain for the past century. It used in the treatment of pain associated with arthritis, neuralgia, migraines, bursitis, dislocation, cancer, back pain, post operative pain, pain following child birth, etc. (Might also be effective in the treatment of severe obsessive-compulsive disorder.) It, like many narcotics, has also been used and abused as a psychotropic substance. Prior to the development of modern psychotropics, narcotic substances were used to treat many conditions. Today, most of these conditions are commonly treated with more effective medications and psychotherapy.

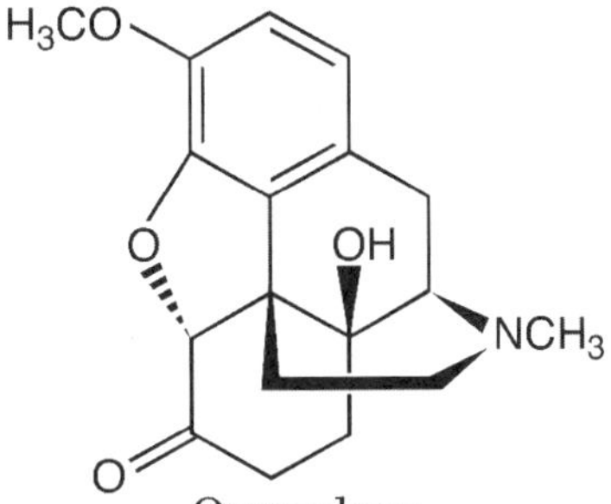

H_3CO OH NCH_3 O O

Oxycodone
(narcotic agonist)

Narcotics can produce euphoria in patients suffering from depression. They have a depressant effect on the central nervous system which allows these drugs to have an anti-anxiety effect. Opium produces sleep and has been used for thousands of years as a hypnotic.

The downside to the wonderful medicinal effects of narcotics is that they cause severe constipation. They are respiratory depressants and can kill by causing respiratory failure. They are addictive and tolerance develops rapidly.

Oxycodone is a semi-synthetic drug. Many semi-synthetic narcotics have less toxic effects than morphine or opium, yet they are poisons like all drugs and have the same ability to addict and kill as their natural parent substances.

The effectiveness and safety of any drug or substance for that matter is dependent on its appropriate use.

At the turn of the 19th century, one and in every three women were addicted to opium and opium products (eg. morphine). It was used to treat depression, anxiety, insomnia, as a cough supressant and for pain relief. The Harrison Drug Act stopped the adulteration of narcotics in food products and controls were placed to allow patients to obtain narcotics only by prescription. People were able to obtain narcotics to treat the same symptoms that they were used prior to the Harrison Drug Act.

Following the passage of the Harrison Drug Act, jail penalties were imposed on those who were addicted to narcotics or in possession of narcotics outside of legal channels. White women remained the largest population of those addicted to these drugs. The primary addicts were physicians, wives of physicians and housewives. When arrested, those wealthy enough were admitted to private rehabilitation hospitals. Individuals who could not afford treatment in private facilities, were jailed or sent to incarceration hospitals such as the federal hospital in Kentucky. Inmates in these detention centers could not leave, they were fenced and caged in, all treated as prisoners; their addiction being the crime. There was a 100% relapse rate with both those jailed and 'treated' in incarceration hospitals. It would not be until the woman's rights movement in the 1960's that attention would be given to treatment of women addicted to drugs.

Where there is war and injustice there will be narcotics. They are used to ease the pain of both psychological and physical injury. Narcotics are used to brunt physical exhaustion and psychological trauma encountered with war. Following the civil war, heroin and morphine addiction were called the 'soldiers' disease,' both drugs were used to treat those injured during the war, at this time, drugs could be obtained over the counter or through mail order without a prescription.

Richard Nixon was the first president to recognize the need for scientific investigations into the biochemistry of addiction and treatment for those who are addicted to narcotics. Only a few patients were treated compared to all those afflicted with the soldiers disease. The fortunate ones were helped by their families and friends. Many war vets would go for a second tour so as not to run out of heroin.

It has been estimated that 20% to 1/3 of all returning Vietnam veterans were addicted to heroin.

In the 1980's several discoveries were made concerning narcotic receptors in the human body. An endogenous (naturally occurring in the body) narcotic substance was discovered called endorphin. The discovery would revolutionize current understandings of addiction and several mental illnesses.

It was found that patients who exhibit self mutilation behavior showed elevated endorphin levels. Patients will cut themselves with knives, bite and tear flesh from themselves. When the patients were given a narcotic antagonist (eg. naltrexone) this self mutilation stopped. Victims of childhood sexual abuse have elevated endorphin levels. It was discovered that individuals who developed PTSD (Post Traumatic Stress Disorder) also had elevated endorphin levels.

Today the drug is being prescribed to patients with PTSD, self mutilation behavior, alcoholism, narcotic addiction, obsessive-compulsive disorder, dermatitis and also reduces flashbacks in victims of trauma. It is not a cure, but a little relief in a world marred by torture, violence and injustice.

Naltrexone crosses the blood barrier and blocks the pain killing effects of narcotics and also induces withdrawal in heroin addicts. Methylnaltrexone is used in combination with narcotics as it blocks narcotic receptors in the intestine and reduces the severe constipation caused by narcotics. Melthylnaltrexone does not cross the blood brain barrier and does not block the pain killing effects of the narcotic.

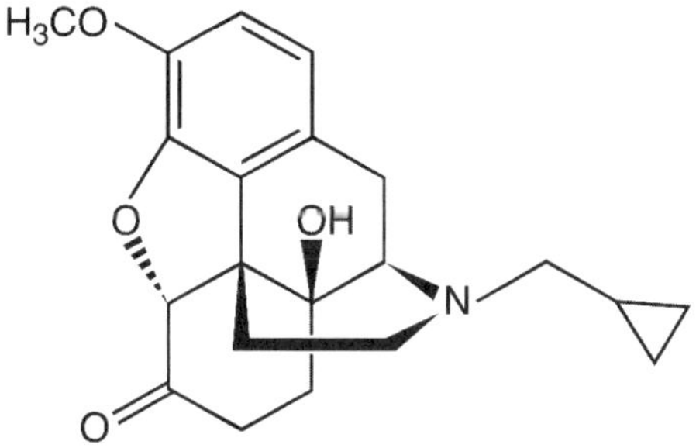

H_3CO OH N O O

Naltrexone
(narcotic antagonist)

Oxycodone has been in the attention of the media for the past year and I speculate will be making the news more until there is a comprehensive patients' rights bill. Patients can become addicted to narcotics if they do not discontinue the narcotics when the pain has subsided. Approximately 75% of people addicted to narcotics are self medicating, yet without help they are likely to turn to street heroin when they can not obtain drugs through legal channels. Street heroin is, in most communities, much less expensive than diverted pharmaceuticals on the street.

The primary source for pharmaceuticals that reach the street is from physicians called 'script doctors.' They are sociopaths that take money to write prescriptions, are generally addicted to drugs themselves, sexually assault patients, commit insurance fraud and are a threat to the safety and welfare of any community.

Physicians who are committing crimes are allowed to do so by the medical community that protects them. So called 'conspiracies of silence' (obstruction of justice) only occur when other physicians have skeletons in their closets and are all parties to insurance fraud and/or human rights violations. Legal actions should be handled through the state attorneys offices or the district attorneys office instead of peer review by medical boards. In areas of the country that have been a haven for script doctors, there is a need for expansion of diversion and insurance fraud units.

"Toughen federal criminal laws and enforcement tools for the intentional health care fraud. Specifically, create a federal health care fraud offense; provide criminal forfeiture and civil injunctive relief for health care fraud offenses; establish health care fraud as a predicate to the Racketeer Influenced Corrupt Organizations Act (RICO); and expand the civil False Claims Act to cover claims presented to health plans...

Patients -- and, in the case of Medicare and Medicaid, taxpayers -- pay a high price for health care fraud and abuse in the form of higher health care costs, higher premiums, and at times, serious risks to patients' health and safety...

In one of the largest fraud cases ever in New Hampshire, a pharmacist stole almost $375,000 from the States's Medicaid program and private health insurance plans. Over a two-year period, the pharmacist systematically billed over one thousand times for prescription drugs that he did not actually dispense....

Since Medicare and Medicaid lose as much as $31 billion annually to fraud and abuse, the savings from reducing fraud in these programs would go far toward paying for much needed reforms in our health care system, such as providing access to health care coverage for the uninsured, prescription drug benefit for the elderly, or long-term care for the elderly and individuals with disabilities."

Source: Senator William S. Cohen, Investigative Staff Report July 7, 1994

When diversion units shut down script doctors, they not only stop the supply of pharmaceuticals on the street, but also fraud being committed against private insurance companies, Medicaid, CHAMPUS and Medicare.

"a White Sulphur Springs, West Virginia, physician was sentenced on October 24, 2000, and will spend more than 2 years in federal prison for Medicaid fraud and for dispensing prescription sedatives and painkillers in exchange for sex."

Source: NDIC Info. Bulletin January 2001.

"A DEA investigation of a prescription drug distribution group led to the identification of the group's supplier, a local Portland (Maine) neurologist. The doctor diverted large quantities of pharmaceuticals, including OxyContin®, to this group in order to support his own crack habit. The neurologist committed suicide before the investigation was completed, but the distribution group was successfully disbanded."

Source: NDIC April 2001

OxyContin® is a time release tablet of oxycodone. It is a major breakthrough in the treatment of pain so that patients do not have to take multiple tablets of oxycodone throughout the day. Most of the oxycodone medications are mixed with acetaminophen or aspirin. For the patient who is in pain, taking multiple tablets of these drugs is common and can lead to liver damage or ulcers. Supposedly, acetaminophen and aspirin are added to narcotics to stop addicts from abusing the drug. The problem is that when cancer patients or patients in pain can't get appropriate treatment from physicians or hospitals then they have to take what they can get. An analogy would be a parent placing a rat trap underneath the cookies in a cookie jar and telling their obese child not to eat any cookies.

Oxycontin® might be a safer choice for any patient on multiple medications (polypharmacy) which may effect the liver.

State consumption statistics indicate that in some states more prescriptions are being filled than the average consumption compared against other states. Florida and NH are two of those states. I interpret this to the fact that in Florida, there are more elderly and cancer patients who need pain relief. In southern NH it is because there are more script doctors.

Narcotics can produce euphoria in patients who are not in pain. Many people become addicted because of this effect. Newer antidepressants maybe more affective for these individuals. Serotonin specific reuptake inhibitors have adverse effects (aggression, sexual dysfunction, sleep disorders etc.) which make them intolerable and ineffective for many patients. Older designed antidepressants are just plain toxic and also produce disease in patients. Drugs which block the reuptake of epinephrine and norepinepherine may have less adverse effects for patients. There are also several medications which increase dopamine in the brain to help people addicted to alcohol and narcotics. Over the past decade, many new and wonderful molecules have been developed, I speculate we will see many more in the near future that will relieve the suffering of the those with biochemical disorders including addictions

It is important for physicians who prescribe any narcotic drugs to have the training to be able to prescribe appropriately. In the state of Florida, there are many elderly cancer patients who are prescribed narcotics. There are many qualified physicians, yet there are physicians who do not have the training or experience to treat patients in pain (eg. Tylenol and codeine for terminal spinal cancer pain with a broken leg).

Hospital physician referral lines knowingly refer patients to physicians on staff who are unqualified to treat a condition or the elderly (false advertising). All Americans must have the right to the National Physicians Database as hospitals conceal when there are dangerous or unqualified physicians on staff.

It is wise for all people to keep medications in the event of an emergency. Medications are good for many years and can be stored in a cool dark place or a refrigerator. A desiccant will absorb moisture and keep the medications dry. Do not store medications in bathroom medicine cabinet as the drugs will absorb water and deteriorate.

Keep all medications out of childrens reach.

Its a crime committed by our society when addicts can not get rehabilitation (methadone) and help with psychological/sociological dysfunction. Addiction destroys the lives of those addicted, and also those who love them. Program admission should be readily available to all those who are addicted or need long term narcotic drugs for pain relief.

NIH Panel Calls for Expanded Methadone Treatment for Heroin Addiction

By Robert Mathias, NIDA NOTES Staff Writer

An expert panel at a National Institutes of Health (NIH) Consensus Development Conference on Effective Medical Treatment of Heroin Addiction has concluded that heroin addiction is a medical disorder that can be effectively treated in methadone treatment programs. The consensus panel strongly recommended expanding access to methadone treatment by eliminating excessive Federal and State regulations and increasing funding for methadone treatment. The conference, which was cosponsored by NIDA, along with the NIH Office of Medical Applications of Research and the NIH Office of Research on Women's Health, was held in Bethesda, Maryland, last November.

Methadone is the medication used most frequently to treat heroin addiction. Outpatient methadone treatment programs administer methadone to reduce patients' cravings for heroin and block its effects, thereby enabling patients to lead productive lives. These programs also may provide counseling, develop vocational skills, and/or provide psychosocial and medical support services to rehabilitate patients. Some patients stay on methadone indefinitely, while others move from with methadone to abstinence.

NIH consensus conferences constitute a science forum where a panel of independent nongovernment experts examines the scientific evidence and makes recommendations on an area of medicine. During the course of the conference on treating heroin addiction, the consensus panel, chaired by Dr. Lewis L. Judd of the University of California at San Diego School of Medicine, focused on determining the effectiveness of methadone treatment. After conducting a thorough review of the accumulated data and listening to expert testimony and public debate on the issues, the panel stated unequivocally that addiction to opiate drugs such as heroin is a disease of the brain and a medical disorder that can be effectively treated. Methadone treatment significantly lowers illicit opiate drug use, reduces opiate-related illness and death, reduces crime, and enhances social productivity, the panel concluded.

Despite methadone's effectiveness, less than 20 percent of the estimated 600,000 heroin addicts in the United States are being treated in methadone treatment programs, the panel noted. Many barriers limit the availability of methadone treatment.

These barriers include unnecessary laws administered by a number of Federal agencies and many State and local governments that burden treatment programs with excessive regulatory requirements and duplicative inspections. Some of these regulations restrict treatment programs' ability to tailor methadone doses to the needs of individual patients. Other regulations require physicians to obtain a special Federal registration to use methadone to treat narcotic addiction, thus limiting the number of physicians who are available to treat heroin addiction. Wider use of methadone treatment also is restricted by a shortage of physicians and other health care professionals who are trained to treat heroin addiction, and inadequate funding to provide methadone treatment slots for all those who require them.

The Recommendations

The panel recommended a number of steps to improve access to methadone treatment for all people addicted to heroin and other opiate drugs. The panel's recommendations include the following:

* eliminating unnecessary layers of Federal and State regulation for methadone and similar opiate treatment medications;

* instituting means other than regulation to improve the quality of methadone treatment, such as accreditation of methadone treatment programs;

* improving the training that physicians and other health care professionals receive in the diagnosis and treatment of patients with heroin addiction; and

* increasing funding for methadone treatment, including providing benefits for methadone treatment as part of public and private health insurance programs.

The panel also recommended that additional research be conducted on factors that lead to heroin use; changes in the brain that occur with repeated heroin use and result in addiction; the neurobiological processes of craving; and the differences among individuals who are able to end opiate addiction and those who cannot. In addition, the panel called for a national study to assess the prevalence of heroin addiction in the United States and for rigorous studies of the financial costs of heroin addiction to society and the cost-effectiveness of methadone treatment.

Source: National Institute on Drug Abuse - NIDA Notes News Volume 12, Number 6 November/December 1997

Prevention and Treatment Programs; Heroin Abuse Declines in Western Europe; Cocaine Abuse Declines in the US

Abuse of heroin (Western Europe) and cocaine (North America), however, is stagnating or declining in some of the main consumer markets:

In the United States cocaine use fell - based on monthly prevalence data revealed in household surveys - by some 70 per cent over the 1985-99 period (from three per cent of the population aged 12 and above to 0.8 per cent), more than overall drug use (representing a fall of 40 per cent).

In Germany, heroin abuse remained stable at 0.2 percent of the general population (aged 18 to 59) over the 1995-97 period.

Surveys in Spain showed a decline in the use of heroin among the general population (aged 15 to 64) from 0.5 percent in 1995 to 0.1 percent in 1999.

Models based on treatment data for Italy indicated a heroin epidemic in the late 1980's, which peaked at around 1991; abuse levels fell thereafter and stabilized at lower levels after 1993.

The mean age in treatment (mostly heroin-related in Europe) increased throughout Western Europe, suggesting that fewer younger users were entering the treatment system. Strong increases in the mean age of people treated (for more than one year) were reported from Greece, Spain, Italy, Portugal, France, Belgium and Denmark.

There was also a strong decline in the incidence of HIV/AIDS cases related to injecting drug use, falling EU-wide from 28 cases per million inhabitants in 1994 to 11 in 1998, with reductions reported by all EU countries. The strongest declines were reported by Spain, Italy and France.

Declines in drug-related death cases (mostly related to abuse of opiates in Western Europe) over the 1992-98 period were reported by France, Spain, Germany, Italy, and if the 1994-98 period is considered, by Austria, Luxembourg and Switzerland.

Prevention and treatment interventions seem to have contributed to the progress made. The 40 per cent decline in overall drug consumption and the 70 per cent decline in cocaine consumption in the United States over the period 1985-99, for instance, went parallel with an increase in demand reduction expenditure (research, prevention and treatment) from $0.9 billion in 1985 to $5.6 billion in 1999 ($20 per inhabitant), a more than four-fold increase after adjusting for inflation.

There is increasing evidence that both prevention and treatment do play a significant role in reducing drug demand:

Following large-scale prevention campaigns in the United States, for instance, the upward trend of drug abuse among 8th graders was reversed.

Follow-up studies in the United Kingdom found that two years after the end of treatment, regular heroin use as well as acquisitive crime were halved; similar studies in the United States also showed that involvement in illegal activities could be halved; weekly heroin and cocaine use were down by as much as two-thirds one year after the end of treatment.

Source: UN ODCCP World Drug Report 2000 - Highlights

High-Dose Methadone Improves Treatment Outcomes

By Patrick Zickler, NIDA NOTES Staff Writer

Methadone has been used effectively for more than 30 years as a treatment for heroin addiction. The medication blocks heroin's narcotic effects without creating a drug "high," eliminates withdrawal symptoms, and relieves the craving associated with addiction. Methadone is administered orally in licensed clinics and its effects typically last 24 to 36 hours.

Although methadone has been used for decades, no clinical consensus has been reached about the most effective daily dose. Many clinics do not adjust dosages according to the needs of individual patients. Instead, they administer fixed doses. One clinic might use doses of 25 milligrams (mg) per day for all patients; others may administer daily doses of 60 mg. "Federal regulations require that a clinic receive a special exemption in order to provide patients with doses greater than 100 mg per day, but no contemporary studies have examined the effectiveness of daily doses greater than 80 mg," says Dr. Eric Strain, a

NIDA-supported researcher at The Johns Hopkins University Medical Center in Baltimore.

Dr. Strain and his colleagues investigated the effectiveness of high-dose -80 to 100 mg per day-methadone treatment and found this dosage to be more effective in reducing heroin use than treatment with a moderate dose of 40 to 50 mg per day. The study involved 192 patients. Sixty-five percent of participants were male; pregnant women were excluded from the study group.

Following a 1-week orientation period, patients receiving high-dose (80-100 mg) methadone treatment had less self-reported heroin use and lower rates of drug-positive urine samples than patients on moderate-dose (40-50 mg) treatment. Urine results are shown as 3-week averages of twice-weekly samples.

During the first week of treatment all patients received 30-mg daily methadone doses. Daily doses were increased until, by the 8th week, half the patients were receiving a moderate dose of 40 to 50 mg per day and the other half were receiving a high dose of 80-to-100 mg per day. These doses were maintained through the study's 30th week. Dosages were then decreased by 10 percent each week during the final 10 weeks of the program. Patients were encouraged to enroll in long-term community-based treatment programs following completion of the 40-week study.

Dr. Strain and his colleagues evaluated the effectiveness of treatment through analysis of twice-weekly observed urine testing, weekly patient reports of heroin use, and the length of time patients remained in treatment. "The high-dose group used opiates significantly less during treatment than did the moderate-dose group on average," Dr. Strain says. "Patients in the high-dose group reported using opiates no more than once a week. The moderate-dose group reported using drugs two to three times per week on average." Among patients who completed the 30-week active phase, 33 percent of high-dose patients remained in treatment throughout a 10-week methadone phase-out, compared with 20 percent of moderate-dose patients. There were no gender-related differences in outcome for high- or moderate-dose groups, and no difference was reported between the high- and moderate-dose patients for side effects such as grogginess or constipation.

In an earlier study, the researchers found that moderate-dose treatment of 50 mg per day was more effective than low-dose treatment of 20 mg per day. "The current study provides strong evidence that we can achieve much better outcomes at dose rates much higher than 50 mg per day," Dr. Strain says.

Dosages exceeding the currently regulated ceiling of 100 mg per day may provide the best result for some patients, Dr. Strain says, but he notes that clinical trials would be needed to support changing this regulation. "The most important aspect of our research from a therapeutic and public health perspective is that methadone treatment over a broad range of doses results in significant clinical improvement for opioid-addicted patients," he says.

Sources:

Strain, E.C.; Bigelow, G.E.; Liebson, I.A.; and Stitzer, M.L.; Moderate- vs high-dose methadone in the treatment of opioid dependence: A randomized trial. Journal of the American Medical Association 281(11):1000-1005, 1999.

Strain, E.C.; Stitzer, M.L.; Liebson, I.A.; and Bigelow, G.E.; Dose-response effects of methadone in the treatment of opioid dependence. Annals of Internal Medicine 119:23-27, 1993. Article Source: National Institute on Drug Abuse - NIDA Notes, Focus on Treatment Research Volume 14, Number 5.

"Office based methadone treatment would represent an enormous step forward in treating heroin addiction," said NIDA Director Alan I. Leshner, Ph.D. "This study shows that practitioners understand that their addicted patients are suffering from a treatable disease, and they are willing to provide that treatment."

Methadone is a synthetic opiate, similar to heroin, that blocks the effects of heroin and eliminates withdrawal symptoms. It has been used effectively and safely in addiction treatment for more than 30 years, and has been shown to increase the retention of patients who enter treatment, reduce rates of intravenous drug use and HIV infection, and reduce criminal activity by allowing patients to enhance their social productivity.

"The principal finding of our study is that these practitioners, who are already caring for the populations and communities most in need of more addiction treatment, are supportive of extending methadone treatment to mainstream medical practice," Dr. Drucker said...

Half of the practioners expressed some concern that the multiple needs of methadone patients would be difficult to meet, but 66 percent said that they would prescribe MMT (methadone maintenance treatment) for their patients, given proper training and support.

"For these practitioners, methadone is not laden with stereotypic fears about bringing drug addicts into their practice," Dr. Drucker said. "They see methadone as another useful tool for managing the overall health of their patients."

Source: NIDA News Release 3/1/2000 Beverly Jackson, Michelle Muth

In Florida, many physicians are afraid to prescribe appropriate schedule 2 and 3 drugs because of an unnecessary fear of harassment from the DEA. This 'fear' appears to be a result of not knowing how to prescribe these drugs and an unwillingness to learn. It is terrible that those who use drugs properly and gain benefit from them are having a hard time getting appropriate medications. Many patients are forced to purchase medications on the street. The crime isn't the drug, its when patients suffer because they can't get medications when they need them.

"Portenoy, a national leader in the field of pain management, has been asked to serve as a consultant to a U.S. Food and Drug Administration panel that will meet in the fall to consider whether oxycodone, the generic name for OxyContin®, and other opioids need more restrictions.

He says patients have reason to worry.

"Because of the pervasive fear of these drugs in this country, what I would call the stigmatism of these drugs, stories about (misuse) may drive regulators and those in law enforcement to take actions that are not warranted and would have the unintended effect of reducing access to patients who need them," Portenoy said."

Source: St. Petersburg Times; 5/27/01; Wes Allison

Narcotics can be used to ease pain and to help those who could benefit from management of their addiction (methadone). It is important for people to educate themselves about narcotics. The majority of people who use narcotics, use them appropriately and effectively. They should not have to suffer for the actions of those who do not.

References:

[Authors not listed]; Inadequate treatment of pain in hospitalized patients; New England Journal of Medicine (1982) July 1;307(1):55-56.

[Authors not listed]; Chronic use of opioid analgesics in non-malignant pain; Pain. (1987) May;29(2):257-262.

[Authors not listed] Special report. Drug theft from hospital pharmacies: lessons from the 'Syracuse scam'. Hosp Secur Saf Manage (1996) Oct;17(6):5-9.

[Authors not listed]; 'ATMs' for dispensing medication, supplies said to cut hospital losses; Hosp Secur Saf Manage. (1997) May;18(1):3-4.

Aceto, M.D., Harris, L.S., Bowman, E.R.; Etorphines: mu-opioid receptor-selective antinociception and low physical dependence capacity; Eur J Pharmacol (1997) Nov 12;338(3):215-223.

Anderson, C.M.; Ibogaine Therapy in Chemical Dependency and Posttraumatic Stress Disorder: A Hypothesis Involving the Fractal Nature of Fetal REM Sleep and Interhemispheric Reintegration; Bulletin of the Multidisciplinary Association for Psychedelic Studies (1998) 8 (1): 5-14.

Baker, Dewleen G; West, Scott A; Orth, David N; Hill, Kelly K; Nicholson, Wendell E; Ekhator, Nosa N; Bruce, Ann B; Wortman, Matthew D; Keck, Paul E; Geracioti, Thomas D.; Cerebrospinal fluid and plasma [beta]-endorphin in combat veterans with post-traumatic stress disorder; Psychoneuroendocrinology (1997) v. 22, no. 7, pp. 517-529.

Barrett, R.P.; Feinstein, C.; Hole, W.T.; Effects of naloxone and naltrexone on self-injury: a double-blind, placebo-controlled analysis; Am J Ment Retard. (1989) May;93(6):644-651.

Baylson, M.M.; Markman, J.L.; Jaipaul, S.C.; A word to the wise on drug diversion; Am Pharm (1992) May;NS32(5):54.

Bills, J. Lyndra; Kreisler, Kevin; Treatment of Flashbacks with Naltrexone; American Journal of Psychiatry (1993) 150 (9): 1430.

Bohus, M.J.; Landwehrmeyer, G.B.; Stiglmayr, C.E.; Limberger M.F.; Bohme, R.; Schmahl, Christian G.; Naltrexone in the treatment of dissociative symptoms in patients with borderline personality disorder: an open-label trial; J Clin Psychiatry (1999) Sep;60(9):598-603.

Bystritsky, A.; Strausser, B.P.; Treatment of obsessive-compulsive cutting behavior with naltrexone; J Clin Psychiatry. (1996) Sep;57(9):423-24

Chapman, P.J.; Ganendran, A.; Scott, R.J; Basford, K.E.; Attitudes and knowledge of nursing staff in relation to management of postoperative pain; Aust N Z J Surg. (1987) Jul;57(7):447-450

Cherny, N.J.; Chang, V.; Frager, G.; Ingham, J.M,.; Tiseo, P.J.; Popp, B.; Portenoy, R.K.; Foley, K.M.; Opioid pharmacotherapy in the management of cancer pain: a survey of strategies used by pain physicians for the selection of analgesic drugs and routes of administration; Cancer. (1995) Oct 1;76(7):1283-1293.

Dabney, D.; Workplace deviance among nurses. The influence of work group norms on drug diversion and/or use; J Nurs Adm. (1995) Mar;25(3):48-55.

Dilworth, N.M.; Children in pain: an underprivileged group; J Pediatr Surg. (1988) Feb;23(2):103-104

Dixon, B.A.; Institutional survey of nurse anesthesia practice in patients receiving opioids via patient-controlled analgesia; Nurse Anesth. (1993) Sep;4(3):112-117.

Evans, C.J., Monteillet-Agius, G., Saliminejad, N., Zaki, P.A.; Opiate drugs: 'guilt by association'. Mol Psychiatry. 2000 Mar;5(2):122-123

Freeman, H.P., Payne, R.; Racial injustice in health care; New England Journal of Medicine (2000) April 6;342(14):1045-1047

Friedman, J.D.; Dello, Buono F.A.; Opioid antagonists in the treatment of opioid-induced constipation and pruritus; Ann Pharmacother (2001) Jan;35(1):85-91

Ford, J.; Murphy, J.E.; Chain pharmacists' attitudes on and awareness of domestic abuse; J Am Pharm Assoc (Wash) (1996) May;NS36(5):323-328.

Gispen, W.H.; Wiegant, V.M.; Bradbury, A.F.; Hulme, E.C.; Smyth, D.G.; Snell, C.R.; de Wied, D.; Induction of excessive grooming in the rat by fragments of lipotropin; Nature (1976) 264: 794-795

Glatt, W.; A new method for detoxifying opioid-dependent patients; J Subst Abuse Treat (1999) Oct;17(3):193-197.

Greenwald, B.D., Narcessian, E.J., Pomeranz, B.A.; Assessment of physiatrists' knowledge and perspectives on the use of opioids: review of basic concepts for managing chronic pain; American Journal Phys Med Rehabil. (1999) Sep-Oct;78(5):408-415

Hackett, T.P.; Pain and prejudice. Why do we doubt that the patient is in pain?; Med Times. (1971) Feb;99(2):130-134

Hao, J.X.; Yu, W.; Xu, X.J.; Evidence that spinal endogenous opioidergic systems control the expression of chronic pain-related behaviors in spinally injured rats; Exp Brain Res. (1998) Jan;118(2):259-268.

Herman, C.M., Zabloski, E.J.; Crimes against pharmacies; Journal of the American Pharmaceutical Association (1977) Jan;17(1):26-9, 32

Herman, B.H.; Hammock, M.K.; Egan, J.; Arthur-Smith, A.; Chatoor, I.; Werner, A.; Role for opioid peptides in self-injurious behavior: dissociation from autonomic nervous system functioning.; Dev Pharmacol Ther. (1989);12(2):81-89

Hill, C.S. Jr.; The barriers to adequate pain management with opioid analgesics; Semin Oncol. (1993) Apr;20(2 Suppl 1):1-5.

Glover, Hillel; Emotional numbing: a possible endorphin-mediated phenomenon associated with post-traumatic stress disorders and other allied psychopathologic states; Journal of Traumatic Stress (October 1992) v. 5, no. 4, pp. 643-675

Ibarra, Paloma; Bruehl, Stephen P.; McCubbin, James A.; Carlson, Charles R.; Wilson, John F.; Norton, Jane A.; Montgomery, Thomas B.; An unusual reaction to opioid blockade with naltrexone in a case of post-traumatic stress disorder. Journal of Traumatic Stress (1994) April v. 7, no. 2, pp. 303-309.

Jacquet, Yasuko, F.; Marks, Neville; Endorphins: Profound Behavioral Effects in Rats Suggest New Etiological Factors in Mental Illness; Science (1976) 194: 630-635.

Jasinski, D.R., Griffith, J.D., Carr, C.B.; Etorphine in man. I. Subjective effects and suppression of morphine abstinence; Clin Pharmacol Ther (1975) Mar;17(3):267-272.

Joranson, D.E., Gilson, A.M.; Pharmacists' knowledge of and attitudes toward opioid pain medications in relation to federal and state policies; J Am Pharm Assoc (Wash) (2001) Mar-Apr;41(2):213-220.

Joranson, David E.; Ryan, Karen M.; Gilson, Aaron M.; Dahl, June L.; Trends in Medical Use and Abuse of Opiod Analgesics; Journal of the American Medical Association (2000) 283 (13): 1710-1714

Jordan, B.A., Trapaidze, N., Gomes, I., Nivarthi, R., Devi, L.A.; Oligomerization of opioid receptors with beta 2-adrenergic receptors: a role in trafficking and mitogen-activated protein kinase activation.; Proc Natl Acad Sci U S A. (2001) Jan 2;98(1):343-348

Judson, B.A.; Goldstein, A.; Symptom complaints of patients maintained on methadone, LAAM (methadyl acetate), and naltrexone at different times in their addiction careers; Drug Alcohol Depend (1982) Oct-Nov;10(2-3):269-82

Judson, B.A.; Goldstein, A.; Naltrexone treatment of heroin addiction: one-year follow-up; Drug Alcohol Depend. (1984) Jul;13(4):357-365.

Kalb, Claudia; Newsweek (2001) April 9: pgs. 45-51.

Kandall, Stephen R.; Women and Addiction in the United States-1920 to the Present; pgs. 53-64.

Khan, K.; Our duty lasts until the end of life; BMJ. (1999) Aug 7;319(7206):343

Kenny, D.E.; Use of naltrexone for treatment of psychogenically induced dermatoses in five zoo animals; J Am Vet Med Assoc. (1994) Oct 1;205(7):1021-1023

Kirschenbaum, H.L., Rosenberg, J.M.; Educational programs offered by colleges of pharmacy and drug information centers within the United States; Am J Pharm Educ. (1984) Summer;48(2):155-157

Knabe, R.; Schulz, P.; Richard, J.; Initial aggravation of self-injurious behavior in autistic patients receiving naltrexone treatment; J Autism Dev Disord. (1990) Dec;20(4):591-593

Knight, A.L, Adelman, A.M., Sobal, J.; House call practices among young family physicians; J Fam Pract. (1989) Dec;29(6):638-42.

Krick, S.E.; Lindley, C.M.; Bennett, M.; Pharmacy-perceived barriers to cancer pain results of the North Carolina Cancer Pain Initiative Pharmacist Survey; Ann Pharmacother. (1994) Jul-Aug;28(7-8):857-862.

Lako, C.J.; Lindenthal, J.J.; Confidentiality in medical practice; J Fam Pract. (1990) Aug;31(2):167-170

Lander, J.; Fallacies and phobias about addiction and pain; Br J Addict. (1990) Jun;85(6):803-809.

Lee, A., Gin, T., Oh, T.E.; Opioid requirements and responses in Asians; Anaesth Intensive Care. (1997) Dec;25(6):665-670.

Liao, Y.; McGee, D.L.; Cao, G.; Cooper, R.S.; Quality of life at the end of life; Journal of the American Medical Association (2000) Sep 27;284(12):1513-1515.

Lienemann, J,.; Walker, F.; Naltrexone for treatment of self-injury; American Journal of Psychiatry. (1989) Dec;146(12):1639-1640.

Maki, D.G.; Klein, B.S.; McCormick, R.D.; Alvarado, C.J.; Zilz, M.A.; Stolz, S.M.; Hassemer, C.A.; Gould, J.; Liegel, A.R.; Nosocomial Pseudomonas pickettii bacteremias traced to narcotic tampering. A case for selective drug; Journal of the American Medical Association (1991) Feb 27;265(8):981-986

McCaffery, M.; Pasero, C.; Stigmatizing patients as addicts; Am J Nurs. (2001) May;101(5):77-8, 81.

McCaffery, M.; Pasero, C.;The merits of methadone; Am J Nurs. (2000) Jul;100(7):22-23

McCaffery, M.; Understanding your patient's pain tolerance; Nursing. (1999) Dec;29(12):17

McGee, Michael D.; Cessation of self-mutilation in a patient with borderline personality disorder treated with naltrexone [letter]; Journal of Clinical Psychiatry (1997 Jan), v. 58, no. 1, pp. 32-33

Morgan, J.P.; American opiophobia: customary underutilization of opioid analgesics; Adv Alcohol Subst Abuse. (1985) Fall-1986 Winter;5(1-2):163-713

Morrison, R.S.; Planning and providing care at the end of life; Hosp Pract (Off Ed) (2000) Oct 15;35(10):61-4, 67-68

Morrison, R.S.; Wallenstein, S.; Natale, D.K.; Senzel, R.S.; Huang LL.; “We don't carry that”--failure of pharmacies in predominantly nonwhite neighborhoods to stock opioid analgesics; New England Journal of Medicine (2000) April 6;342(14):1023-1026.

Mullahy,C.M.;Ethics-until the end of life.Case Manager.(1999)Sep-Oct;10(5):4, 6

Nemes, J.; Fighting drug abuse in operating rooms; Mod Healthc. (1991) Jul 29;21(30):60, 62

Nordenberg, T.; Pharmacy chief turns medicine thief; FDA Consumer (1999) Nov-Dec;33(6):35.

Nicholson, Ann-Marie; The Agony of Relief; Painkillers are Scarce When You Live in the Hood; The Source; July (2000) no. 130, 79-80.

Orentlicher, D.; Caplan, A.; Legislation and end-of-life care; Journal of the American Medical Association (2000) Jun 14;283(22):2933-2935

Packer, J.; GAO rips VA over 'large quantities' of stolen drugs; Mod Healthc. (1991) Jun 24;21(25):8.

Pasero, C.L.; McCaffery, M.; Transdermal fentanyl for chronic pain; Am J Nurs 1997 Nov;97(11):17-18.

Perry, S.W.; Irrational attitudes toward addicts and narcotics; Bull N Y Acad Med. (1985) Oct;61(8):706-727.

Przewlocka, B.; Lason, W.; Stress prevents the chronic ethanol-induced delta opiod receptor supersensitivity in the rat brain; Pol J Pharmcol. Pharm (1990) Mar-Apr;42(2):137-142.

Ranelli, P.L., Coward, R.T.; Residential differences in the use of pharmacies by older adults and their communication experiences with pharmacists; J Rural Health. (1996) Winter;12(1):19-32.

Saiz, Jose Carlos Bouso; Rodríguez, Pedro Antonio Sopelana; Proposal for a Study with MDMA and Post Traumatic Stress Disorder in Spain; Bulletin of the Multidisciplinary Association for Psychedelic Studies (1999) 9: (3), pp. 11-14.

Sells, D. Jr.; On drug diversion in health care; Hosp Secur Saf Manage. (1995) Mar;15(11):11-13.

Sial, V.A.; Moss, A.H.; Pain management for end-of-life care; W V Med J. (2000) Sep-Oct;96(5):556-558

Silverman, S.I.; Responding to search warrants; Healthc Hazard Mater Manage (1999) Jan;12(5):1-5.

Simpkins, J.W.; Smulkowski, M.; Dixon, R.; Tuttle, R.; Evidence for the delivery of narcotic antagonists to the colon as their glucuronide conjugates; J Pharmacol Exp Ther (1988) Jan;244(1):195-205.

Smith, K.C.; Pittelkow, M.R.; Naltrexone for neurotic excoriations; J Am Acad Dermatol. (1989) May;20(5 Pt 1):860-861

Starck, P.L., Sherwood, G.D., Adams-McNeill, J., Thomas, E.J.; Identifying and addressing medical errors in pain mismanagement; Jt Comm J Qual Improv. (2001) Apr;27(4):191-199.

Volpicelli, Joseph; Balaraman, Geetha; Hahn, Julie; Wallace, Heather; Bux, Donald; The role of uncontrollable trauma in the development of PTSD and alcohol addiction; Alcohol Research and Health, (1999) v. 23, no. 4, pp. 256-262

Walters, A.S.; Barrett, R.P.; Feinstein, C.; Mercurio, A.; Hole, W.T.; A case report of naltrexone treatment of self-injury and social withdrawal in autism; J Autism Dev Disord. (1990) Jun;20(2):169-176.

Weinstein, S.M., Laux, L.F., Thornby, J.I., Lorimor, R.J., Hill, C.S. Jr, Thorpe, D.M., Merrill, J.M.; Physicians' attitudes toward pain and the use of opioid analgesics: results of a survey from the Texas Cancer Pain Initiative; South Med J. (2000) May;93(5):479-487.

Yuan, C.S.; Foss, J.F.; Oral methylnaltrexone for opioid-induced constipation; Journal of the American Medical Association (2000) Sep 20;284(11):1383-1384.

Yuan, C.S.; Foss, J.F.; O'Connor, M.; Osinski, J.; Karrison, T.; Moss, J.; Roizen, M.F.; Methylnaltrexone for reversal of constipation due to chronic methadone use: a randomized controlled trial; Journal of the American Medical Association (2000) Jan 19;283(3):367-372.

Yuan, C.S., Foss, J.F., Osinski, J.; Toledano, A.; Roizen, M.F.; Moss, J.; The safety and efficacy of oral methylnaltrexone in preventing morphine-induced delay in oral-cecal transit time; Clin Pharmacol Ther (1997) Apr;61(4):467-475

Yuan, C.S.; Foss, J.F.; O'Connor, M.; Toledano, A.; Roizen, M.F.; Moss. J.; Methylnaltrexone prevents morphine-induced delay in oral-cecal transit time without affecting analgesia: a double-blind randomized placebo-controlled trial; Clin Pharmacol Ther (1996) Apr;59(4):469-75

Suggested Readings:

Impact of Prescription Drug Diversion Control Systems on Medical Practice and Patient Care: NIDA Research Monograph 131 (1993)

Substance and Shadow: A History of Women and Addiction in the United States-1850 to the Present by Stephen R. Kanadall

The Rights of the Critically Ill by John A. Robertson; pub. by Bantam Book in arrangement with the American Civil Liberties Union: 1983, ISBN: 0-553-23137-5

Shivitti by Ka-Tzetnick 135633. pub. by Gateways Consciousness Classics; 1998; ISBN: 0-89556-113-1

Marijuana Myths Marijuana Facts by Lynn Zimmer and John P. Morgan, pub. by Lindesmith Center; 1997; ISBN: 0-9641568-4-9

The Basketball Diaries by Jim Carroll; published by Penguin Books, 1978; ISBN: 0140100180

Janos Kaby: The Life of an Inventor by John J. Kabay; (1990) ISBN: 0 646 01672 5

Poppy: the genus Papaver - (Medicinal and aromatic plants; industrial profiles; v.3) by Jeno Bernáth; published by Harwood Academic Publishers; Amsterdam; ISBN 90-5702-271-0

Poppies: A Guide to the Poppy Family in the Wild and in Cultivation by Christopher Grey-Wilson; published by Timber Press; Portland Oregon; (19??) ISBN: 0881925039

Opium Poppy; Botany, Chemistry and Pharmacology; by L.D. Kapoor; pub. by Haworth Press, 1995; ISBN: 0-7890-0202-7

Annotated Bibliography on Opium and Oriental Poppies and Related Species; by James A. Duke; Charles R. Gunn, Elmar E. Leppik, Clyde F. Reed, Marie L. Solt, and Edward E. Terrell; pub. by U.S. Department of Agriculture, Agricultural Research Service (ARS-NE-28); published December 1973.

Narcotic Antagonists: Naltrexone Progress Report (NIDA Research Monograph 9) (1977)

Narcotic Antagonists: The Search for Long-Acting Preparations (NIDA Research Monograph 4) (1978)

Buprenorphine: An Alternative Treatment for Opioid Dependence (NIDA Research Monograph 121) (1992)

Discovery of Novel Opioid Medications (NIDA Research Monograph 147) (1995)

Mechanisms of Tolerance and Dependence (NIDA Research Monograph 54) (1984)

Etiology of Drug Abuse: Implications for Prevention (NIDA Research Monograph 56) (1985)

Relapse and Recovery in Drug Abuse (NIDA Research Monograph 72) (1986)

Progress in Opioid Research - 1986 Narcotics Research Conference (NIDA Research Monograph 75) (1986)

Opioid Peptides: Molecular Pharmacology, Biosynthesis, and Analysis (NIDA Research Monograph 70) (1987)

Opioid Peptides: Medicinal Chemistry (NIDA Research Monograph 69) (1987)

Opiate Receptor Subtypes and Brain Function (NIDA Research Monograph 71) (1988)

Opioids in the Hippocampus (NIDA Research Monograph 82) (1988)

Opioid Peptides: An Update (NIDA Research Monograph 87) (1989)

Anatomy of a Scientific Discovery, by Jeff Goldberg; (1988) pub. by Bantam Book; ISBN: 0 553 17616 1

GLOBAL NARCOTICS PRODUCTION

The Suppression of Poppy Cultivation in the United States

Should it be necessary for the United States, in a time of crisis, to produce its own opiates, it is thought that about 600 pounds of poppy-seeds could be obtained per acre, and about 400 pounds of dried capsule chaff. At 0.5 to 0.3 per cent morphine content in the chaff, a little over some 13,000 to 22,000 acres would be needed to fill the needs of the United States for morphine, codeine, etc.,-425,000 ounces in terms of morphine. The minimum area needed, 13,000 acres, would yield about 7,800,000 pounds of poppy-seed, as compared with normal imports of 6 million to 8 million pounds. More seeds could be used for oil. The requirements of the United States for the two products of the poppy plant could therefore very well be brought into balance, on perhaps 15,000 to 20,000 acres, if domestic cultivation should ever be necessary.

The United States, however, has no present intention of entering the field of poppy cultivation. On the contrary, this field was abandoned as a matter of national policy, and commercial poppy cultivation suppressed even during the war: for it is the conviction of the narcotics authorities of the United States that only by striking at the source can the opium evil finally be overcome. It may be that in some countries the poppy can be grown for seed alone, or for seed and alkaloids, without the danger of narcotic addiction spreading among the population. Certain it is, however, that, in some countries, opium is produced far in excess of legitimate needs. It is the belief of the United States that the only way to conquer the opium evil is by restricting, and, where necessary, completely abolishing, the cultivation of the opium poppy plant itself. The narcotics authorities of the United States have expressed their satisfaction that the United States can contribute, by its own sacrifice and example, to this end. Source: Bulletin on Narctoics (1950/01/01)

World Consumption of Morphine in 1950 5615 kg.
World Consumption of Morphine in 1954 5150 kg.
World Consumption of Metadon in 1954 553 kg.
World Consumption of Morphine in 1999 245.3 tons
Sources: Bulletin on Narcotics 1956, Isuue 3; INCB 2000

US Population 1950: 152,271,417 (July 1, 1950)
US Population 1954: 163,025,854 (July 1, 1954)
US Population 2001: 284,837,915 (Aug 06 2001)
Source: US Census Bureau

Global Production and Consumption of Derivatives of Opium Alkaloids, 1957-1961 in Kilograms

		1957	1958	1959	1960	1961
		Kilograms-Kilogrammes-Kilogramos				
Dihydrocodeine	Production	1963	2516	2352	2884	3002
	Consumption	2001	2370	2078	2457	2685
Pholcodine	Production	948	1215	1353	1565	1612
	Consumption	953	863	1249	1507	1557
Hydrocodone	Production	1301	1432	1258	1041	765
	Consumption	1036	1053	1106	825	817
Oxycodone	Production	344	462	520	647	475
	Consumption	435	426	453	508	470
Benzylmorphine	Production	89	102	119	81	117
	Consumption	80	56	80	79	83
Hydromorphone	Production	88	94	25	75	91
	Consumption	89	76	64	86	64
Thebacon	Production	140	188	147	150	58
	Consumption	130	128	131	130	111
Dihydromorphine	Production		22	49	73	27
Acetyldihydrocodeine	Production	6	6	7	3	11
	Consumption	4	8	3	6	10
Nicomorphine	Production		2	3	4	7
	Consumption		1	2	3	3
Hydromorphinol	Production					5
Oxymorphone	Production		1	8	14	3
	Consumption			2	5	2
Normorphine	Production			3		

Consumption of methadone, which reached a maximum of 570 Kg. in 1954, has since decreased. This trend was apparent in 17 of the 20 countries in which annual consumption has reached 1 kg. at least once; in ten countries it remained stationary, leaving only two countries in which it increased. These variations resulted in a fall of 212 kg. between 1954 and 1961, which brought the total down to 358 kg. in the latter year. Between 1954 and 1961 production also decreased by 233 kg., the totals for those two years being 608 and 375 kg. respectively.
Source: Bulletin on Narcotics 1963 Issue 1,
Work of the Permanent Central Opium Board in 1962

The United States continued to be the largest consumer of oxycodone (11.6 tons), accounting for 90 percent of the global total. Over the last 20 years, global manufacture of oxycodone increased gradually, from an average of 2.1 tons per annum at the beginning of the 1980's to 11.5 tons in 1998. In 1999, it reached an all-time high of 17.6 tons. The rising trend has again reflected ongoing developments in the United States, the leading manufacturer, where oxycodone has been increasingly manufactured to meet growing demand, particularly since 1994.
Source: INCB Narcotics 2000

Learning to Make Opiates Without Flowers

In the early 1970's, a severe opium shortage was created by increased demand, poor poppy crops, a Turkish ban on poppy cultivation, and the Soviet Union's entry as a buyer of opium on the world market. In 1973, 45% of the United States' strategic stockpile of opium had to be released for domestic use. Finding a way to manufacture totally synthetic opium products from readily available materials became imperative.

On January 22, 1979, Dr. Kenner Rice of the LMC discovered the critical chemical reaction enabling large-scale production of totally synthetic morphine, codeine, and thebaine, the three basic raw materials in opium. As shown in his laboratory journal, the initial sign of success was the identical chromatographic behavior of Dr.Rice's product and an authentic sample from opium. Dr. Rice's method, now internationally known as the NIH Total Opiate Synthesis, is still the only practical process available for making large quantities of opium products from synthetic materials, guaranteeing reliable supplies of opiate pain relievers. Source: Laboratory of Medicinal Chemistry, National Institute of Diabetes and Digestive and Kidney Diseases.

Poppy cultivation under properly controlled conditions so as to meet the world's requirements of opium for medical and scientific purposes

(Twenty-sixth session of the Commission on Narcotic Drugs)

According to the request made at its Third Special Session, the Commission had at its disposal to study that question a note describing important developments which had taken place within the year, the Report of the International Narcotics Control Board setting out certain elements of the problem and details of the scientific research initiated by the UN Narcotics Laboratory...

As for the scientific research, it included investigations on *Papaver somniferum* as well as *Papaver bracteatum*: international collaboration in that research work had been established on a broad scale, and important investigations were being carried out in many countries. For *Papaver somniferum*, projects included research on the improvement of the yield of phenanthrene alkaloids from the opium poppy and also on the use both of lanced and unlanced poppy straw as an important source of these alkaloids. As for *Papaver bracteatum*, research was carried out on the most suitable conditions for the cultivation with a high yield of thebaine, also on methods for the determination of thebaine in the various parts of the plant, etc...

Present research into obtaining codeine from *Papaver bracteatum* should be vigorously pursued.. 1975/01/01

Global Consumption of Opiates 1984-1998

Morphine consumption underwent a steady and constant increase during the period 1984-1998, from an average of 2.2 tons per annum before 1984 to 20.5 tons in 1998. In 1999, morphine consumption fell for the first time in 15 years, to 19.5 tons, a decline mainly attributable to the United States. In view of the increasing use of oxycodone as an analgesic for the treatment of moderate and severe pain in that country, which accounted for 90 per cent of global oxycodone consumption, it is likely that global consumption of morphine will remain at the current level of 20 tons in the years to come.

Utilization of Opiate Raw Materials

The amounts of opium used for the extraction of alkaloids fluctuated widely over a period of 20 years (1980-1999), between a maximum of 109.3 tons in morphine equivalent in 1991 and a minimum of 46.9 tons in 1989. Following a continuous increase during the 1995-1998 period, utilization of opium fell to 85.4 tons in morphine equivalent in 1999, whereas utilization of concentrate of poppy straw continued its upward trend initiated in 1986, reaching 245.5 tons in morphine equivalent in 1999. In general, the patterns of use reflect the trend towards a larger proportion of the alkaloids being extracted from concentrate of poppy straw than from opium. The growing demand for thebaine, particularly in the United States, led to the increase in the utilization of concentrate of poppy straw manufactured from a new variety of opium poppy with high thebaine content in Australia.

Stocks of Opiate Raw Materials

The increased production and reduced exports in 1999 led to a substantial increase in global stocks of opium at the end of that year, reaching 122 tons in morphine equivalent. Of that total, 95 tons, or 78 per cent, were held by India. The remainder was held, in descending order, by Japan (17 tons), the United States (7 tons), France (1.3 tons) and China (1.1 tons), in morphine equivalent. Global stocks of concentrate of poppy straw also continued to rise, amounting to 57 tons in morphine equivalent, as compared with 47 tons in 1998. Nevertheless, the stocks were still far below the current level of annual utilization. The United States held the largest stocks in 1999, with 21 tons (37 per cent) in morphine equivalent, followed by Turkey with 10 tons (17 per cent), Australia with 9 tons (16 per cent) and France with 7 tons (13 per cent). Source: Narcotics 2000 Part 4, pp. 77-78.

Production of opiate raw materials[a], a consumption of opiates and balance, 1985-2000

(Area harvested in hectares; production, consumption and balance in tonnes of morphine equivalent)

Item	1985	1986	1987	1988	1989	1990	1991	1992	1993	1994	1995	1996	1997	1998	1999	2000
Australia Area																
Harvested:	4851	3994	3274	3462	5011	5581	7155	8030	6026	6735	8139	8360	9520	11491[b]	13553[c]	20645[d]
Production:	49.4	38.5	31.8	38.5	38.8	43.0	67.5	89.8	66.9	66.0	55.6	69.0	54.1	79.5	84.0	120.2
France Area																
Harvested:	4029	3200	3300	3113	2644	2656	3598	3648	4158	4431	4918	5677	6881	7884	7913	7819
Production:	20.7	15.7	16.6	21.4	13.4	19.5	30.2	21.8	28.8	32.9	48.9	47.3	52.0	64.8	79.0	64.0
India Area																
Harvested:	25153	23811	22823	19858	15019	14253	14145	14361	11907	12694	22798	22596	24591	10098	29163	29700
Production:	86.8	82.6	84.5	70.2	59.3	52.8	47.4	54.7	41.9	51.5	88.8	92.1	110.3	29.3	118.3	143.3
Spain Area																
Harvested:	4042	3458	3252	2935	2151	1464	4200	3084	3930	2539	3622	1180	1002	1640	3913	5698
Production:	11.2	5.6	12.3	10.8	5.7	8.0	24.2	12.8	9.0	5.2	4.2	4.4	1.9	7.5	18.0	23.9
Turkey Area																
harvested:	4902	5404	6137	18260	8378	9025	27030	16393	6930	25321	60051	11942	29681	49207	87193	25787
Production:	9.2	8.4	9.2	24.7	7.2	13.3	57.9	18.7	7.8	41.1	75.2	16.1	38.3	86.7	97.1	38.4
Other countries Area																
Harvested:	--	--	--	--	--	--	--	--	--	--	--	--	--	--	--	--
Production:	34.6	27.1	30.3	36.9	18.4	38.0	31.2	14.9	13.2	21.5	25.5	16.9	6.1	7.3	10.3	11.0
Total																
Area Harvested:		39867	38786	47628	33203	32979	56128	45516	32951	51720	9952	849755	71675	80320	141715	89649
Production: (1)	211.9	177.9	184.7	202.5	142.8	174.6	258.4	217.7	167.6	218.2	298.2	245.8	4272.7	275.1	406.7	400.8
Total																
Consumption(2):	202.1	203.2	206.9	200.9	204.3	196.1	217.8	212.4	236.6	225.7	237.8	246.5	241.0	236.8	245.3	240.0
Balance ((1) Minus (2)):	9.8	-25.3	-22.3	1.6	-61.5	-21.5	40.6	5.3	-69.0	-7.5	60.3	-0.8	31.7	38.2	161.4	160.8

Note: [a] Opium or concentrate of poppy straw. [b] Including 809 hectares of a new variety of *Papaver somniferum* with a high thebaine content. [c] Including 1,978 hectares of a new variety of *Papaver somniferum* with a high thebaine content. [d] Including 5,479 hectares of a new variety of *Papaver somniferum* with a high thebaine content. Source: INCB March 2001 (1987-2000 figures), INCB 1999 (1986 figures), INCB 1998 (1985 figures), India Production figures (1986-1998) were increased in 1999 INCB report.

MANUFACTURE OF OTHER NARCOTIC DRUGS
FABRICATION DES AUTRES STUPÉFIANTS
FABRICACIÓN DE OTROS ESTUPEFACIENTES

1. Derivatives of opium alkaloids - Dérivés des alcaloïdes de l'opium Derivados de los alcaloides del opio

	1994	1995	1996	1997	1998
	Kilograms-Kilogrammes-Kilogramos				
Acetyldihydrocodeine-Acétyldihydrocodéine-Acetildihidrocodeína	9	13	--	10	--
Dihydromorphine-Dihidromorfina	249	92	117	262	430
Heroin-Héroïne-Heroína	193	423	420	304	188
Hydrocodone-Hidrocodona	8382	10700	10407	12651	16934
Hydromorphone-Hidromorfona	436	485	822	702	1023
Nicocodine-Nicocodina	12	14	--	14	14
Nicomorphine-Nicomorfina	41	--	72	--	51
Oxymorphone-Oximorfona	2	7	4	40	55
Thebacon-Thébacone-Thebacón	--	84	--	161	--

2. Synthetic opiods-Opiacés synthétiques-Opiáceos sintéticos

	1994	1995	1996	1997	1998
	Kilograms-Kilogrammes-Kilogramos				
Alfentanil	19	22	41	20	2
Anileridine-Anilérídine-Anileridina	125	104	177	142	163
Bezitramide-Becitramida	12	--	28	--	--
Dextromoramide-Dextromoramida	114	89	35	34	--
Difenoxin-Difénoxine-Difenoxina	--	9	--	4	--
Dipipanone-Dipipanona	57	73	69	85	--
Fentanyl-Fentanil	170	133	187	203	374
Ketobemidone-Cétobémidone-Cetobemidona	249	203	276	377	339
Levorphanol-Lévorphanol-Levorfanol	8	6	12	7	9
Methadone intermediate-Méthadone, intermédiaire de la-Metadona, intermediairio de la-	4757	8400	6578	8404	11074
Normethadone-Norméthadone-Normetadona	--	54	--	--	--
Pethidine intermediate A-Péthidine, interméd. A de la-Petidina, intermed. A de la	2019	2981	1004	2073	1562
Phenazocine-Phénazocine-Fenazocina	--	--	5	5	--
Piritramide-Piritramida	396	391	395	--	400
Sufentanil	1	4	3	1	3
Tilidine-Tilidina	16926	15712	19253	28033	27816
Trimeperidine-Triméperidine Trimeperidina	363	326	336	148	9

Source: INCB Narcotic Drugs 1999. Cultivation of *Papaver Somniferum* for the Production of Opium, Statistics from 1994-1998.

Narcotics and Narctoic Antagonists from Thebaine

by Anthony John Fist et al., May 30, 2000

"The 14-hydroxymorphinans, such as, oxycodone, naloxone, naltrexone, nalbuphine and nalmefene are important opiate derivatives due to their behavior as potent analgesics and/or narcotic antagonists. The most practical synthetic routes to the preparation of these pharmaceuticals have utilized the alkaloid, thebaine, as a starting material. Other important opiate derivatives such as the ring-C bridged compounds buprenorphine and etorphine are also most practically prepared from thebaine...

Oxycodone is a product sold for use as an analgesic and its production consumes large amounts of thebaine...

A second reason for the limited availability of thebaine, and its high cost, is that the primary source of thebaine is extraction from the poppy plant, *Papaver somniferum*. Morphine is the major alkaloid that accumulates in capsules of *Papaver somniferum*. Thus, the supply of thebaine is to a great degree limited to some fraction of the demand for morphine...

Oripavine has not been used as a starting material for the 14-hydroxymorphinans in any practical sense because it is not recoverable from *Papaver somniferum* in any practical yield. Thus, there is now no real shortage of this material, but only because there has never developed any demand for it..."

While thebaine has been obtained as a by-product during the extraction process from opium, it is mainly obtained, in the United States, from concentrate of poppy straw of a new variety of *Papaver somniferum* L., cultivated in Australia. Thebaine is not itself used in therapy, but it is an important material for the manufacture of a number of opoids, namely oxycodone, oxymorphone, etrophine and buprenophine, the later substance being under the control of the 1971 Convention. Thebaine is also the starting material for the syntheses of substances not under international control, such as the derivatives naloxone, naltrexone, nalorphine and nalbuphine, some of which are used in the tratment of opiate poisoning and opiate addiction.

Having fluctuated widely between 6 and 10 tons during the period 1980-1996, global manufacture of thebaine has increased progressively over the last three years, amounting to 28.4 tons in 1999, and increases of 27 per cent over the previous year. That increase was exclusively attributable to the United States, which reported the manufacture of 21.6 tons, accounting for 76 per cent of the global total in 1999. Source: INCB 2000

Thebaine from Oriental Poppies

Thebaine is found in traces in many species of Papaver. Thebaine is a major alkaloid in both Garden Poppies (*Papaver somniferum*) and *Papaver orientale var. bracteatum* (also called the Great Red Oriental). Several other varieties of *Papaver orientale* also contain thebaine as the major alkaloid. A new strain of garden poppy was developed in Tasmania which produces more thebaine than the original garden poppy and is grown alongside the opium poppy fields of Tasmania. The Great Red Oriental (*Papaver bracteatum*) also called the Scarlet Poppy and the Blood Poppy has been evaluated as a thebaine source as oxycodone demands are putting a strain on thebaine supplies. Oriental poppy pods are one third the size of Garden poppies and produce one third the amount of seeds. Although Oriental poppies have not been developed for thebaine or seed production, labor costs are much lower for Orientals as they are perennial (zones 5-8; will not flower without winter cold) and Garden poppies are annual and have to be replanted every year.

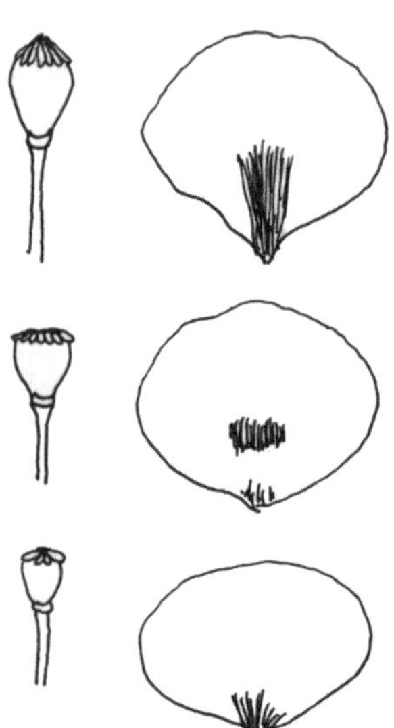

In the Great Red Oriental, thebaine concentration reaches a peak in capsules 3 to 4 weeks (latex 28-53% thebaine) after the petals open and then two weeks later it peaks again. Fully mature capsules (dried) produce higher yields as thebaine is 'unbound' at this stage and is more completely extracted, plus seeds can be used for food. The alkaloid yields are from 0.32% to 3.75% thebaine for capsules (dried capsules weigh from 2.5 to 9 grams each). Alkaloid production increases with the age of plants. Plants which are several years old (3-4 years) produce more flowers and contain higher concentrations of thebaine than younger plants. Pretreatment of seeds with colchicine increases thebaine production in plants.

The United States, France and England grow Scarlet Poppies for horticultural purposes, but this meager harvest will not sustain a nation in case of a war, epidemic, nuclear or biological attack. A few acres of poppies may sustain a small town with medications both for pain and PTSD patients, but not the nation.

Capsule on left. Petals on right. Top: *Papaver bracteatum.*
Middle: *Papaver pseudo-orientale.* Bottom: *Papaver orientale.*

In long term survival of your family, the nation and the world may depend on a few flowers growing in your garden. According to DEA intelligence there is no cultivation of opium in the northeast of the US. Although Garden Poppies can be lanced to produce opium, it is very labor intensive. The few *somniferum* poppies that grow in grandmothers' gardens could not support the needs of a patient in severe pain never mind a community after a major emergency.

Modern narcotics are produced by processing multi-tons of poppy straw. This method was discovered by János Kabay to prevent the diversion of narcotics to illicit narcotics brokers. This method is one of the greatest discoveries in the manufacture of narcotics. Following a major catastrophe, plague, terrorist attack or meteor striker; the entire US stockpile of narcotics would disappear in a few days. There would be no pain relief for small communities unless they are cultivating fields of poppies now and have the knowledge to process them.

Timely provision of controlled drugs in acute emergency situations

"The application of the export and import authorization system makes the quick international transportation of controlled drugs to sites of acute emergencies virtually impossible. Recognizing the difficulty involved, the Board in its report for 1994 proposed that the control obligations could be limited to the competent authorities of exporting countries in such situations. That proposal was endorsed by the Commission on Narcotic Drugs at its thirty-eighth session."

Source: INCB Annual Report 1995

Analogs, homologs and congeners of etorphine have been found that are 8000 times more activie compared to morphine. The problem with etorphine type molecules is that they are so potent that they have to be evenly tritrated into a inert carrier. An example of this would be much like the tritration of LSD into an inert carrier. This is done by diffusing the drug into a solvent and reabsorbed into an inert carrier. Doses would have to have to be uniform much in the way that LSD-25 is on gel sheets or blotter paper. (see LSD-25 & Tryptamine Syntheses).

At 0.025, 0.050, and 0.100 mg, etorphine has been found to have morphine effects. It is a fast acting, short duration narcotic providing 2 hour pain relief equal to morphine. It has been patented for use in a transdermal patch much like that of fentyl patches. It might be the only safe way in which the drug could be administered and provide slow release for sustained pain relief.

REFERENCES

Asgharian, R.; Nasseri, P.; Lalezari, I.; *Papaver bracteatum* Lindl: Population Arya II; Journal of Pharmaceutical Sciences (1974) 63:1331.

Barton, D.H.R.; Kirby, G.W.; Steglich, W.; Thomas, G.M.; Battersby A.R.; Dobson, T.A.; Ramuz, H.; Investigation on the Biosynthesis of Morphine Alkaloids; Journal of Chemical Society (1965) 2423-2438.

Boden, M. Richard; Gates, Mrashall; Ho, Siew Peng; Sundararaman, P.; Derivatives of the Thebaine Anion. 1. Structure of Metopon. A Direct Demonstration; Journal of Organic Chemistry (1982) 47: 1347-1349.

Bonner, Robert M.; Rapoport, Henry; Delta-7 Desoxymorphine; Journal of the American Chemical Society (1951) 5485.

Brown, Ivor, Martin-Smith, M.; Oxidation Products from Codeine; Journal of the Chemical Society (1960) 4139-4140.

Conroy, Harold; Neopine; Journal of the American Chemical Society (1955) 77: 5960-5966.

Dauben, William, G.; Basking, Craig, P.; van Riel, Herman, C.H.A.; Facile Synthesis of Codeine from Thebaine; Journal of Organic Chemistry (1979) 44 (9); 1567-1568.

Edward E. Smissman-Bristol-Myers Squibb Award Address. The role of concepts in structure-activity relationship studies of opioid ligands; Journal of Medicinal Chemistry (1992) May 29;35(11):1927-1937.

Etorphine pgs 41-42; also see Opiod Analgesics pgs 75-81; The Extra Pharmacopea by Martindale.

Goodrich, P.G.E.; Accidental self-injection; The Veterinary Record (1977) 100 (21): 458-459

Hardy, D.G.; Bentley, K.W.; Novel Analgesics and Molecular Rearrangements in the Morphine-Thebaine Group. I. Ketones Derived from 6,14-endo-Etheotetrahydrothebaine; Journal of the American Chemical Society (1967) 89 (13) 3267-73.

Hauser, Frank, M.; Chen, Tek-Kuei Chen, and Carroll, Frank I.; 14-Hydroxycodeinone. An Improved Synthesis; Journal of Medicinal Chemistry (1974) 17: 1117.

Helliwell, K.; Fairbairn, J.W.; Papaver bracteatum Lindley: Thebaine Content in Relation to Plant Development; J. Pharm. Pharmac (1977) 29: 65-69.

Hayashi, Goro; Inoue, Hirozumi; Oine, Toyonari: Kugita, Hiroshi; 3-Alkyl-3-phenylpiperidine Dervatives as Analgesics. II; ???? (1965) 8: 313-316.

Heydenreich, Kaethe; Pfeifer, S.; Alkaloids of the genus Papaver. IX. Bractavine, a new Papaver alkaloid; Chemical Abstracts (1965) 63: 16660 a-b.

Hite, Gilbert; Smissman, Edward, E. Smissman; The Quasi-Favorskii Rearrangement. I. The Preparation of Demerol and ß-Pethidine; Journal of Organic Chemistry (1959) 81: 1201-1203.

Horn, Alan S.; Rodgers, John R.: Structural and Conformatinal Relationships between Enkephalins and the Opiates; Nature (1976) 260: 795-797.

Iijima,Ikuo; Minamikawa, Jun-ichi; Jacobson, Arthur E.; Brossi, Arnold; Rice, Kenner, C.; Studies in the (+)-Morphinan Series. 5. Synthesis and Biological Properties of (+)-Naloxone; Journal of Medicinal Chemistry (1978) 21(4): 398-400.

Immobilon: Curiously Strong; Lancet (1977) 2: 178.

Jaffarian, S.; Aynehchi, Y.: determination of Thebaine in Varous Parts of *Papaver bracteatum* Lindl. During the Growing Season; Lloydia (1973) 36: 427-429.

Janssen, Paul A.J.; Niemegeers, Carlos J.E.; Van Bever. Willem F.M.; Synthetic Analgesics. Sythesis and Pharmacology of the Diastereoisomers of N-[3-Methyl-1-(2-phenylethyl)-4-piperidyl]-N-phenyl-propanamide and N-[3-Methyl-1-(1-phenylethyl)-4-piperidyl]-N-phenylpropanamide; Journal of Medicinal Chemistry (1974) 17(10): 1047-1051.

Küppers, F.J.E.M. et al; Alkaloids of *Papaver bracteatum*: Presence of Codeine, Neopine and Alpinine; Phytochemistry (1976) 15; 444-445.

Lalezari, I.; Shafiee, A.; Nasseri-Nouri, P.; Isolation of Alpinigenine from *Papaver bracteatum*; Journal of Pharmaceutical Sciences (1973) 62: 1718.

Lavie, David: Meshulam, Haim; The Alkaloidal Constituents of *Papaver bracteatum* Arya II; Phytochemistry (1980) 19: 2633-2635.

Levy, A.; Palevitch, D.; Lavie, D.; Genetic Improvement of *Papaver bracteatum*: Heritability and Selection Response of Thebaine and Seed Yields; Journal of Medicinal Plant Research (1981) 43; 71-76.

Lewis, John W.; Ring C-Bridged Derivatives of Thebaine and Oripavine; Advances in Biochemical Psychopharmacology (1974) 8: 123-136.

Lister, Robert, E.; Structure-activity requirements in some novel thebaine derived analgesics, Journal of Pharm. Pharmacol (196) 16, 364-366.

López, Dolores; Quinoá, Emilio; Riguera, Ricardo; The [4 + 2] Addition of Singlet Oxygen to Thebaine: New Access to Highly Functionaized Morphine Derivatives via Opiod Endoperoxides; Journal of Organic Chemistry (2000) 65: 4671-4678.

Lousberg, J.J. Ch.; Theuns, H. Leo; Theuns, Hubert, G.; Search for New Natural Sources of Morphinans; Economic Botany (1986) 40(4): 485-497.

Marynanoff, Bruce E.; Simon, Eric J.; Gioannini, Theressa; Gorissen, H.; Potential Affinity Labels for the Opiate Receptor Based on Fentanyl and Related Compounds; Journal of Medicinal Chemistry (1982) 25: 913-919

Morris, R.W.; Dobberstein, R.H.; Wu, Fen-Fen; The Effects of Selected Fungicides and Insectides on Growth and Thebaine Production of *Papaver bracteatum*; Lloydia (1978) 41(4):355-360.

Nyman, U.; Bruhn, J.G.; P*apaver bracteatum*- a Summary of Current Knowledge; Journal of Medicanal Plant Research (1979) 35 (2): 97-117.

Phillipdon, J. David; Sariyar, Günay; Macrantaline and Macrantoridine, New Alkaloids from a Turkish Sample of *Papaver Pseudo-Orientale*; Phytochemistry (1977) 16; 2009-2013.

Pless, J.; Roemer, D.; Structure Activity Relationship of Orally Active Enkephalin Analogues as Analgesics; Life Sciences (1979) 24: 621-624

Rapoport, Henry; Synthesis of Thebaine and Oripavine from Codeine and Morphine; Journal of Medicinal Chemistry (1975) 18(11): 1074-1077.

Rapoport, Henry; Reist, Helen N.; A Method for Preparing Codeinone; Journal of the American Chemical Society (1955) 77: 490-491.

Rapoport, Henry; Horn, Jerold S.; Hodges, Craig, C.: Morphinan Alkaloids in *Papaver bracteatum*: Biosynthesis and Fate; Phytochemistry (1977) 16: 1939-1942.

Rapoport, Henry; Stermitz, Frank R.; The Biosynthesis of Opium Alkaloids.

Alkaloid Interconversions in *Papaver somniferum* and *P. orientale*; Journal of the American Chemical Society (1961) 83: 4045-4050.

Roemer, Dietmar; Buescher, Heinz H.; Hill, Ronald C.; Pless, Janos; Bauer, Wilfried; Cardinaux, Francis; Closse, Annemarie; Hauser, Daniel; Huguenin, Rene; A Synthetic Enkephalin Analogue with Prolonged Parenteral and Oral Analgesic Activity; Nature (1977) 268: 547-549.

Santavy, F.; Preininger, V.; Nemeckova, A.; Isolation and identification of alkaloids from *Papaver orientale, P. rhoeas*, and other Papaver Species; Chemical Abstracts (1967) 105072-105074t.

Sharghi, N.; Lalezari, I.; *Papaver bracteatum* Lindl., a Highly Rich Source of Thebaine; Nature (1967) 1244

Shen, K.F., Crain, S.M.; Specific N- or C-terminus modified dynorphin and beta-endorphin peptides can selectively block excitatory opioid receptor functions in sensory neurons and unmask potent inhibitory effects of opioid agonists.; Brain Res (1995) Feb 27;673(1):30-38.

Shilling, W.L.; Homeyer, A.H.; Isolations and Purification of Neopine (1947) 12: 356-358.

Small, Lyndon; Fitch, Howard, M.; Smith, William E.; The Addition of Organomagnesium Halides to Pseudocodeine Types. II. Preparation of Nuclear Alkylated Morphine Derivatives; Journal of the American Chemical Society (1936) 58: 1457-1463.

Small, Lyndon; Lutz, Robert E.; Reduction Studies in the Morphine Series. IX. Hydroxycodeinone: Journal of Organic Chemistry (1939) 4: 220-228.

Soudijn, Willem; Lobbezoo, Marinus W.; Opiate Receptor Interaction of Compounds Derived from or Structurally Related to Fentanyl; Journal of Medicinal Chemistry (1981) 24: 777-782

Steele, Melanie J.; Fairbairn, J.W.; Bound Forms of Alkaloids in *Papaver somniferum* and *P. bacteatum*; Phytochemistry (1980) 19: 2317-2321

Tao, P.L., Law, P.Y., Loh, H.H.; Decrease in delta and mu opioid receptor binding capacity in rat brain after chronic etorphine treatment; J Pharmacol Exp Ther (1987) Mar;240(3):809-816.

Teakle, J.A.; Rees, R.B.; Handling Immobilon; The Veterinary Record (1976) 98 (19): 390

Theuns, Hurbert G.; van Dam, Jan E. G.; Luteijn, Jan M.; Salemink, Cornelis A.; Alkaloids of *Papaver bracteatum*: 14-ß-Hydroxycodeineone, 14-ß-Hydroxycodeine and N-Methylcorydaldine; Phytochemistry (1977) 16: 753-755.

Vincent, P.G.; Bare, C.E.; Gentner, W.A.; Thebaine Content of Selections of *Papaver bracteatum* Lindl. at Different Ages; Journal of Pharmaceutical Sciences (1977) 66 (12): 1716-1719.

White, Peter T.; Raymer, Steve; The Poppy-For Good and Evil; National Geographic (1985) February pgs. 140-189.

Whittle, B.A.; Volans, Glyn, N.; Accidental injection of Immobilon; British Medical Journal (1976) ii, 472-473.

Wunderly, S.W.; Brochemann-Hanssen, E.; Biosynthesis of Morphine Alkaloids in *Papaver bracteatum* Lindl.; Journal of Pharmaceutical Sciences (1978) 67(1):103-106.

Zee, S.H.; et al.; Preparation of Fentanyl from Phenethylamine and Methyl Acrylate; Natl. Sci. Counc. Monthly, ROC (1981) 9(5): 387-397

OXYCODONE
(14-Hydroxydihydrocodeinone; Dihydrohydroxycodeinone; Eucodal; Dihydro-oxycodeinone)

Pharmacology of Oxycodone

by Hugo Krueger, Nathan B. Eddy and Margaret Sumwalt

Narcotic Effect (described in some instances as depression or motor paralysis) **Man:** A narcotic effect was seen (Freund and Speyer, 1917; Hesse, 1917; Merck, 1919; Mayer, 1927; Boyer, 1929); with 5-30 mg. T, in 300 cases (Falk, 1917); with 5.0-7.5 mg. T (Eibuschitz, 1927).

Analgesia Man: An analgesic effect was seen (Merck, 1919; Mayer, 1927; Boyer, 1929; Mutch, 1934); with 5-30 mg. T, sc (Falk, 1917); with 5-20 mg. T (Keim, 1923); with 10 mg. T, o (Heinroth, 1926).

Straub Tail Reaction Mouse: The tail reaction was seen (Okuda, 1931, 1932; Schübel, 1934; Juan, 1937); in 29 out of 50 animals with 1.4 mg. K, sc, in 44 out of 50 animals with 2.5 mg. K, sc (Keil and Kluge, 1934).

Respiration Man: The respiration decreased (Mayer, 1927; Boyer, 1929). Cough was relieved (Hecht, 1923; Mayer, 1927; Boyer, 1929).

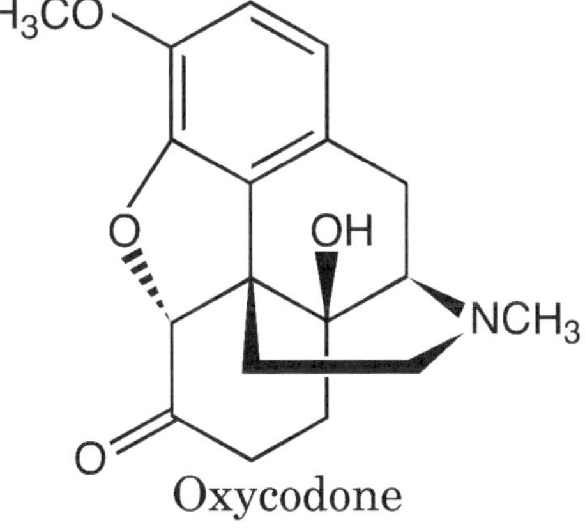

Oxycodone

Metabolism Man: An addict to eucodal, receiving 450 mg. T, sc, daily, showed no evidence of liver damage (Haug, 1934).

Blood Pressure Man: The circulatory changes were insignificant (Mayer, 1927).

Source: The Pharmcology of the Opium Alkaloids; Part 1 & 2 (1941)

T=per animal (total dose); K=per kilogram; o=oral; v=intravenous; sc=subcutaniously; m= intramuscular; p= intraperitoneal; r= rectal

Heart Man: The circulatory changes were insignificant (Mayer, 1927). Eucodal was no more harmful to the heart than morphine (Boyer, 1929).

Gastrointestinal Tract Man: The flow of bile into the duodenum diminished with 20 mg. T, sc and afterward neither subcutaneous injection of hypophysin, nor placing oil in the duodenum increased the flow (Schöndube and Lürmann,1927). Constipation was seen (Alexander, 1920); constipation was less with eucodal than with morphine (Boyer, 1929).

Other Smooth Muscle Man: The action of eucodal on the uterus was "unsatisfactory" (Falk, 1917).

Toxicity Man: Patients, presumably not addicted, survived 40 mg. and 100 mg. T, o; in the case when 100 mg. was taken, the stomach was washed (von Wild, 1924).

Tolerance and Addiction Man: Tolerance developed (Hecht, 1923; Hildebrandt, 1929); to a daily dose of 200 mg. T, in one case and 300 mg. T in another (König, 1919); of 300-350 mg. T (Frensdorf, 1924); of 2 g. T (Klee and Grossmann, 1925); of 2.4 g. T (Lemperg, 1926). Addiction developed (references on Tolerance, above; also Alexander, 1920; Meyer, 1924; Stern-Piper, 1925; Berliner, 1926; Wolff, 1928; Rosenfeld, 1928; Grunthal and Hoefer, 1929; Hoefer, 1929; Menninger-Lerchenthal, 1930; Schottky, 1931; Dansauer and Rieth, 1931; Haug, 1934; Meyer, 1936, Pilcz, 1937). Addiction acquired to morphine was supported with about one and a half times as much eucodal, administered at the same intervals of time; after withdrawal of the substituted eucodal the syndrome of abstinence resembled that following withdrawal of morphine (Himmelsbach, Eddy, and Davenport, 1938). In a eucodal addict, the threshold for pain was higher than in normal individuals; during the first 5 days of withdrawal the threshold dropped below normal; during the next month it approached normal (Grünthal and Hoefer, 1929). An addict to eucodal, receiving 450 mg. T, sc, daily, showed no evidence of liver damage (Haug, 1934). In a case addicted to eucodal, the sedimentation rate of the blood was normal (Schottky, 1931); in 6 cases addicted to eucodal the sedimentation rate increased when the drug was withdrawn (Stern-Piper, 1925).

Fate of Eucodal Man: Eucodal was recovered from the urine of addicts (Panse 1933); was looked for vainly in the urine of an addict (Schübel, 1934).

References

Ahlgren. Gunnar. (1925) Zur Kenntnis der Tierischen Gewebsoxydation sowie ihrer Beeinflussung durch Insulin, Adrenalin, Thyroxin und Hypophysepräparate. Lund. Skandin. Arch. f. Physiol., **47**, Suppl. 171.

Alexander, Alfred. (1920) Uber Eukodalismus.München. med. Wchnschr., **67**, 873.

Berliner, Max. (1926) Uber Eukodalismus. Wien. klin. Wchuschr., **39**, 1045.

Boyer, Paul. (1929) Sur quelques nouveaux dérivés des alcaloïdes de l'opium (eucodal, dicodide et dilaudide). Bull. méd., Par., **43**, 393-402.

Dansauer, Friedrich and Rieth, Adolf. (1931) Uber Morphinismus bei Kriegsbeschädigten. Nach amtlichen Unterlagen hearbeitet. Arbeit und Gesundheit Schriftenreihe zum Reichsarbeitsblatt. Issued under the auspices of the Reichsarbeitsministerium. Berlin.

Eibuschitz, Robert. (1927) Vorsicht mit Eukodal. Wien. klin. Wchnschr., **40**, 1231.

Falk, Edmund. (1917) Eukodal, ein neues Narkotikum. München. med. Wchnschr., **64**, 381.

Frensdorf. (1924) Uber Eukodalismus. München. med. Wchnschr., **71**, 751.

Freund, Martin and Speyer, Edmund. (1917) Uber Dihydrooxykodeinonchlorhydrat. München. med. Wchnschr., **64**, 380.

Grünthal, E. and Hoefer, P. (1929) Untersuchungen über akute und chronische Morphinwirkungen. Klin. Wchnschr., **8**, 104-107.

Haug, K. (1934) Die Leberfunktion beim Missbrauch von Opiaten und beim chronischen Gebrauch von Schlafmitteln in hohen Dosen. Monatschr. f. Psychiat. u. Neurol., **89**, 23.

Hecht, Paul. (1923) Uber Klinische Prüfung von Hustenmitteln. aus der Morphingruppe.Klin. Wchnschr. **2**, 1069.

Heinroth, Hans. (1926) Uber die Wirkung verschiedener Arzneimittel auf die Schmerzempfindlichkeit der Zahnpulpa. Arch. f. exper. Path. u. Pharmakol., **116**, 245.

Hesse, Walter. (1917) Eukodal als Narkotikum.Zentralbl. f. innere Med., **38**, 819.

Hildebrandt, Fritz. (1929) Gewöhnung an Gifte. Handb. d. norm. u. path. Physiol., **13**, 833-879.

Himmelsbach, Eddy, and Davenport (1938) Studies on drug addiction, with special reference to chemical structure of opium derivatives and allied synthetic substances and their physiological action. Pub. Health Rep., Suppl. No. 143.

Hoefer, Paul. (1929) Uber die Beeinflussung der Hautsinnesqualitäten durch Morphin und ähnliche Präparate, zugleich ein Beitrag zur Kenntnis des Morphinismus. Ztschr. f. Biol., **89**, 21.

Jüan, Shuhfarng. (1937) Pharmakologisches Studium der Thebainderivrate. III-VI. Folia pharmacol. japon., **23**, 233-247; **24**, 168-183. Ab.: Jap. J. M. Sc., IV, Pharmacology, **11**, (22), 1938.

Keil, W. and Kluge A. (1934) Uber die Anwendung des Mäuseschwanzphänomens zur Auswertung von Morphin- und Skopolaminpräparaten. Arch. f. exper. Path. u. Pharmakol., **174**, 493.

Keim, P. (1923) Uber das Dihydrooxykodeinonchlorhydrat (Eukodal). Munchen. med. Wchnschr., **70**, 466.

Klee, Ph. and Grosslnann. (1925) Uber die klinische Brauchbarkeit des Cholins. München. med. Wchnschr., **72**, 251.

König. (1919) Eukodalismus. Berl. klin. Wchnschr., **56**, 320.

Lernperg, Fritz. (1926) Tod clurch Eukodalismus. Zentralbl. f. innere Med., **47**, 57.

Mayer, Richard F. (1927) Vergleichende Beobachtungen über die Wirkung der wichtigsten Narcotica der Opiumgruppe. München. med. Wchnschr., **74**, 1657.

Menninger-Lerchenthal, E. (1930) Eukodalismus. Jahrb. f. Psychiat. u. Neurol., **47**,177.

Merck, E. (1919) Eukodal. Pharm. Ztg., **64**, 264. Ab.: Chem. Ab., **13**, 3272.

Meyer, Fritz M. (1936) Einige zahlenmässige Ergebnisse an 90 Morphinkranken. Ztschr. f. d. ges. Neurol. u. Psychiat., **154**, 499.

Meyer, Max. (1924) Uber Eukodalismus. Deutsche med. Wchnschr., **50**, 194.

Mutch, N. (1934) Proprietary remedies, with special reference to hypnotics. Brit. M. J., **1**, 319.

Okuda, Sozaburo. (1931) Vergleichende Untersuchungen der verschiedenen Arzneimittel der Morphingruppe hinsichtlich der Schwanzreaktion bei Mäusen. Jap. J. M. Sc., IV, Pharmacology, **5**,16.

Okuda, Sozaburo. (1932) Vergleichende Untersuchungen der verschiedenen Arzueimittel der Morphingruppe hinsichtlich der Schwanzreaktion bei Mäusen. II. Mitt. Folia pharmacol. japon., **13**, 30. Ab.: Ber. ü. d. ges. Biol., Abt. B, **65**, 819.

Panse, Friedrich. (1933) Ein einfache, klinisch brauchbare Methode des Nachweises von Opiaten im Harn der Morphinisten. Monatschr. f. Psychiat. u. Neurol., **84**, 151. Ab.: Deutsche med. Wchnschr., **58**, 1444, 1932.

Pilcz, Alexander. (1937) Arztliches über Rauschgifte. Wien. med. Wchnschr., **87**, 998.

Rosenfeld, M. (1928) Repetitorium der praktischen Psychiatrie. Deutsche med. Wohnschr., **54**, 967, 998.

Schöndube. W. and Lürmann, O. (1927) Uber die Wirkung des Morphiums auf die Gallenwege. München. med. Wchnschr., **74**, 1906.

Schottky, Johannes. (1931) Die Blulkörperchensenkung bei Geistes- und Nervenkranken. Ztschr. f. d. ges. Neurol. u. Psychiat., **133**, 631.

Schübel, Konrad. (1934) Uber die Ausscheidung des Eukodals. Arch. f. exper. Path. u. Pharmakol., **177**, 34.

Stern-Piper, Ludwig. (1925) Untersuchunge über die Senkungsgeschwindigkeit des Blutes bei chronischem Morphinismus und Eukodalis mus. Jahresvers. d. südwestdtsch. Psychiatr.-Vereinig., Frankfurt; am Main, October 25 and 26, 1924. Zentralbl. f. d. ges. Neurol. u. Psychiat., **40**, 722. Klin. Wchnschr., **4**, 548.

v. Wild. (1924) Eukodalvergiftung. München. med. Wchnschr., **71**, 453.

Waller, A. D. (1919) Concerning emotive phenomena. Part III. The influence of drugs upon the electrical conductivity of the palm of the hand. Proc. Roy. Soc. Lond., **91**, 32.

Wolff, P. (1928) Zur Behandlung und Bekämpfung der Alkaloidsuchten (Morphinismus, Kokainismus usw.). Deutsche med. Wchuschr., **54**, **7**, 51, 134, 224, 266, 349, 387.

14-Hydroxycodeinone → (sodium hydrosulphite) → Oxycodone

Preparation of Oxycodone (in English and German)

by Martin Freund (1924) US 1,479,293

10 grams oxycodeinon (14-hydroxycodeinone) are heated with a solution of 20 grams sodium hydrosulphite ($Na_2S_2O_4$) in 60 mL. water. After a short time complete solution takes place. Upon supersaturating with soda or ammonia 6 grams oxycodone are separated in crystalline form.

Dihydrooxycodeinon (Oxycodone)... crystallizes from alcohol in long jagged columns melting at 222° C. and yields well crystallized salts. Its hydrochloride $C_{18}H_{20}NO_4 \bullet HCl$ crystallizes from water or diluted alcohol in columns melting at 268 to 270° C. Its free base is precipitated from solutions of the salts by ammonia, soda or alkalies; it is in-soluble in excess of alkalies.

by Martin Freund and Edmund Speyer (1916) DE 296916

10 g Oxycodeinon werden mit einer Lösung von 20 g Natriumhydrosulfit in 60 ccm Wasser gekocht, wobei nach kurzer Zeit alles gelöst ist. Beim Ubersättigen mit Soda oder Ammoniak fallen 6 g Dihydrooxycodeinon inkristallinischem Zustande aus.

References

Freund, Walter (1924) Product of Reduction of Oxycodeinon and Process of Preparing the Same; Merck Index 13th edition (1996) Oxycodone; Dihydrothebenine from thebenine and sodium hydrosulfite, see Speyer and Rosenfeld, Ber (1925) **58**, 1120.
Note: Other sulfites might also work. See page 47.

14-Hydroxycodeinone from Thebaine and Hydrogen Peroxide (in English)

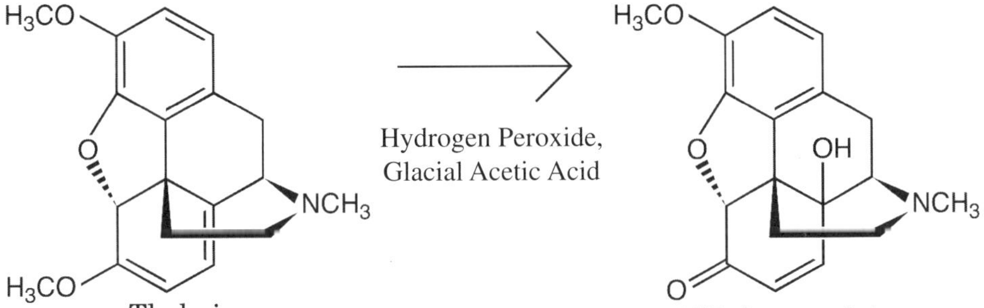

H_3CO ... NCH_3 ... H_3CO

Hydrogen Peroxide, Glacial Acetic Acid

H_3CO ... OH ... NCH_3 ... O

Thebaine (Paramorphine) 14-Hydroxycodeinone

Research on this reaction was done by Robert E. Lutz and Lyndon Small. It is based on the method of Freund and Speyer. The project was funded by The Rockeffer Foundation, University of Michigan, U.S. National Research Council, U.S. Public Health Service, and the U.S. Bureau of Narcotics. The original paper was authorized by the Surgeon General of the Public Health Service.

50 Grams of thebaine are mixed with 200 mL. of glacial acetic acid. The solution is rapidly heated to boiling with a Bunsen burner. The flame is immediately removed when the solution reaches boiling. 25 mL. of 30% hydrogen peroxide is added to the solution. The reaction occurs quickly (comes to a boil) and is maintained by heating for another ten minutes. The mixture is poured onto a quantity of ice and neutralized with concentrated ammonia (ice addition). A crude dark-brown solid is filtered from the solution. Trituration of the product with several portions of ethanol removes the resinous impurtities. The yield ranges from 36-40% theoretical. Fel'dman and Lyutenberg report a yield of 76.5% theoretical. The product is brown and can be futher purified by transforming into the hydrochloride. Base: m.p. 275°-276° [α]25/D=-111° (10% acetic acid, c=0.90). Hydrochloride dihydrate: m.p. 272°-274° [α]24/D=-89 (water, c=0.86). Monohydrate salt: [α]20/D=-149.7

References

Fel'dman; Lyutenberg (1945) J. Applied Chem. (U.S.S.R.) **18**, 715
Freund; Speyer (1914) Z. angew. Chem. **27**, i, 250.
Freund; Speyer (1914) D. R.-P. 286,431; Frdl. **12**, 750; Houben, **4**, 572.
Freund; Speyer (1916) J. prakt. Chem. **94**, 135.
Gulland; Robinson (1925) Mem. Proc. Manchester Lit. Phil. Soc., **69**, 79
Lutz, Robert; Small, Lyndon (1939) Journal of Organic Chemistry, **4**, 220-
Schöpf; Borkowsky (1927) Ann., **452**, 211.

14-Hydroxycodeinone from Thebaine and Hydrogen Peroxide (in German)

by Martin Freud und Edmund Speyer
1914 DE 286,431

H_3CO NCH_3 H_3CO Thebaine (Paramorphine)

Hydrogen Peroxide, Glacial Acetic Acid

H_3CO OH NCH_3 O 14-Hydroxycodeinone

100 g Thebain werden in etwa 400 ccm Eisessig gelöst und zu der heißen Lösung 50 ccm 30 prozentige Wasserstoffsuperoxydlösung zugegeben, wobei sofort eine heftige Reaktion eintritt. Nach deren Beendigung wird die Lösung mit 400 ccm Wasser versetzt und mit Ammoniak übersättigt. Die ausgeschiedene Base wird abfiltriert, mit heißem Wasser, dann mit Alkohol gewaschen und aus Alkohol unter Zusatz von wenig Chloroform umkristallisiert; Zersetzungspunkt 275°. Die Ausbeute beträgt etwa 70 g (das gleiche Oxydationsprodukt bildet sich beim Erhitzen von festem Thebainchlorhydrat mit 30 prozentiger Wasserstoffsuperoxydlosung oder bei der Oxydation des Thebains mit Kaliumbichromatlösung bei Gegenwart von verdünnter Schwefelsäure). Die Base gibt gut kristallisierte Salze. Das Chlorhydrat $C_{18}H_{19}NO_4$ HCl + H_2O kristallisiert aus Wasser in Saulen vom Zersetzungspunkt 285 bis 286°. Die Basc liefert ein Oxym von der Zusammensetzung $C_{18}H_2ON_2O_4$ und dem Zersetzungspunkt 279 bis 280° und ein Acetylderivat $C_{18}H_{18}(CO\ .\ CH_3)NO_4$ Vom F. 185 bis 186°.

Preparation of 14-Hydroxycodeinone from Thebaine and Sodium Dichromate (in English)

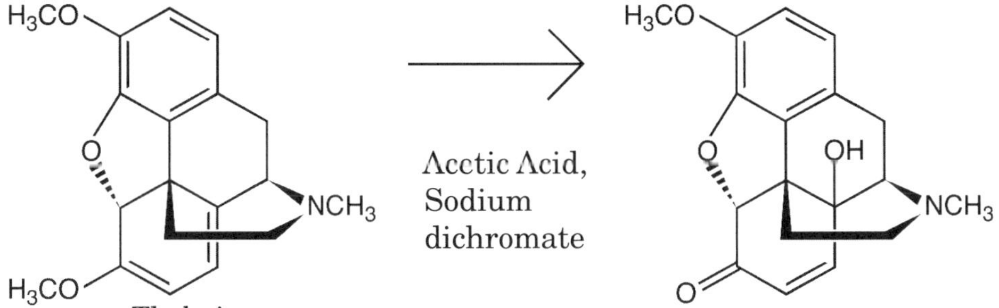

Thebaine (Paramorphine) → 14-Hydroxycodeinone

Acetic Acid, Sodium dichromate

by Lyndon F. Small and Robert E. Lutz (1932)

HYDROXYCODEINONE: (B=$C_{18}H_{19}O_4N$); prep. by treatment of thebaine with 30% hydrogen peroxide in acetic acid, or with potassium dichromate and sulphuric acid.

20 grams thebaine in 80 g. water with 25 g. acetic acid is treated cold with a solution of 20 g. $Na_2Cr_2O_7$ in 25 g. water. An oily ppt. forms, which becomes cryst. after short warming. The mixture is heated to 80° with stirring until the solid goes into solution; the temperature rises spontaneously to 90°. After short standing, the base is precip. from the cold solution as the dichromate by adding excess of chromic acid solution.

Cryst. from alcohol with a little chloroform, plates, decomp. 275°; sol. chloroform, ligroin, ethyl acetate, sparingly in alcohol, insol. in ether or water. Stable to strong acid or alkali.

—HYDROCHLORIDE, B•HCl+H_2O, decomp. 285° to 286°; $[\alpha]2_D$= 149.7° (water, C=2.502)

References

Freund; Speyer (1914) Z. angew. Chem. **27**, i, 250.
Freund; Speyer, (1916) D.R-P. 296,916
Freund; Speyer (1916) J. prakt. Chem. **94**, 135.
Freund; Speyer, D.R-P. 286431; Frdl. **12**, 750; Houben **4**, 572.
Freund; Speyer, Frdl. **13**, 880.
E. Merck, D.R-P. 411530; Frdl. **15**, 1516.

Preparation of 14-Hydroxycodeinone from Codeine or Codeinone and Sodium Dichromate (in German)

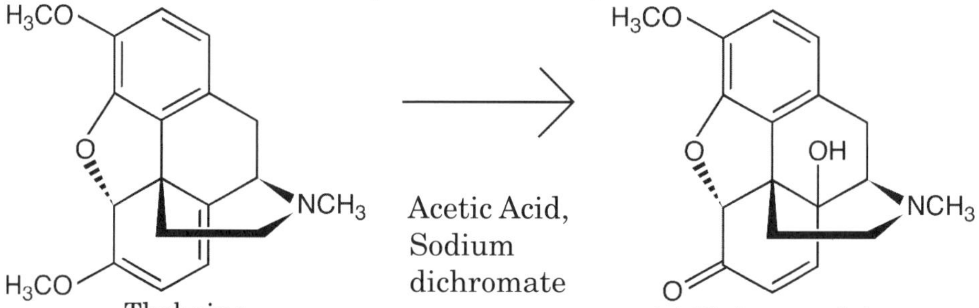

Thebaine (Paramorphine) → Acetic Acid, Sodium dichromate → 14-Hydroxycodeinone

by Firma E. Merk, Chemische Fabrik in Darmstadt
DE 411530 (1923)

20 Teile Kodein werden in 80 Teilen Wasser unter Zusatz von 25 Teilen Eisessig in Lösung gebracht und die abgekühlte Flüssigkeit mit einer Lösung Von 20 Teilen Natriumbichromat in 25 Teilen Wasser versetzt. Es entsteht ein öliger Niederschlag, der nach kurzem Erwärmen fest und kristallinisch wird. Das Reaktionsgemisch wird auf dem Wasserbade langsam unter ständigem Rühren auf 80° erwarmt, wobei sich der Niederschlag auflöst. Nunmehr unterbricht man das Erwämen; infolge einer Nachreaktion steigt die Temperatur bis etwa 90°.

Nach kurzem Stehen kühlt man stark ab und fällt die neugebildete Base durch Zusatz von überschüssiger Chromsaurelösung als Bichromat. Die aus dem Bichromat in üblicher Weise isolierte Base kristallisiert aus Alkohol in Blättchen vom Zersetzungspunkt 273° und zeigt die Eigenschaften des von Freund und Speye r beschriebenen Oxykodeinons.

Teile Kodeinon werden in 80 Teilen Wasser unter Zusatz von 25 Teilen Eisessig in Lösung gebracht und dann eine Lösung von 8 Teilen Natriumbichromat in 25 Teilen Wasser hinzugegeben. Der weitere Verlauf der Reaktion gestaltet sich, wie in Beispiel 1 angegeben. Man erhält eine Ausheute von 8 bis 10 Teilen Oxykodeinon.

Preparation of 14-Hydroxycodeinone from 8:14-dihydroxydihydrocodeinone

8:14-Dihydroxydihydrocodeinone → 14-Hydroxycodeinone

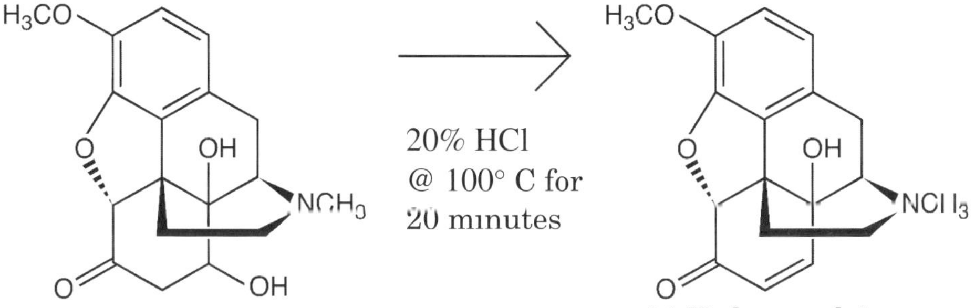

20% HCl
@ 100° C for
20 minutes

14-Hydroxycodeinone is prepared by heating 8:14-dihydroxydihydrocodeinone with 20% HCl for 20 minutes at 100° C.

References: Vieböck (1934) Ber. **67**, 197

Preparation of 8:14-dihydroxydihydrocodeinone from 8-(or 14-) Acetyl-8:14-dihydroxydihydrothebaine

8- (or 14-) Acetyl-8:14-dihydrothebaine → 8:14-Dihydroxydihydrocodeinone

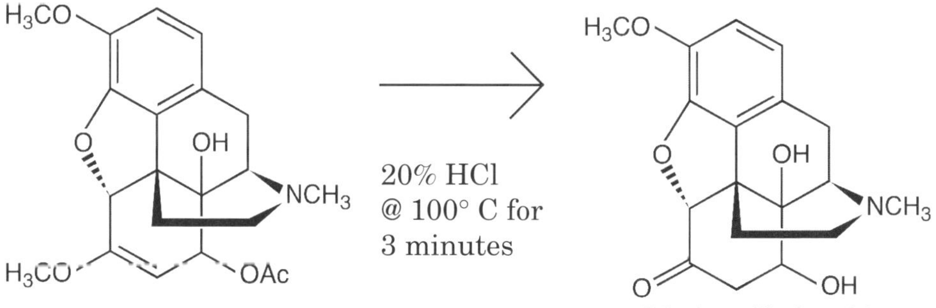

20% HCl
@ 100° C for
3 minutes

8:14-Dihydroxydihydrocodeinone is prepared by heating 8- (or 14-) acetyl-8:14-dihydroxydihydrothebaine with 20% HCl for 3 minutes at 100° C.

References: Vieböck (1934) Ber. **67**, 197

Preparation of 8-(or 14-) Acetyl-8:14-dihydroxydihydrothebaine from Thebaine

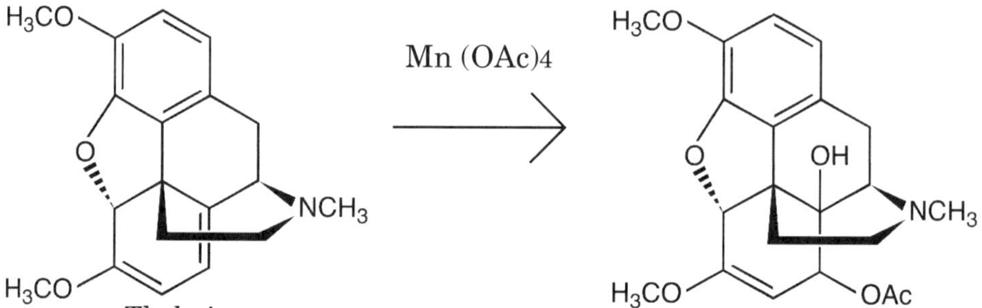

Mn (OAc)4

Thebaine
(Paramorphine)

8- (or 14-) Acetyl-8:14-dihydrothebaine

8- (or 14-) Acetyl-8:14-dihydrothebaine canbe produced from the oxidation of thebaine with manganic acetate.

References: Vieböck (1934) Ber. **67**, 197

ETORPHINE
Process of Purifying Oripavines

by William R. Hydro,
assignor to the United States of America
as represented by the Secretary of the Army
US 3,763,167

ABSTRACT OF THE DISCLOSURE

The process of purifying oripavines, tranquilizers for animals, comprisng the contacting highly colored oripavines with a liquid comprising an immiscible solvent and aqueous solution of sulfur containing compounds, separating the solvent phase with subsequent drying and recovering the oripavines.

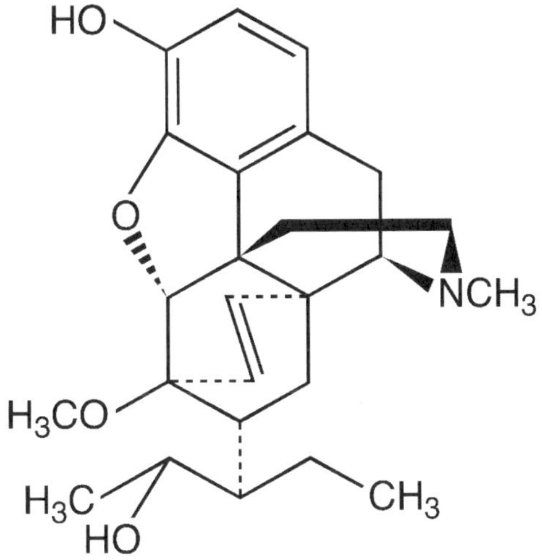

DEDICATORY CLAUSE

The invention described herein may be manufactured, used, and licensed by or for the Government for governmental purposes without the payment to me of any royalty thereon.

Etorphine

SPECIFICATION

This invention relates to a novel process for preparing orpavines in higher yields.

The object of this invention is to utilize sulfur containing compounds as the purification vehicle in preparing oripavines.

It is a further object of this invention to employ a less cumbersome purification process.

This invention relates to a novel purification process for 7-α(1-hydroxy-1, 4-dimethylpentyl)-6, 14-endoethenotetrahydrooripavine and 7-α(1-hydroxy-1-methylbutyl)-6, 14-endoethenotetrahydrooripavine.

These compounds have been reported in a series of papers by K. W. Bentley et al., J. Am. Chem. Society 89, (1967), pages 3267 et seq. K. W. Bentley et al. purified the oripavines utilizing refluxing conditions of aqueous 2-ethoxyethanol and activated charcoal treatment followed by the recrystallization in hot aqueous 2-ethoxyethanol.

The oripavines of Bentley et al. supra, have been employed as tranquilizers in gas propelled dart guns to subdue wild animals thus enabling their capture without harm and transport to a game reserve or for examination and care by a veterinary. In addition, the oripavines can be administered subcutaneously by a veterinary.

Pharmacological evaluation of 7-α(1-hydroxy-1, 4 -dimethylpentyl)-6, 14-endoethenotetrahydrooripavine and 7-α(1- hydroxy-1-methylbutyl)-6, 14-endoethenotetrahydrooripavine for potency was determined by administering intravenously various proportions (mg./kg.) of the compounds in mice using the method described in "The Search For and Selection of Toxic Chemical Agents for Weapons Systems," disclosed in the Edgewood Arsenal, Maryland Publication (CRDL SOP 70-3 May 6, 1965). LD50 is the lowest dose in milligrams of compound per kilogram of animal required to be lethal in 50% of the tested animals. MED50 is the minimum effective dose in milligrams of compound per kilogram of animal required to give any visible physiological effects (e.g. decreased locomotive activity, aimless wandering and glossy-eyed stare in 50% of the tested animals). The quotient of the ration LD50/MED50 described in Table 1 below in the margin of safety, that is, the higher numerical quotient, the greater the proportion of agent can be used before causing death and therefore a more effective tranquilizing agent.

TABLE I

	ED50	MED50	LD50/MED50
Compound:			
A	8.9	0.00075	12,000
B	20.0	0.00056	36,000

Note: A= 7-α(1-hydroxy-1, 4 -dimethylpentyl)-6, 14-endoethenotetrahydrooripavine;
B= 7-α(1-hydroxy-1-methylbutyl)-6, 14-endoethenotetrahydrooripavine

THE GENERAL PROCEDURE

Thebaine was reacted with methyl vinyl ketone forming 7-α-acetyl-6,14-endoethenotetrahydrothebaine, thevinone. Then the Grignard reaction of said thevinone with n-propylmagnesium iodide or isoamylmagnesium bromide (other alkylmagnesium halides can also be utillized if desired) gave the corresponding thebaines (a) 7-α(1-hydroxy-1-methylpentyl)-6, 14-endoethenotetrahydrothebaine and (b) 7-α(1-hydroxy-1, 4-dimethylpentyl) -6, 14-endoethenotetrahydrothebaine. The aforesaid compounds (a) and (b) were O-demethylated in the 3-position to the corresponding crude (c), 7-α(1-hydroxy-1-methylbutyl)-6, 14-endo-ethenotetrahydrooripavine and (d) 7-α(1-hydroxy-1, 4- dimethylpentyl)-6, 14-endoethenotetrahydrooripavine. The product (c) and (d) were extracted with ether. The ethereal extract was shaken at room temperature with an aqueous solution containing 0.5 to 4.0 g of a sulfur containing compound. The ether extract containing the decolorized product was evaporated giving rise to a solid which is dissolved in 2-ethoxyethanol at 60° C. or below, then adding water to effect precipitation of the final orpavines.

The purification step at room temperature is carried out in a solution compompsing 80-120 mL. of water and, 0.5 to 4.0 g. of a sulfur containing compound of an alkali metal, i.e. Na or X, salt of metabisulfite, bisulfite, sulfite, hydrosulfite or thiosulfate followed by recrystallization in 2-ethoxyethanol at a temperature of 60° C. or below. In this invention, it is critical for the purification procedure that ambient conditions are maintained during the step employing the aqueous solution comprising the sulfur containing compound and that the temperature of the 2-ethoxyethanol not rise above 60° C. in the recrystallization step in order to achieve the high yields.

EXAMPLE 1

(a) A solution comprising thebaine, paramorphine (141.7 g.) and 425 ml. methyl vinyl ketone was refluxed for about 1 hour. Excess ketone was removed by distillating for about 1 hour from a hot water bath followed by distillation at 150 mm. pressure. The hot reacted mixture, a dark brown colored syrup, was dissolved in hot methyl alcohol followed by rapid cooling giving rise to fine brown crystals. Recrystallization from methyl alcohol afforded fine white crystals, M.P. 114.5°-118° C. Infared analysis confirmed the proposed structure of 7-α-acetyl-6,14-endoethenotetrahydrothebaine.

Analysis.-Calcd. for $C_{23}H_{27}NO_4$, (percent): C, 72.42; H, 7.13; N, 3.67; O, 16.78. Found (percent): C, 72.1; H, 7.3; N, 3.6; O, 16.8.

(b) Magnesium (8.35 g.) was treated to remove grease by washing with ether and drying overnight in vacuo at 85° C. The magnesium was covered with sodium-dried ether, heated to reflux with vigorous stirring, followed by the addition of a solution of 58.5 g. of freshly distilled n-propyl iodide in 400 mL. of sodium dried ether over 1 hour period and refluxed an additional 40 minutes.

A filtered solution comprising 50.0 g. of 7-α-acetyl-6, 14-endoetheno-tetrahydrothebaine, from (a) supra in 250 mL. of sodium-dried benzene was added over a period of 20 minutes forming a reaction mixture which was refluxed for an additional 30 minutes. The reaction vessel was cooled to 0° C. and the reacted mixture, black, was decomposed with a solution comprising 22.4 g. of ammonium chloride in 75 mL. of water. The organic layer, upper, was removed leaving a paste-like residue which was washed three (3) times with 50 mL. portions of benzene and the combined said portions were washed three (3) times with water, dried over anhydrous magnesium sulfate, filtered and evaporation of the pale yellow portions in vacuo afforded 54.6 g. of white solid which was recrystallized ftom ethyl alcohol yielding 25.3 g. of white cystals, M.P. 173°-176° C. The infrared analysis confirmed the proposed structure of 7-α(1-hydroxy-1-methylbutyl)-6, 14-endoethenotetrahydro-thebaine.

Analysis.-Calcd. for $C_{26}H_{35}NO_4$ (percent): C, 73.38; H, 8.29, N, 3.29, O, 15.04. Found (percent): C, 73.5; H, 8.0; N, 3.3; O, 15.2

(c) In accordance with the procedure as outlined in (b) supra, with the exception of substituting 52.0 g. of freshly distilled isoamyl bromide for the n-propyl iodide 43.8 g. crude end-product was obtained which was recrystallized 4 times from ethyl alcohol giving rise to fine white crystals, M.P. 126°-127° C. The infrared analysis confirmed the proposed structure of 7-α(1-hydroxy-1, 4-dimethylpentyl)-6, 14-endoethenotetra-hydrothebaine.

Analysis.-Clcd. for $C_{28}H_{39}NO_4$ (percent): C, 74.14; H, 8.67; N, 3.09; O, 14.11. Found (percent): C, 74.2; H, 8.2, N, 3.2; O, 14.1.

EXAMPLE 2

(a) A stirring solution comprising bubbling a stream of nitrogen through 300 mL. of diethylene glycol in a container was heated to and discontinued at 55° C., adding 120 g. of potassium hydroxide forming a mixture which was heated to 200° C., adding 16.0 g. of 7-α(1-hydroxy-1, 4-dimethylpentyl)-6, 14-endoethenotetrahydrothebaine, Example 1(c), then fitting the container with a condenser and heating to 203°-205° C. for about 1.25 hours resulting in O-demethylation in the 3-position which was considered complete when a one mL. sample of the reacted mixture, dark reddish-brown colored solution, diluted with 10 mL. of water producing a clear, homogeneous solution. The reacted mixture was cooled to 100° C., diluted with water to five times its volume and filtering through diatomaceaus earth, Celite, producing a clarified dark reddish-brown solution, adding a precipitating soution comprising 125.0 g of ammonium chloride in 375 mL. water forming the insoluble desired product which was extracted once in 500 mL. diethylether, and if desired the ether extract can be further treated with water, the diethylether extract, dark reddish-brown solution, was shaken with a solution comprising 0.5 to 4.0 g. sodium metabisulfite in 100 mL. of water for about 3-6 minutes with the ethereal phase converting to a very pale yellow color. The ethereal phase was washed with water, separated, dried over anhydrous magnesium sulfate, filtered, and evaporated in vacuo to give 12.4 g. (80.0%) of a pale yellow solid, M.P. 200°-202° C. Three recrystallizations were carried out with the yellow solid the steps comprising the adding 90-110 mL. of the 2-ethoxyethanol warmed to 60° C. or lower sufficient to dissolve the yellow solid, then adding about 35 to 40 mL. of water to the ethanol solution for the formation of pale yellow crystals 9.5 g. (61.3%), M.P. 200°-204° C. The infrared analysis confirmed the proposed structure of 7-α(1-hydroxy-1, 4-dimethylpentyl)-6, 14-endoethenotetrahydrooripavine

Analysis.-Calcd. for $C_{27}C_{37}NO_4$ (percent): C, 73.77; H, 8.49; N, 3.19; O, 14.56. Found (percent): C, 73.9; H, 8.4; N, 3.1; O 14.5.

(b) The procedure in (a) was repeated with the substitution of sodium bisulfite, sodium hydrosulfite, sodium sulfite or sodium thiosulfate for the corresponding metabisulfate with the decolorization of the ethereal solution and solid as described in Table 1.

TABLE 1.

COLOR OF ETHER EXTRACT CONTAINING COMPOUND AFTER TREATMENT

Sulfur compound	Ethereal solution	Solid
Sodium metabisulfite	Very pale yellow	Pale yellow.
Sodium bisulfite	Very pale yellow	Pale yellow.
Sodium hydrosulfite	Colorless	Snow white.
Sodium sulfite	Colorless	Snow white.
Sodium thiosulfite	Dark yellow	Light yellow.

EXAMPLE 3

(a) The procedure in Example 2 was followed with substituting 7-α(1-hydroxy-1-methylbutyl)-6, 14-endoethenotetrahydrothebaine, Example l(b), for the corresponding 7-α(1-hydroxy-1, 4-dimethylpentyl)-

6, 14-endoethenotetrahydrothebaine. After the precipitation step with the aqueous ammonium chloride solution and the separated diethylether extract, the etheral extract, reddish-brown color, was shaken for 3-6 minutes with a solution comprising 3.2 g. of sodium metabisulfite in 100 mL. of water with the ethereal phase converting to a pale yellow color. The latter ethereal phase was also treated as in Example 2. The recrystallization from aqueous 2-ethoxyethanol yield 3.8 g. (24.6%) of white crystals, M.P. 214°-217° C. The infrared analysis confirmed the proposed structure of 7-α(1-hydroxy-1-methylbutyl)-6, 14-endoetheno-tetrahydrooripavine.

Analysis.-Calcd. for $C_{25}H_{33}NO_4$ (percent): C, 72.96; H, 8.08; O, 15.15. Found (percent): C, 72.8; H, 8.0; O, 15.6.

(b) The procedure in (a) was repeated with the substitution of sodium bisulfite, sodium hydrosulfite, sodium sulfite or sodium thiosulfate for the corresponding metabisulfite with the decolorization of the ethereal solution.

Example 4, below, illustrates the purification procedure described in the series of paper by K. W. Bentley et al., J. Am. Chem. Soc., Vol. 89 (1967), page 3267 et al.

EXAMPLE 4

Employing the general procedure, that is, proportions, reactants and conditions as set forth in above Example 2, up to and including the diethylether extract, dark reddish-brown extract from the insoluble product precipitated by the aqueous ammonium chloride step, was washed with water dried over anhydrous magnesium sulfate and evaporation of the ether leaving a very dark brown solid. Refluxing, about 30 minutes, a solution comprising the latter dark brown solid, 2-ethoxyethanol and activated charcoal, filtering, washing the charcoal cake with boiling temperature (135° C.) 2-ethoxyethanol, combining and washings, and then adding water to the boiling 2-ethoxyethanol washings to effect crystallization and yielding 9.4 g. (60%) of a dark brown solid and recrystallization of the later brown solid from refluxing activated charcoal and 2-ethoxyethanol and precipitation upon the water addition yielding 4.2 g. (27.1%, a medium brown colored solid, M.P. about 198°-202° C., 7-α(1-hydroxy-1, 4-dimethylpentyl)-6, 14-endoethenotetrahydro-oripavine.

References :US 3,433,791; US 3,442,900; US 3,464,992; US 3,464,994; US 3,474,101; US 3,562,279 Canada 487,263

THEBAINE

Discovery and chemical properties

By Lyndon F. Small and Robert E. Lutz

Thebaine was discovered in 1835 by Pelletier and Thiboumery (1) (2) who believed it to be an isomer of morphine, and gave it the name "Paramorphine." The name thebaine was introduced by Couerbe (3) (4) (*cf.* Kane (5)). The correct composition of the base, corresponding to the formula $C_{19}H_{21}O_3N$ was first determined by Anderson (6) (7), whose analyses were later confirmed by those of Hesse (8) and Beckett and Wright (9).

The separation of thebaine from opium extract usually takes place after morphine, codeine, narcotine, and papaverine have been removed. The alcoholic mother liquor from which narcotine and papaverine have crystallized is concentrated and taken up in acetic acid. Basic lead acetate is added to alkaline reaction, whereby narcotine and resinous materials are precipitated; the filtrate is freed from lead with sulphuric acid, and the crude thebaine precipitated with ammonia (7).

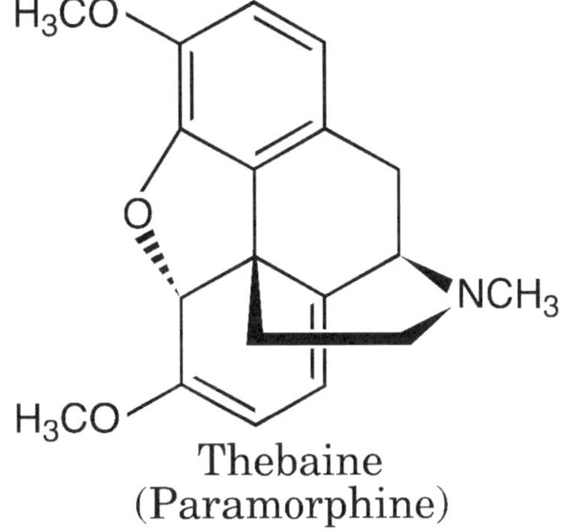

Thebaine (Paramorphine)

Hesse (8) treated the mother liquors from morphine-codeine separation with excess of alkali, and dissolved the heavy precipitate in dilute acetic acid; narcotine and most of the other alkaloids remain undissolved. By addition of tartaric acid to the acetic acid solution, the thebaine was precipitated as the sparingly soluble acid tartrate. Plugge's (10) method makes use of thebaine salicylate. A review of these separations, as well as the description of a new method, which depends upon the differences in basicity of the opium alkaloids, is given in the discussion by Kanewskaja (11); see also Ishikawa (12). Gulland and Robinson (13) have observed cryptopine as an impurity in commercial thebaine.

Source: Chemistry of the Opium Alkaloids (1932)

Thebaine occurs chiefly in *Papaver somniferum*, where it appears to be the last alkaloid formed by the growing plant (14). The amounts found in opium vary from 0.2% to 0.3% (15) to 0.8% (16) or 1%. Gadamer and Klee (17) (18) observed that thebaine is present in *Papaver orientale* during the period of growth, but appears to be changed to the isomer, isothebaine, as the plant withers. Isothebaine is an isoquinoline derivative of the apomorphine type.

Thebaine crystallizes from alcohol in shining leaflets, from dilute alcohol in rectangular plates (6), often associated in tufts more or less radiating from a center (Deane and Brady (19), illustration). Thebaine melted and cooled forms highly refracting biaxial crystals; at low temperatures it crystallizes in two kinds of spherulites (20). Thebaine crystallized from solvents has the density 1.305 (1.282) (21), the refractive indices 1.63 and 1.69 (14), and melts at 193° (8).

Blyth (22) observed sublimation of thebaine at 135° under atmospheric pressure in needlelike crystals; at higher temperatures, cubes and prisms were formed. Sublimation and micro sublimation in vacuum are described by Kempf (23) and Heiduschka (24). Vacuum sublimed thebaine melts at 192.5° (196.2° corr.) (23).

The thermochemistry of thebaine has been studied by Leroy (25) (26) who found the heat of combustion at constant volume to be 2439.9 Cal., at constant pressure 2441.8 Cal.; this is in good agreement with the values expected of a dimethyl ether of morphine less two hydrogen atoms.

The absorption spectrum of thebaine was investigated by Hartley (27) and Kitasato (28), the ultraviolet spectrum by Steiner (29) .

Thebaine is levorotatory; in 97% alcohol, Hesse (30) found $[\alpha]^{15}_{D}$= -218.64° (p=2). The rotatory power is affected but little by change in concentration, but decreases rapidly with rise in temperature. In chloroform, $[\alpha]^{22.5}_{D}$= -229.5° (p=5). Thebaine hydrochloride in aqueous solution gives the value $[\alpha]^{15}_{D}$= -163.66° (p = 2).

Thebaine is a strong monoacid base, whose salts with strong acids are stable and neutral in reaction. An aqueous suspension of the base turns litmus blue (8), or helianthin to yellow; the aqueous suspension does not affect phenolphthalein, but addition of water to alcoholic thebaine solution containing phenolphthalein gives a rose color (26).

Thebaine is soluble in alcohol, ether, benzene, chloroform (2) (7) (8), aniline, pyridine, or piperidine (31), practically insoluble in water, ammonia, or alkalies (6). One part of thebaine dissolves in 140 parts of ether (10°) (8) in 10 parts of cold alcohol (2), in 59 parts of amyl alcohol (32), 19 parts of benzene (32), 18 parts of chloroform, or 11.1 parts of pyridine (20° to 25°) (33) ; it is insoluble in petroleum ether (34).

The following reactions have been proposed for the identification or detection of thebaine :

Thebaine color and precipitation tests

Reagent	Reaction	Observer
Conc. H_2SO_4	Red, becoming yellow	Hesse (8); Reichard (35).
Conc. H_2SO_4 containing HNO_3.	Red, yellow in thin layers	Couerbe (3).
Conc. HNO_3	Colorless, 10 min. yellow, 60 min. dark yellow	Reichard (35).
Conc. HCl	Yellow to greenish	Do. (35).
Marquis' reagent	Red	Pfister (36).
Fröhde's reagent	do.	Do. (36).
Mandelin's reagent	do.	Do. (36).
2% aqueous furfurol	Transient red	Do. (36).
Magnol (basic magnesium hypochlorite)	Alkaloid in 3 c. c. acetic acid cont. 0.2% magnol, and layered onto conc. H_2SO_4, forms a red ring; after 24 hours the test shows a layer of the color Scharlach G over a yellow zone over a broad Scharlach G ring over a yellow layer.	David (37).
$ZnCl_2$ in dil. HCl	Reagent is added to the dry hydrochloride, and evaporated on porcelain to dryness on the water bath: Yellow.	Jorissen (38); Czumpelitz (39).
K_2CrO_4	Precip. scales of $B_2H_2CrO_4$	Plugge (40) (41).
$K_2Cr_2O_7$	Precip. needles of $B_2H_2Cr_2O_7$	Plugge (40).
$K_3Fe(CN)_6$ or $K_4Fe(CN)_6$.	Precip. of hydroferri- or hydroferro-cyanide	Plugge (40) (41).
PbO_2, H_2SO_4	Thebaine is boiled with PbO_2 in acetic acid, filtered, and the filtrate treated with excess conc. H_2SO_4: filtrate is orange-red, turning golden-yellow when the H_2SO_4 is added.	Deér (42).
Iodine chloride	Yellow precip. which gives off iodine vapor on boiling in water.	Dittmar (43).
$SbCl_3$	Weak blue color, which disappears on warming	Smith (44).

The sensitivity of thebaine to a large number of precipitants is given by Kerbosch (14). Wagenaar (45) claims that precipitation as the free base is more delicate than as the salicylate, acid tartrate, or periodide.

Bibliography (Thebaine)

(1) Pelletier, J. Pharm. (2) **21**, 555 (1835); Compt. rend. **1**, 11 (1835).
(2) Pelletier, Ann. **16**, 38 (1835).
(3) Couerbe, Ann. chim. phys. (2) **59**, 136 (1835).
(4) Couerbe, Ann. **17**, 166 (1836).
(5) Kane, Ann. **19**, 7 (1836).
(6) Anderson, J. prakt. Chem. **57**, 358 (1852).
(7) Anderson, Ann. **86**, 179 (1853).
(8) Hesse, Ann. **153**, 47 (1870).
(9) Beckett and Wright, J. Chem. Soc. **29**, 652 (1876).
(10) Plugge, Rec. trav. chim. **6**, 157 (1887).
(11) Kanewskaja, J. prakt. Chem. (2) **108**, 247 (1924).
(12) Ishikawa and Maruta, Bull. Hyg. Research Inst. (Japan) **35**, 19 (1929).
(13) Gulland and Robinson, J. Chem. Soc. **123**, 1007 (1923).
(14) Kerbosch, Arch. Pharm. **248,** 536 (1910).
(15) Dragendorff, Die Heilpflanzen, p. 249, (Enke, Stuttgart, 1898).

(16) Machiguchi, J. Pharm. Soc. Japan **529**, 185 (1926); Chem. Abst. **20**, 2725 (1926).
(17) Gadamer and Klee, Z. angew, Chem. **26**, 625 (1913).
(18) Klee, Arch. Pharm. **252**, 211 (1914).
(19) Deane and Brady, J. Chem. Soc. **18**, 34 (1865).
(20) Gaubert, Compt. rend. **156**, 1161 (1913).
(21) Schröder, Ber. **13**, 1075 (1880).
(22) Blyth, J. Chem. Soc. **33**, 313 (1878).
(23) Kempf, J. prakt. Chem. (2) **78**, 201 (1908).
(24) Heiduschka and Meisner, Arch. Pharm. **261**, 102 (1923).
(25) Leroy, Compt. rend. 129, 220 (1899).
(26) Leroy, Ann. chim. phys. (7) 21, 87 (1900).
(27) Hartley, Phil. Trans. Roy. Soc. London **176**, 471 (1885).
(28) Kitasato, Acta Phytochim. **3**, 175-258 (1927); Chem. Abst. **22**, 1779 (1928).
(29) Steiner, Bull. soc. chim. biol. **6**, 231 (1924).
(30) Hesse, Ann. **176**, 189 (1875).
(31) Merck's Index, Merck and Co., **1930**, 4th ed.
(32) Kubly, Jahresber. Fortschr. Chem. **1866**, 823.
(33) Dehn, J. Am. Chem. Soc. **39**, 1399 (1917).
(34) Taylor, Allen's Comm'l. Organ. Anal. **6**, 363 (1912).
(35) Reichard, Pharm. Zentralhalle, **47**, 623 (1906).
(36) Pfister, Chem. Ztg. **32**, 1494 (1908).
(37) David, Pharm. Ztg. **70**, 969 (1925).
(38) Jorissen, Z. anal. Chem. **19**, 357 (1880).
(39) Czumpelitz, Arch. Pharm. (3) **19**, 63 (1881); Pharm. Post **14**, 47 (1881).
(40) Plugge, Arch. Pharm. (3) **25**, 793 (1887).
(41) Plugge, Rec. trav. chim. **6**, 209 (1887).
(42) Deér, Pharm. Monatsh. **6**, 117 (1925).
(43) Dittmar, Ber. **18**, 1612 (1885).
(44) Smith, Ber. **12**, 1420 (1879); Chem.News **40**, 26 (1879).
(45) Wagenaar, Pharm. Weekblad 64, 472 (1927).

Pharmacology of Thebaine

Thebaine is not a narcotic, but in its effects on the system is closely analogous to strychnine, producing tetanic spasms in a dose of 60 mg. (E. Fullerton Cook and Eric W. Martin (1948))

by Hugo Krueger, Nathan B. Eddy and Margaret Sumwalt

Nervous System and Skeletal Muscle: Although thebaine may be slightly depressant and analgesic, its predominant tendency without doubt is excitant, often convulsant. Man is the only animal studied in which this type of effect is not recorded; he probably was spared the giving of large enough doses.

Central Nervous System: Narcotic Effect Man: Drowsiness was seen with 20-97 mg. T, sc (Harley, 1871). An hypnotic effect of at least some slight degree was seen in 19 out of 25 cases (Fronmüller, 1869). A soporific effect was looked for vainly (Rabuteau, 1872); in children with 500 mg. T, o (Bouchut, 1872).

Analgesia Man: An analgesic effect was seen (Rabuteau, 1872); an "anodyne effect" upon a case of sciatica was seen (Harley, 1871). Analgesia was looked for vainly, and a very slight hyperalgesia was seen with 10 mg. T, sc (Macht, Herman and Levy, 1915, 1916). Analgesia was looked for vainly in children with 500 mg. T, o (Bouchut, 1872). Slight local analgesia was seen in hand, lips, or tongue, with direct application of 5 percent solution (Macht, Johnson and Bollinger, 1916a).

Effect on the Pupil Man: Myosis was seen with 1 drop of 2.5 percent (Bono, 1979).

Metabolism: The body temperature increases in most animals with sufficient doses of thebaine.

Man: The glycosuria due to epinephrine was not affected with thebaine (Lewysohn, 1914). The cicatrization of ulcerated neoplastic growths of skin was not affected with thebaine applied locally, the author attributing this failure to the lack of hyperglycemic effect of thebaine (Gomès Da Costa, 1932). The urinary output of urea increased from a normal of 60 mg. per 100 g. of body weight per 24 hours to 76 mg. with 10 mg. T, sc (Fubini, 1880, 1888) .

Emesis Man: Nausea or vomiting was seen in 3 out of 25 cases (Fronmüller, 1869). Emesis was looked for vainly in a single patient with 20-100 mg. T, sc (Harley, 1871).

References

Bono. 1886 Le chlorhydrate de thebaine dans quelques affections du nerf optique. Nouv. remédes, **2**, 120. Ab.: J. Am. M. Ass., **6**, 376.

Bouchut, E. 1872 Recherches thérapeutiques sur les substances et sur les alcaloides tirés de l'opium tels que la morphine, la codéine, la narcéine, la thébaine, la narcotine, la papavérine, la méconine, l'acide opianique. Bull. gén. de thérap., **82**, 289-30l, 337-347. Compt. rend. Acad. d. sc., **74**, 1289-1290.

Fubini, S. 1880 Ueber den Einfluss der wichtigsten Opium Alcaloide auf die Menge des vom Menschen in 24 Stunden ausgeschiedenen Harnstoffs. Centralbl. f. d. med. Wissensch., **18**, 773.

Fubini, S. 1888 Uber den Einfluss einiger Opium-Alkaloide auf die Menge des durch die Nieren ausgeschiedenen Harnstoffes. Untersuch. z. Naturl. d. Mensch. u. d. Thiere, **13**, 3.

Fronmüller. 1869 Klinische Studien über die schlafmachende Wirkung der narkotischen Arzneimittel. Eriangen.

Gomés Da Costa, S. F. 1932 L'action de quelques substances hypoglycémiantes sur les cancers ulcérés de la peau. Bull. de l'Ass. franc. p. l'étude du cancer, **21**, 700.

Harley, John. l871 On the action and use of the opium alkaloids cryptopia and thebaia. St. Thomas's Hosp. Rep., **2**, n.s., 123.

Lewysohn, Georg. 1914 Uber die Hemmungswirkung der Opiumalkaloide auf experimentell erzeugte Glykosurien. Dissertation. Breslau. Ab.: Jahresb. ü. d. Leistung . . . d. ges. Med., **1**, 185.

Macht, David I., Herman, N. B. and Levy, Charles S. 1915 A quantitative study of cutaneous analgesia produced by various opium alkaloids. Proc. Nat. Acad. Sc., **1**, 582.

Macht, David I., Herman, N. B., and Levy, Charles S. 1916 A quantitative study of the analgesia produced by opium alkaloids, individually and in combination with each other, in normal man. J. Pharmacol. & Exper. Therap., **8**, 1. Ed.: J. Am. M. Ass., **66**, 1389.

Macht, David I., Johnson, S. L., and Bollinger, H. J. 1916a On the peripheral action of the opium alkaloids. Effect on the sensory nerve terrninals. J. Pharmacol. & Exper. Therap., **8**, 451.

Rabuteau. 1872 Recherches sur les propriétés physiologiques et thérapeutiques de divers principes immédiats de l'opium. Gaz. hebd. de méd., **9**, 2.s., 264-268. 295-298. Monit. scient., **14**, 578-590. Ab.: Am. J. Pharm., **45**, 76, 1873; Am. J. M. Sc., **65**, 241, 1873.

The Dependence Potential of Thebaine

United Nations: Report of a WHO Advisory Group*
Creation Date: 1980/01/01

Introduction

This study was initiated by WHO when concern was expressed by the UN Commission on Narcotic Drugs about the intention to utilize, instead of *Papaver somniferum*, the poppy species *Papaver bracteatum* with its main constituent thebaine as raw material for the manufacture of opioid agonists, especially codeine and antagonists (1). The subject had temporarily aroused considerable concern. The increasing world-wide legitimate demand for codeine would have had to be met by either the increased production of alkaloids from *Papaver somniferum* with the ensuing increased risk of its diversion into illicit channels or, preferably, the cultivation of the species *bracteatum*, instead of *somniferum*, provided that thebaine had no, or at least appreciable lower, dependence and abuse potential than the opium alkaloids, morphine and codeine.

The present report addresses itself to the question of the pharmacological profile of thebaine with particular reference to its dependence potential. No documented information was available on the occurrence of abuse of thebaine or *Papaver bracteatum*.

With financial support from the United Nations Fund for Drug Abuse Control (project No. ACB-90117) a literature review and a study of the dependence potential of thebaine was carried out by WHO, Division of Mental Health, with the assistance of a Group of Advisors, several of whom contributed ad hoc experimental work. *

Data available prior to this study

Chemistry

Thebaine is one of the phenanthrene alkaloids contained in the opium poppy and constitutes usually about 0.3 to 1.5 per cent of opium, but figures up to 6 per cent have been reported. Thebaine is the major alkaloid in Papaver bracteatum and can readily be extracted from the capsules and roots of that plant.

Thebaine is dehydromorphine 3,6-dimethyl ether. Its hydrochloride salt is sparingly soluble in water up to about 8 w/v%. Thebaine can be converted into drugs of abuse, such as oxycodone and hydrocodone. Furthermore, a series of thebaine derivatives with very high analgesic potency, such as acetorphine and etorphine (known as "Bentley compounds") has been developed. However, there are considerable problems in connexion with the conversion of thebaine into these substances, especially into the Bentley compounds.

An Expert Group was convened by the United Nations Narcotics Laboratory in January 1976 to consider the feasibility of the conversion of thebaine into drugs of abuse and the potential of abuse (2). Having evaluated the problems associated with the possible use of thebaine in the production of such drugs, the Expert Group considered that these are not such that they should prejudice the manufacture of thebaine and its use as a commercial source of therapeutically useful substances.

General pharmacology Most of the facts were obtained from two extensive reviews (3, 4) Unless otherwise indicated.

Central nervous system. The predominant effect of thebaine is central nervous system stimulation. In the mouse, rabbit, cat and dog, hyper-irritability and increase in motor activity as well as reflex excitability were observed at doses around 2-10 mg/kg s.c. or i.m. The Straub-tail reaction was noted only occasionally. In rabbits, thebaine antagonized the effects of phenobarbital and potentiated those of caffeine.

Convulsions were observed in almost all species of animals including the skate, frog, sparrow, pigeon, mouse, guinea pig, rabbit, cat and dog. In the rhesus monkey, transient tremors, restlessness, hyper-irritability and convulsions were observed (5). The convulsive doses were around 20 mg/kg s.c. in mice, rabbits, cats, dogs and rhesus monkeys.

Naloxone, a known morphine-antagonist, antagonized the convulsions induced by thebaine in mice (convulsive dose 7.4 mg/kg i.v.). However, it was 10 times less effective against thebaine than it was against heroin. In mice, treated with 30 mg/kg of thebaine s.c., neither sotalol nor propanolol changed the survival rate; propanolol (25 mg/kg s.c.) prevented the tonic phase of the convulsions, but did not prevent death.

The respiratory effect of the drug was usually observed to be stimulatory in mice, rabbits, cats and dogs. In rabbits, thebaine in doses of 2 mg/kg antagonized the respiratory inhibition caused by 5 mg/kg of morphine. Mixtures of narcotine (15 mg/kg i.v.)and thebaine (1 mg/kg i.v.) strongly stimulated respiration.

The analgesic effect varied, depending on the investigator, method applied and animal species. While positive effects were reported for mice and cats, some reports were negative for mice and dogs. A "narcotic" effect, as judged by the over-all depressive manifestation including drowsiness was not observed in the mouse, guinea pig, rabbit, cat or dog.

Electrophysiologically, the spasmolytic effect of thebaine was different from that of morphine and codeine, but similar to that of strychnine.

Cardiovascular system. Decreased blood pressure and heart rate in the dog were reported in several studies. In one study with anaesthetized dogs, a fall in blood pressure, continuing for 1-3 hours was reported.

Gastro-intestinal system. Many studies indicated an increase in the tone and activity of the intestine in situ by thebaine. In the isolated intestine of the guinea pig, however, the tone diminished and peristalsis was inhibited. In anaesthetized rats, thebaine had no effect on the central vagal stimulation of pancreatic secretion induced by 2-deoxy-D-glucose in doses up to 17 mg/kg s.c. Inhibition of this stimulation has been suggested to be specific for morphine agonists.

Biochemical pharmacology

Thebaine caused a slight decrease in heart and brain catecholamine levels. It had an inhibitory effect on human, guinea pig and horse cholinesterase, as well as on human procain-esterase; neither lactic and citric acid, nor glucose dehydrogenases were inhibited.

Toxicity

Thebaine is far more toxic than morphine. The LD 50 in mice is 31 mg/kg s.c. and 20 mg/kg i.p.; other authors have reported an intraperitoneal LD 50 of 42 mg/kg in mice (7). In rabbits, the intravenous LD 50 is 3-4 mg/kg and is dependent on the age of the animals (7). In the dog the lethal doses are reported to be 10-30 mg/kg s.c. and 5-7 mg/kg i.v. (3). In chicken embryo, thebaine has been reported to induce pseudo-hyperfeminization.

Tolerance and dependence

The only documented indication for tolerance was the report that in anaesthetized dogs, a single dose of thebaine decreased the blood pressure for 1-3 hours; after that, it did not change significantly with additional doses of thebaine, nor with morphine (3). However, this may be more indicative of tachyphylaxis than of tolerance.

The physical dependence potential of thebaine had not been systematically investigated, but was believed to be non-existent until it was first reported at the 5th International Congress of Pharmacology in San Francisco in 1972. Rhesus monkeys manifest severe withdrawal signs upon abrupt withdrawal following intravenous self-administration of thebaine at a daily dose level of 10-30 mg/kg for one month. However, thebaine not only failed to suppress the morphine withdrawal signs in monkeys physically dependent on morphine, but served to precipitate the signs as well (5). Such seemingly contradictory effects are known with many of the partial antagonists.

The reinforcing effect of thebaine was not evident in the cross self-administration experiments, but was clearly demonstrated in a continuous intravenous self-administration experiment (5). The average daily doses ingested were 20-35 mg/kg at a unit dose of 1 mg/kg/injection. During the active self-administration period, no marked drug effects were observed.

Metabolic studies

The metabolism of thebaine in rats has been studied by Misran et al. (8, 9). In the urine from rats treated with thebaine at a single subcutaneous dose of 5 mg/kg, several metabolites, though only in residual amounts, were found by thin-layer chromatography. The possibility that these metabolites were codeinone, codeine, morphine and

14-hydroxycodeinone was suggested. The investigators discussed the possible cause of the difference in the dependence potential of thebaine between the rat and the rhesus monkey and attributed it to different metabolic pathways of thebaine.

Data collected in this study

General pharmacology

Studies on isolated organ preparations. The morphine-like character of the guinea pig ileum and the mouse vas deferens by Kosterlitz (10). In the former preparation the maximum inhibiting potency of thebaine was 0.32 ± 0.07 per cent of that of morphine, was much slower in onset, and only partially reversed by naloxone. A similar profile was obtained with the mouse vas deferens preparation. The very weak morphine-like action of thebaine and its incomplete reversal by naloxone as shown in these tests permit the interpretation that these are not specific morphine-like effects.

Analgesic tests in mice. Aceto et al. (11) reported that thebaine was inactive as an analgesic in the tail-flick and phenylquinone abdominal stretching tests. It was also inactive as an antagonist of morphine in the tail-flick test. Thebaine was active in the hot place (ED 50=8.2 mg/kg s.c.) and Nilsen (ED 50=4.4 mg/kg s.c.) tests. However, doses in the higher range of the dose responses curves produced convulsions.

Gross behavioural observation of acute effects of thebaine in rhesus monkeys. In a preliminary test for a tolerance study, Yanagita and Miyasato (12) studied the effects of single intravenous injections of thebaine to rhesus monkeys. The results were: no effect at 1.0 mg/kg; tremor at 2.0 mg/kg; and convulsions and drowsiness at 4.0 mg/kg. The convulsions occurred a few minutes after the injection, but drowsiness followed much later, becoming prominent about 2 hours after administration and continuing for another 2 hours. This delayed onset of the depressant effect may be attributed to the metabolic breakdown of thebaine.

Behavioural pharmacology

Operant behavioural effects of thebaine in rats. Takada et al. (13) studied the operant behavioural effects of thebaine, pentazocine and codeine in rats using FR 30 and DRL 20 seconds schedules with food reinforcement. At subcutaneous doses of up to 16 mg/kg, thebaine did not exert much influence on responding generating by the FR 30 schedule, but did depress the responding at 64 mg/kg. In the DRL experiment, thebaine increased the number of responses at 16 mg/kg and shortened the modal inter-response time at 4 mg/kg but not at 16 mg/kg. Since 64 mg/kg is a near-lethal dose, the effect observed in the FR experiment may be unspecific. In contrast, a mild stimulatory effect by the drug was observed in the DRL experiment. In these experiments the order of potencies was pentazocine-codeine-thebaine.

Effect of thebaine on food-reinforced responding in rhesus monkeys. Hartel et al. (14) studied the effects of thebaine on food-reinforced responding rhesus monkeys, and their modification by nalaxone. A chain DRO 30 seconds FR 30 schedule was used. Saline as well as 0.32 and1.0 mg/kg thebaine had no effect on the response rates during the FR component of the schedule while 3.2 mg/kg of thebaine reduced them. Naloxone had no influence on the above results. It was concluded that naloxone does not antagonize the effects of thebaine on operant responding for food.

Tolerance

In an attempt to produce tolerance to the convulsant effect of thebaine in rhesus monkeys, Yanagita and Miyasato (12) repeatedly administered 2 mg/kg of thebaine 6 to 24 times daily for 6 weeks or longer to 4 monkeys by programmed injection through intravenous in-swelling catheters. Every two weeks the monkeys were challenged with 4 mg/kg of thebaine which is the convulsant dose. No evidence for the development of tolerance to the convulsant effect of thebaine was obtained.

Physical dependence studies in dogs. Gilbert and Martin (16) studied the physical dependence potential of thebaine in chronic spinal dogs. In the first experiment, thebaine or naloxone were given to morphine dependent and non-dependent dogs. Thebaine did not precipitate morphine withdrawal signs. In the second experiment, dogs were chronically treated with thebaine or morphine, and challenged with naloxone or naltrexone. Thebaine was administered intravenously, initially at 1 mg/kg/day and finally at 22.5 mg/kg/day divided over 24 injections.

Naltrexone produced very mild withdrawal signs in the thebaine-treated animals. Thus, unlike the findings reported for the rhesus monkey, in the dog the physical dependence potential of thebaine was found to be very low and its antagonistic action lacking.

Substitution studies in morphine dependent monkeys. Aceto et al. (11) and Swaine et al. (17) investigated the ability of thebaine to substitute for morphine in physically dependent rhesus monkeys. Subcutaneous doses up to 9.6 mg/kg failed to support physical dependence on morphine. This confirms the previous report by Yanagita (5).

Development of physical dependence on thebaine by subcutaneous administration in rhesus monkeys. Yanagita et al. (18) studied the physical dependence potential of thebaine in rhesus monkeys by subcutaneous injections of the drug at doses of 3 mg/kg every six hours for 31 days. In confirmation of a previous study (5) with intravenous self-administration, definite withdrawal signs were observed in the monkeys upon abrupt withdrawal of thebaine and also following the administration of naloxone.

Development of physical dependence on thebaine by intravenous self-administration in rhesus monkeys. In the course of a continued intravenous self-administration experiment with thebaine, Hartel et al. (14) attempted to precipitate withdrawal signs by administering naloxone at 1.0 mg/kg to three monkeys. The monkey which ingested thebaine at the highest daily close level (about 30 mg/kg/day) manifested severe withdrawal signs including retching, acute sensitivity to abdominal pressure and violent thrashing about in her cage. The animal was found dead the next morning, clearly not due to convulsions or thebaine overdose. However, the two remaining monkeys did not manifest any withdrawal signs following naloxone injection.

Reinforcing effect

Experiment of cross and continuous self-administration of thebaine in rhesus monkeys. Hartel et al. (14) conducted experiments with both cross and continuous intravenous self-administration of thebaine in rhesus monkeys. In the cross self-administration experiments saline or thebaine in unit doses ranging from 0.0003 to 1.0 mg/kg/infusion were substituted for codeine, but little, if any, reinforcing effect was demonstrated with thebaine. In the continuous self-administration experiment, an increase in the injection rate was observed in three out of four monkeys when they were allowed to take thebaine instead of saline. When each response was followed by the injection of 1.0 mg/kg of thebaine, the animals self-administered an average of 15-32 mg/kg/day. When the number of responses required for each injection was increased to 10 the number of injections earned decreased in two of the animals but increased in the third. In all instances, however, the lever-press responding generated by thebaine was higher than that obtained with saline. This definitely demonstrates that thebaine can serve as a reinforcer in the rhesus monkey.

Progressive ratio experiment in rhesus monkeys. Yanagita and Miyasato (19) assessed the reinforcing intensity of thebaine by the progressive ratio technique in rhesus monkeys. In this experiment, the ratio of lever-presses to injections gradually increased by a factor of 4/2 after each injection. When the number of lever-presses for the last 48 hours diminished to less than 50 per cent of the number required for the next injection, the monkeys were considered to have reached the breaking point. Using these procedures two monkeys were tested with low and high unit doses of thebaine (0.25 and 1.0 mg/kg/inj) and of pentazocine (0.06 and 0.25 mg/kg). The final ratios obtained with the high unit doses of thebaine and pentazocine were respectively 1,900 and 1,900 in one monkey and 2,260 and 2,610 in the other. Thus it was found that the reinforcing intensity of thebaine in rhesus monkeys is high and comparable to that of pentazocine.

Metabolic studies

Yanagita et al. (20) studied the metabolism of thebaine using urine obtained from rhesus monkeys treated with thebaine at single subcutaneous doses of 8 mg/kg. Thebaine and its metabolites were extracted from the urine and separated by thin-layer chromatography. Five spots including thebaine itself were detected, and their RF values were 0.39 (M 1),0.23 (M 2) and 0.1-0.2 (M 3 and M 4). M 1 has been identified as oripavine by gas chromatographic-mass spectrographic analysis. Later, a supply of authentic oripavine (provided through the courtesy of Mr. K. C. Reid of MacFarlan Smith Limited, United Kingdom) was compared with and found to be identical to M 1 in mass spectra, GC-retention time and TLC-Rf values. M 2 appeared to be a codeine-like substance, but has not yet been identified because of its very limited availability. M 3 was positive in the colour reaction with phosphomolybdic acid-ammonium hydroxide and nitroprusside, indicating the existence of a phenolic functional group and a secondary amine group. The chemical structure of M 3 has since been identified as nororipavine by GC-mass spectrographic analysis, M 4 has not yet been identified.

Discussions and conclusions

Thebaine was long believed to have no morphine-like agonistic properties and many studies, old and recent, are supportive of this view. However, it is now evident that it has a meaningful dependence potential, both physical and psychological, when large doses are ingested over a certain period in the rhesus monkey. As one of the causes of these discrepancies, contamination by morphine-like substances of thebaine used for the monkey studies was suspected. Since, however, in the analysis by Dr. Jacobson (National Institutes of Health, USA), the sample was found to be free from significant impurity, the species differences in metabolism of thebaine might well explain the discrepancy as already postulated by some investigators. There are some findings which tend to support the idea that the agonistic property of thebaine in rhesus monkeys may be attributable to its metabolites:

1. Thebaine is devoid of opiate agonistic effects as shown in the guinea pig ileum longitudinal muscle and the mouse vas deferens.

2. The depressant effect on the gross behaviour of rhesus monkeys appears after a time delay in contrast to the immediate onset of the stimulating and convulsant effects.

3. The reinforcing effect, which has been found to be equally strong as that of pentazocine, could not be demonstrated in cross self-administration experiments, probably because of the delayed onset of the agonistic effects.

4. The initiation of self-administration requires a longer time period with thebaine than with other opioids.

Some metabolites of thebaine, such as oripavine, nororipavine and probably codeine, are detectable in the urine of the rhesus monkey. The question arises as to whether these metabolites have a dependence potential and are biosynthesized in sufficient quantities to produce dependence.

In this connexion the pharmacological profile and dependence potential of oripavine deserve particular attention because:

1. Oripavine may be the pharmacologically most active metabolite of thebaine;

2. it may be biosynthesized by ingestion of other opium alkaloids as well; and

3. it may become available in the future as a therapeutic agent or a substance of abuse.

For these reasons, the Group concluded:

1. that thebaine has a meaningful dependence potential, both physical and psychological, when large doses are ingested over a certain period in the rhesus monkey;

2. it is desirable to investigate the dependence potential of oripavine in view of its being a most active metabolite of thebaine; and

3. the findings in this study apply to animals; whether or not they would apply to humans requires further study. From the monkey studies it would appear that large doses of thebaine are necessary to produce dependence. It is unlikely that comparable doses could be given to humans experimentally or would be self-administered in an abuse situation.

References

001) The Dependence Potential of Thebaine; Report of a WHO Advisory Group, Consolidated report of the Consultations held in Geneva, 11-22 October 1976, 3-4 October 1977, 25-26 September 1978 and 24-25 September 1979.

002) The Feasibility of the Conversion of Thebaine into Drugs of Abuse and of Potential Abuse. Report of an Expert Group, MNAR/4/1976 (Geneva, United Nations Narcotics Laboratory, Division of Narcotic Drugs, 1976).

003) H. Kruger, N. B. Eddy and M. Sumwalt, eds., The Pharmacology of the Opium Alkaloids, U.S. Public Health Service, Public Health Report, Supplement No. 165 (Washington, DC, Government Printing Office, 1941).

004) J. Kettenes-Van Den Bosch, C.A. Salemink and I. Khan, The Biological Activity of the Alkaloids of Papaver Bracteatum Lindl, MNH/79.31 (Geneva, World Health Organization, 1979).

005) T. Yanagita, "An experimental framework for evaluation of dependence liability of various types of drugs in monkeys", Bulletin on Narcotics , vol. 25, No. 2 (1973), pp. 57-64.

006) V. Preininger, "The pharmacology and toxicology of the alkaloids from the plants of the family Papaveraceae", Acta Universitatis Palackianae Olomucensis, Facultatis Medicae , vol. 61, 1972, pp. 213-254 and references cited therein.

007) A. P. Corrado and V. G. Long, "An electrophysical analysis of the convulsant action of morphine, codeine and thebaine", Archives internationales de pharmacodynamie et de therapie , vol. 132, 1961, pp. 255-269.

008) A. L. Misra, R. B. Pontani and S. J. Mule, "Pharmacokinetics and metabolism of (3H) thebaine", Xenobiotica, vol. 4, 1974, p. 17.

009) A. L. Misra, R. B. Pontani and S. J. Mule, "Relationship of pharmacokinetic and metabolic parameters to the absence of physical dependence liability with thebaine (3H)", Experientia, vol. 29, 1973, p. 1108.

010) H. W. Kosterlitz, personal communication.

011) M. D. Aceto and others, "Dependence studies of new compounds in the rhesus monkey", Proceedings 39th Annual Scientific Meeting, Committee on Problems of Drug Dependence (Cambridge, Mass., 1977), p. 586.

012) T. Yanagita and K. Miyasato, "An attempt to produce tolerance to convulsant effect of thebaine in rhesus monkeys", Annual Report of Preclinical Research Laboratories (Central Institute for Experimental Animals, 1977).

013) K. Takada and K. Ando, "Behavioural effects of thebaine in rats", Annual Report of Preclinical Research Laboratories (Central Institute for Experimental Animals, 1977).

014) C. R. Hartel, J. H. Woods and C. R. Schuster, "Behavioural effects of thebaine in the rhesus monkey", submitted to Psychopharmacology.

015) L. S. Harris and others, personal communication.

016) P. E. Gilbert and W. C. Martin, "The pharmacology of thebaine in the chronic spinal dog", Drug and Alcohol Dependence , vol. 3, 1978, pp. 139-142.

017) H. H. Swain, C. L. Fly and M. H. Seevers, "Evaluation of new compounds for morphine-like physical dependence in the rhesus monkey", Proceedings of the 39th Annual Scientific Meeting, Committee on Problems of Drug Dependence (Cambridge, Mass., 1977), pp. 614.

018) T. Yanagita and others, "Dependence potential of brotebanol, codeine and thebaine tested in rhesus monkeys", Bulletin on Narcotics, vol. 29, 1977, pp. 1 and 33.

019) T. Yanagita and K. Miyasato, "Progressive ratio test in intravenous self administration of thebaine and pentazocine in rhesus monkeys", Annual Report of

Preclinical Research Laboratories (Central Institute for Experimental Animals, 1977), Proceedings 40th Annual
Meeting, Committee on Problems of Drug Dependence.

020) T. Yanagita, Y. Yamazoe and H. Numata, "Thebaine metabolites in the urine of rhesus monkeys (Part 1)", Annual Report of Preclinical Research Laboratories (Central Institute for Experimental Animals, 1977), Proceedings 40th Annual Scientific Meeting, Committee on Problems of Drug Dependence.

*** This paper has been prepared by a WHO Advisory Group comprised of:**

Dr H. Halbach, Honorary Professor of Pharmacology, University of Munich, Munich, Federal Republic of Germany;

Dr Louis S. Harris, Chairman, Department of Pharmacology, Medical College of Virginia, Virginia Commonwealth University, Richmond, USA;

Dr J. Knoll, Professor and Head, Department of Pharmacology, University of Semmelweis, Medical School, Budapest, Hungary;

Dr O. O. Ogunremi, Chairman, Department of Psychiatry, University of Ifc, Ifc, Nigeria;

Dr Omal ElGarem, Professor and Head of the Psychiatric Department, Faculty of Medicine, Alexandria University, Alexandria, Egypt;

Dr C. R. Schuster, Director, Research Centre Studying Drug Dependence and Abuse, The University of Chicago, Department of Psychiatry, Chicago, Illinois, USA (Chairman);

Dr R. Willette, Chief, Research Technology Branch, Division of Research, National Institute on Drug Abuse, 5600 Fishers Lane, Rockville, USA

Dr T. Yanagita, Director, Preclinical Research Laboratories, Central Institute for Experimental Animals, 1433 Nogawa, Kawasaki, Japan (Rapporteur).

Representatives of the United Nations:

Dr George M. Ling, Director, UN Division of Narcotic Drugs, United Nations, Vienna International Centre, A-1400 Vienna, Austria, and

Dr O. Braenden, Chief, UN Narcotics Laboratory, United Nations, Vienna International Centre, A-1400 Vienna, Austria.

Representative of the International Narcotics Control Board:

Dr T. L. Chrusciel, Professor of Pharmacology, Deputy Director, Institute for Drugs, Research and Control, 30/34 Chemska Street, 00-725 Warsaw, Poland.

Secretariat:

Dr Inayat Khan, Senior Medical Officer, Division of Mental Health, World Health Organization,Geneva, Switzerland (Secretary).

Dr D. R. Jasinski, Director, National Institute on Drug Abuse, Addiction Research Centre, Lexington, Kentucky, USA, who did not participate also contributed to this report.

Thebaine Extraction and Purification

By Howard Ellis Jones GB 1,586,626 (1961)

Thebaine has become an important starting material for the synthesis of various pharmaceuticals, including codeine, oxycodone, and hydrocodone. Thebaine is naturally present in various poppy plant materials in relatively low concentrations. Accordingly, recovery of thebaine form such materials is difficult, time and energy consuming, and expensive.

Originally, thebaine was obtained as a by-product during the extraction of morphine from *Papaver somniferum*. It was then found that thebaine is present in higher concentrations in *Papaver bracteatum* than in other poppy plants such as the somniferum variety. Thus, recent attentions have focused on the bracteatum variety as a source for thebaine. However, even in *Papaver bracteatum*, thebaine is present in concentrations of only 3-6% in the ripened seed pods, and in even lower concentrations in other plant parts. The importance of developing an efficient process for extraction of thebaine in high yields and purity is apparent.

One of the earliest processes developed for extraction of thebaine from *Papaver bracteatum* is described in East German Patent No. 112,648, granted April 20, 1975 to H. Bohm et al. Bohm's process involves harvesting, drying the roots and/or poppy heads, dry grinding of the plant parts to a powder, moistening the powder with Na_2CO_3 solution, and extracting with methylene chloride under reflux, evaporating the extract to dryness under vacuum, stirring the residue with 1% sulfuric acid, filtering the aqueous phase, adjusting the pH to about 9-10 with ammonia, and filtering the precipitate. The sulfuric acid-ammonia-filtration sequence is repeated, and the precipitate is then dried.

The filtrates are extracted with ether to recover thebaine not precipitated by the ammonia. The product obtained is crude thebaine which must be further purified before use in the preparation of pharmaceuticals.

Additional developments in this area by Fairbairn and Caldwll have been published in Untied Nations Reports. Fairbairn describes an analytical procedure for determination of thebaine in *Papaver bracteatum* (U.S. Reports, ST/SOA/SER. J/3; October 16, 1973) and starts with *Papaver bracteatum* plant material that is air dried and powdered. He then extracts four times with progressively smaller amounts of

MeOH/NH_4OH (98:2), collects the separated supernatant, concentrates the supernatant by evaporation, dilutes the concentrate with acetic acid, cools, filters and washes the filter with additional acetic acid. The filtrates are combined, made basic with NH_4OH, extracted three times with $CHCl_3$, and the combined $CHCl_3$ extracts are evaporated to dryness. The thebaine thus produced is then ready for chromatagraphic analysis.

Caldwell describes another assay procedure for determination of thebaine in *Papaver bracteatum* which is similar to Fairgbairn's procedure in that both use a MeOH/NH_4OH (98:2) extractant. Caldwell merely agitates plant material with MeOH/NH_4OH extractant for 20 minutes with occasional ultrasonification, separates by centrifuge, and then analyzes samples of the liquid layer for thebaine content by liquid chromatography.

According to the present invention we now provide a process for extraction of thebaine from *Papaver bracteatum* which comprises contacting *Papaver bracteatum* plant material in particulate form with an extraction solvent comprising methanol, 5 to 15% by weight of water and sufficient of a weak base to free that portion of the thebaine which is apparently bonded to an acidic substrate in the plant tissue, while maintaining a temperature below 50° C.

The process of the present invention provides great improvement over previously known processes, particularly with regard to process efficiency and purity of product. In addition, the present process eliminates many of the disadvantages of the previously known processes with respect to material handling, occupational safety and health of personal operating the production facilities, and environmental exposure.

The process of the present invention utilizes, in a preferred embodiment, simultaneous grinding and extraction of plant materials, including the capsules and, optionally, the uppers stems of *Papaver bracteatum*. The extraction stage is preferably run countercurrent, thereby reducing problems of solvent handling and recovery, and also permitting the use of smaller, vessels. Extraction efficiency can approach 99% and overall yields of pure product can exceed 80%. A flow diagram of a preferred embodiment of the overall process is shown below.

Preferably the *Papaver bracteatum* plant material in particulate form is of a particle size of less than 1.25 mm. diameter, and the process further comprises forming a thebaine sale solution by acidification of the thebaine resulting form the contacting to a pH of 4-7 with a dilute aqueous acid having a pKa of 5 or less, filtering acid-soluble impurities out of the solution, contacting the filtered solution with activated charcoal, removing the charcoal, adjusting the pH of the solution to about 9-10, and separating the thebaine thus precipitated.

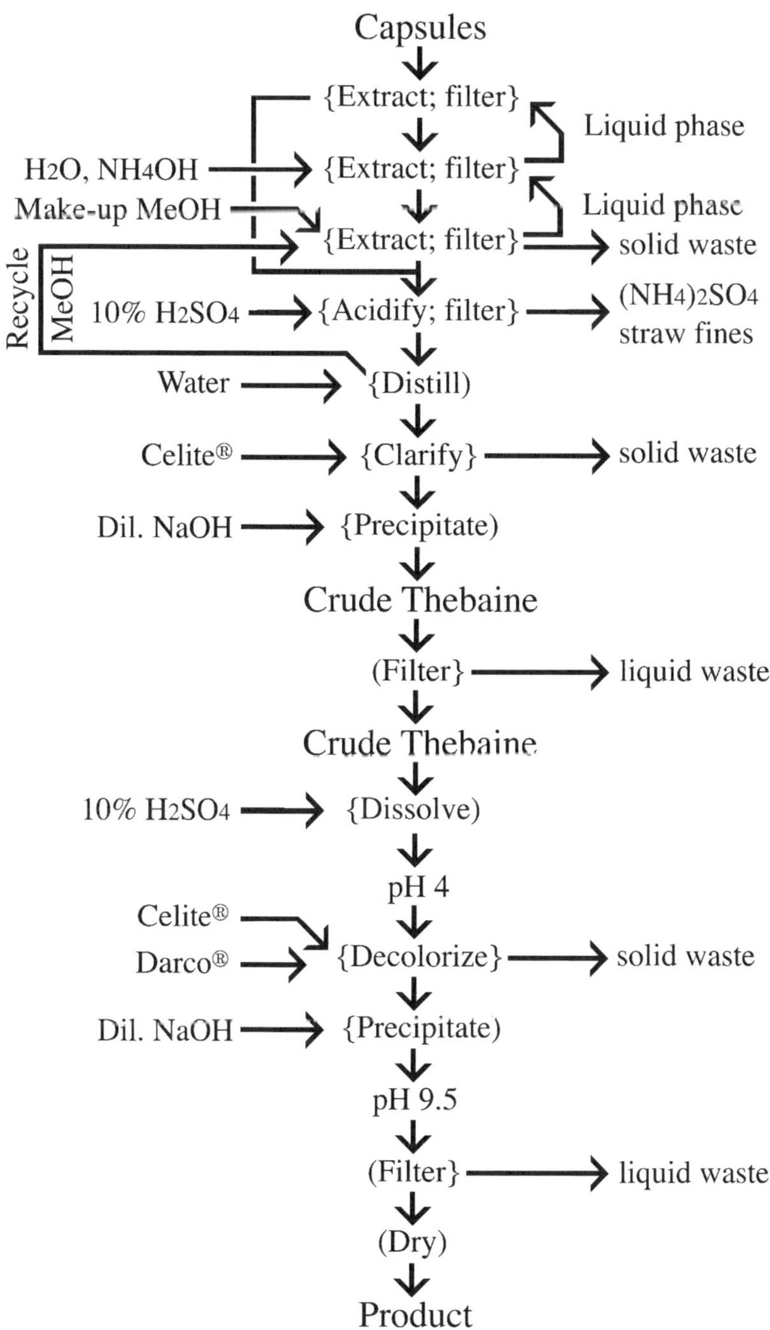

A preferred embodiment of the process of the present invention will now be described.

The process utilizes countercurrent batch extraction of thebaine from plant material and simultaneous grinding and leaching. The *Papaver bracteatum* is ground in a liquid medium to a particle size of less than 1.25 mm in diameter using a high-intensity mixer which cuts and shreds the plant tissues while temperature is maintained below 50° C. At the same time, the high degree of turbulence promotes rapid mass transfer of thebaine form the interior of the plant matter to the surface and across the liquid film boundary into the body of the extraction liquid. The health and explosion hazards encountered are avoided by this wet-grinding procedure.

The extraction solvent is methanol. A small concentration of weak base with a pKb 1.4-5 is added to free that portion of the thebaine which is apparently loosely bonded to an acidic substrate in the plant tissue. Ammonia and calcium hydroxide are preferred. Extraction efficiency is significantly improved by the inclusion of 5% to 15% water in the solvent mixture, in accordance with the invention. The extraction is preferably performed as a batch, multi-stage (e.g. three-stage), countercurrent extraction.

The thebaine is isolated in semi-pure form by transferring into an aqueous medium as the sulfate salt, filtering out acid-insoluble impurities, and precipitation with base.

Final purification is usually achieved by redissolving the thebaine in dilute sulfuric acid, treating with activated charcoal, and reprecipitating with base. The pure thebaine is isolated by filtration. If necessary, ultra-pure thebaine is obtained by redissolving in dilute acid and repeating the charcoal treatment.

The accompanying drawing summarizes one embodiment of the process of the present invention; “Celite” and “Darco” are registered Trade Marks.

Referring to the accompanying drawing the process is operated as follows (all parts and percentages are by weight unless stated otherwise):

Step 1

The plant parts are previously field- or kiln-dried to contain less than 20% water. The capsules, with seeds removed, and, optionally, the upper portion of the stem are charged to a high-intensity mixing vessel, such as an industrial laboratory blender, equipped with a jacketed container for removal of mechanical heat by water cooling, or a similarly constructed production size vessel, such as a Daymax® mixer.

The mixture is maintained at a temperature below 50° C. Three to six parts by weight of solvent consisting essentially of methanol and 0.1% to 2% of a base, preferably ammonium or calcium hydroxide, are added. This solvent also contains 5-15% water. To increase operation efficiency and overall economy, this solvent will have been used in the second extraction of a previous batch of capsules and will contain about 0.3 to 0.5% thebaine. This mixture is stirred for about 5 to 25 minutes, preferably about 15 minutes, to create a slurry during which time the plant material will be reduced in particle size so that it passes a 10-mesh sieve (U.S. Series #10 screen; 2 mm opening) with most of tho particles being less than 0.5 mm in size. After initial size reduction in a high intensity mixer, the resulting slurry is pumped through an in-line wet pulverizer or disintegrator fitted with a screen with 0.5 mm to 1.25 mm diameter perforations. This will assure that no particles above such diameter will survive. This is particularly important because after extraction, smaller particles hold substantially less residual thebaine than larger particles. The slurry is then passed to a basket centrifuge or filter to separate the partially exhausted, ground plant material from the solvent.

Step 2

The filter cake from Step 1 is recharged to the mixing vessel where it is combined with wash liquor from the previous batch. Make-up water, base, and alcohol are added to give the concentration range specified above. The mixture is agitated as before for 5 to 25 minutes. Substantial additional thebaine is extracted even though there is relatively little size reduction. Optionally, the slurry can be passed through the pulverizer as before and filtered. This filtrate is set aside to serve as the initial extraction medium for the next batch of capsules.

Step 3

The resulting pulp or marc is given a final wash in a mixing vessel for 2 to 10 minutes with 3 to 6 parts of methanol per part initial dry capsule charge. The slurry is again filtered and wash serves as part of the extraction medium for the second extraction of the next batch of capsules to be processed. The exhausted plant material now contains less than 0.2 parts thebaine per 100 parts of dry marc. The recovery based on 4% thebaine in the initial charge is over 95%. The wet cake can be dried to recover methanol; it can be incinerated to take advantage of its high fuel value; or the wet or dried cake can be composed.

Step 4

The extract from Step 1 is acidified to a pH of 4 to 7, preferably 4 to 5 with dilute acid, preferably sulfuric acid and is filtered to remove precipitated ammonium or calcium salts and any finely divided plant material.

Step 5

The methanol is removed by vacuum distillation, preferably in a fractionating column. All or a portion of the heat and the water needed to replace the methanol may be added by direct injection of steam. Water is added to provide a dilution of about 50 parts water per part of expected thebaine and the pH is adjusted to within the rage of 2.0 to 4.0 by the addition, if necessary, of a water-soluble acid having a pKa of 5.0 of less.

Step 6

Diatomaceous earth filter aid is added in the amount of 1 to 5 parts per 100 parts of solution, and the solution is filtered to remove acid-insoluble pigments.

Step 7

Semi-pure thebaine is precipitated by adjusting the pH to 9 to 10 with the addition of an aqueous base such as an alkali metal hydroxide or ammonium hydroxide. A 10% solution of sodium hydroxide is preferred.

Step 8

The thebaine is collected on a filter and washed with a little water.

Step 9

The wet thebaine is dissolved in an aqueous acid having a pKa of 5.0 or less, such as sulfuric acid, at a pH of 3 to 5. A pH of 4.0 is preferred. Water is added to give a strength of about 50 parts water per part thebaine.

Step 10

One-half part of activated charcoal, such as Darco® G-60, per part thebaine is added to absorb the remaining impurities. The mixture is stirred for 10 minutes to 30 minutes. Fifteen minutes is preferred. One-half part diatomaceous earth filter aid per part thebaine is advantageously added and dispersed, and the solution is filtered.

Steps 11-13

The pH of the filtrate is adjusted to 9 to 10 as in Step 7. The precipitated thebaine is collected, washed with water, and dried. The above purification may be repeated if necessary to produce thebaine of very high purity, greater than 99%.

EXAMPLE 1

Extraction of Crude Thebaine from *Papaver bracteatum*

The following materials were charged to a Waring Blender® equipped with a jacketed, stainless steel mixing chamber.

100 parts	*P. bracteatum* capsules assaying 3.5% thebaine
366 parts	methanol
46 parts	water
3.6 parts	conc. ammonium hydroxide.

The mixture was blended at high speed for 15 minutes with cooling water flowing through the jacket to absorb mechanical heat. The slurry was centrifuged and the filtrate saved. The centrifuged cake was repulped in the blender for 15 minutes with an identical second batch of solvent mixture, again centrifuged, and then repulped a third time in 450 parts of methanol. After a final centrifugal filtration, all the filtrates were combined.

The damp filter cake was vacuum dried at 60° C. The dry cake weighed 74 parts and analyzed as containing 0.04% thebaine. A calculation shows that 99% of the original thebaine was extracted.

The combined filtrates weighing 1061 parts were acidified to a pH of 4.5 with 16.3 parts of 25% H_2SO_4 and evaporated in vacuo to recover methanol while simultaneously adding 300 parts of water. The aqueous residue was acidified to pH 2, and filtered through diatomaceous earth to obtain a clear amber solution. Acid insoluble residue and alkaloids amounting to 1.69 parts were removed in the filtration.

The pH of the solution was adjusted to 9.5 by the gradual addition with stirring of 17.2 parts of 10% NaOH thereby precipitating crude thebaine. The solids were collected on a filter and dried to a weight of 3.143 parts, which assayed as 92.3% thebaine. The overall calculated yield was 83% based on the content of the original capsules.

EXAMPLE 2

The following materials were charged to a Waring Blender® and stirred at high speed for 15 minutes at 32° C to 34° C.

100 parts	*P. bracteatum* capsules assaying 3.5% thebaine
356 parts	methanol
48 parts	water
2 parts	calcium hydroxide.

The slurry was centrifuged, then re-extracted twice more with identical mixtures of fresh solvents and calcium hydroxide. The combined filtrates were acidified to a pH of 4.5 with 4.6 parts of 25% H_2SO_4, concentrated under vacuum while adding 300 parts of water, filtered through diatomaceous earth to remove 0.6 parts of solid impurities, and adjusted to a pH of 9.5 with the addition of 6.4 parts of 10% NaOH. The resulting crude thebaine, after collecting on a filter and drying, weighed 3.09 parts and analyzed as 98% thebaine. The calculated overall yield is 86.5%.

The dried pulp weighed 81 parts and analyzed as 0.13% thebaine. It is calculated that 87% of the thebaine was extracted from the capsules.

EXAMPLE 3

Countercurrent batch extraction

To a Daymax® high intensity mixer were charged 4.55 parts of capsules of *P. bracteatum* poppy (assaying 3.5% thebaine), 16.84 parts filtrate (analyzing 0.17% thebaine) from the second extraction of a previous batch of capsules, and 1.36 parts of make-up methanol. The mixture was mixed for 15 minutes at 13° C to 15° C then discharged through a Rietz disintegrator for further size reduction and centrifuged. The partially extracted poppy meal was next re-extracted for 15 minutes with 17.18 parts of wash liquor form the third extraction of the previous batch of capsules containing trace quantities of thebaine, plus 1.18 parts of additional water and 0.64 parts of concentrated aqueous ammonia, and centrifuged. For a final extraction, the pulp was mixed with 15.9 parts of pure methanol, centrifuged, and rinsed in the rotating centrifuge with 2.27 parts of fresh methanol, 6.23 parts of wet pulp, which dried to 2.95 parts and analyzed 0.15% as thebaine, was recovered. A calculation shows that 97% of the original thebaine in the capsules was removed.

EXAMPLE 4

Ten parts of crude thebaine, prepared as in Example 1 and analyzing 92% pure, was added to 916 parts of water in a beaker, 6.5 parts of 25% sulfuric acid was then added. After stirring briefly, a clear amber solution of the sulfate salt of thebaine was obtained. Filter acid and Darco® G-60 decolorizing charcoal were added. The mixture was stirred 15 minutes and filtered. The filtrate was made alkaline to pH 9.5 by the slow addition of 10% NaOH. The resulting precipitate was collected on a filter, washed with a little water and dried. 8.79 parts of nearly white product, which exhibited a melting point of 194° C indicating a purity of over 98%, was obtained.

Extraktion von rohem Thebain aus *Papaver bracteatum*

DE 2808905

BEISPLEL 1

Die folgenden Materialien wurden in einen WaringMischer gegeben, der mit einer ummantelten Mischkammer aus nichtrostendem Stahl versehen war:

100	Teile *P. bracteatum*-Kapseln mit 3,5% Thebain
366	Teile Methanol
46	Teile Wasser
3,6	Teile konzentriertes Ammoniumhydroxyd

Das Gemisch wurde 15 Minuten bei hoher Geschwindigkeit gemiscbt, während Kühlwasser durch den Mantel geleitet wurde, um mechanische Warme zu absorbieren. Die Aufschlämmung wurde zentrifugiert und das Filtrat gewonnen. Der beim Zentrifugieren erhaltene Kuchen wurde im Mischer erneut 15 Minuten mit einer gleichen zweiten Charge des Lösungsmittelgemisches angeteigt, erneut zentrifugiert und dann ein drittes Mal in 450 Teien Methanol aufgeschlämmt. Nach einer abschließenden Filtration durch Zentrifugieren wurden alle Filtrate verelnigt. Der feuchte Filterkuchen wurde im Vakuum bei 60° C getrocknet. Der trockene Kuchen wog 74 Teile und enthielt laut Analyse 0,04% Thebain. Eine Rechnung ergibt, daß 99% des ursprünglichen Thebains extrahiert worden waren.

Die vereinigten Filtrate in einer Menge von 1061 Teilen wurden mit 13,6 Teilen 25%iger H_2SO_4 auf pH 4,5 angesäuert, zur Rückgewinnung des Methanols im Vakuum eingedamp, während gleichzeitig 300 Teile Wasser zugesetzt wurden. Der wassrige Rückstand wurde auf pH 2 angesäuert und durch Diatomeenerde filtriert, wobei eine klare, bernsteinfarbene Lösung erhalten wurde. Ein in Säure unlöslicher Rückstand und Alkaloide, die lt 69 Teile ausmachten, wurden bei der Filtration entfernt.

Die Losung wurde auf pH 9,5 eingestellt, indem 17,2 Teile 10%iges NaOH allmählich unter Rühren zugesetzt wurden, wodurch rohes Thebain ausgefallt wurde. Die Feststoffe wurden abfiltriert und bis zu einem Gewicht von 3,143 Teilen getrocknet. Die Analyse ergab 92,3% Thebain. Die berechnete Gesamtausbeute betrug 83%, bezogen auf den Thebaingehalt der ursprünglichen Kapseln .

BEISPLEL 2

Die folgenden Materialien wurden in einen WaringMischer aufgegeben und mit hoher Geschwindigkeit 15 Minuten bei 32° bis 34°C gerührt:

100 Teile Kapseln von *P.bracteatum*, 3,5% Thebain
356 Teile Methanol
48 Teile Wasser 2 Teile Calciumhydroxyd

Die Aufschlämmung wurde zentrifugiert und dann noch zweimal mit gleichen Gemischen aus frischen Lösungsmitteln und Calciumhydroxyd extrahiert. Die vereinigten Filtrate wurden mit 4,6 Teilen 25%iger H_2SO_4 auf pH 4,5 angesäuert, unter Vakuum eingeeng während 300 Teile Wasser zugesetzt wurden, zur Entfernung von 0,6 Teilen fester Verunreinigungen durch Diatomeenerde filtriert und durch Zusatz von 6,4 Teilen. 10%igem NaOH auf pH 9,5 eingestellt. Das erhaltene rohe Thebain wog nach Isolierung auf einem Filter und Trocknen 3,09 Teile und enthielt laut Analyse 98% Thebain. Die berechnete Gesamtausbeute betrug 86,5%.

Der getrocknete Rückstand wog 81 Teile und enthielt laut Analyse 0,13% Thebain. Eine Rechnung ergibt, daß 97% des Thebains aus den Kapseln extrahiert worden waren.

BEISPLEL 3

Chargenextraktion im Gegenstrom

In eien Intensivmischer "Daymax" wurden 4,55 Teile Kapseln der Mohnsorte *P. bracteatum* (laut Analyse 3,5% Thebaine), 16,84 Teile Filtrat (laut Analyse 0,17% Thebaine), aus der zweiten Extraktin einer vorherigen Chartge von Kapseln und 1,36 Teile Methanol zur Ergänzung gengebe. Das Gemisch wurde 15 Minuten bei 13° bis 15°C durchgemischt, dann zur weiteren Zerkeinerung durch einen Rietz-Zerkleineror ausgetraben und zentrifugiert. Das teilweise extrahierte Kapselmehl wurde anschlieBend erneut 15 Minuten mit 17,18 Teilen Spurenmengen von Thebain enthaltender Waschflüssigkeit aus der dritten Extraktion der vorherigen Charge von Kapseln, 1,18 Teilen zusätzlichem Wasser und 0,64 Teilen konzentriertem wässrigem Ammoniak extrahiert und zentrifugiert. Für eine abschließende Extraktion wurde der Rückstand mit 15,9 Teilen reinem Methanol qemischt, zentrifugiert und in der laufenden Zentrifuge mit 2,27 Teilen frischem Methanol gespült. 6,23 Teile nasser Rückstand, der auf 2,95 Teile getrochknet wurde und laut Analyse 0,15% Thebaine enthielt, wurden gewonnen. Eine Berechnung zeigty, daB 97% des ursprünglichen Thebains in den Kapseln entfernt worden waren.

BEISPLEL 4

10 Teile rohes Thebain, das auf die in Beispiel 1 beschriebene Weise hergestellt worden war und dessen Analyse eine Reinheit von 92% ergob, wurden zu 916 Teilen Wasser in einem Becherglas gegeben. Dann wurden 6,5 Teile 25%ige Schwefelsäure zugesetzt. Nach kurzem Rühren wurde eine klare bernsteinfarbvene Lösung des Sulfatsalzes von Thebain erhalten. Dann wurden Filterhilfsmittel und Entfärberkohle "Darco G-60" zugesetzt. Das Gemisch wurde 15 Minuten gerührt und filtriert. Das Filtrat wurde durch langsame Zugabe von 10%igem NaOH bis pH 9,5 alkalisch gemacht. Die hierbei gebildete Fällung wurde abfiltriert, mit wenig Wasser gewaschen und getrocknet. Hierbei wurden 8,79 Teile eines fast weißen Produkts mit einem Schmelzpunkt von 194°C, der eine Reinheit von memr als 89% anzeigte, erhalten.

Papaver Somniferum Strain with High Concentration of Thebaine and Oripavine

by Anthony John Fist; Christopher James Byrne and Wayne Lyle Gerlach

There is disclosed an improved poppy straw of a stably reproducing *Papaver somniferum* for the extraction of thebaine and/or oripavine, the threshed straw having thebaine and oripavine constituting about 50% by weight or greater of the alkaloid combination consisting of morphine, codeine, thebaine and oripavine...

Recovering thebaine and/or oripavine from either the dried straw or from the opium of *Papaver somniferum* is a process well established in the art. Until now, thebaine has been extracted from this plant as a part of the process of extracting morphine and codeine. In one process, the straw is treated with a small amount of lime and water to soften the capsules and to form a free base of the alkaloids. Countercurrent extraction of the softened straw with methanol, ethanol or other suitable solvent forms a solvent/water extract or "miscella" containing the alkaloids, with morphine at a concentration of about 1 g/L where the straw is from standard *Papaver somniferum*. The volume of the miscella is reduced about 30 x under vacuum to produce an aqueous concentrate. Thebaine is extracted from aqueous concentrate using a liquid/liquid extraction with toluene, adjusting pH for the best separation of thebaine. The thebaine is recovered from the toluene. Of course, recovering thebaine from the improved *Papaver somniferum* provided herein will be facilitated by the fact that the concentration of the thebaine in the miscella will be much higher than that of other alkaloids and thus can be more easily collected by precipitation. Also, in the substantial absence of morphine and codeine, the thebaine might be directly extracted from the straw using toluene. In the case of oripavine, it has not been separately recovered on a commercial scale, however, oripavine may be recovered from an aqueous concentrate by adjusting to basic pH and extracting with organic solvent such as toluene. The oripavine will remain in the aqueous layer and the thebaine will be found in the organic solvent. The oripavine can then be recovered from the aqueous phase by adjusting the pH to precipitate the oripavine.

Source: US 6,067,749 References: Aceta Pharmaceutica Nordica, vol. 4(I), 1992, Wold, J.K. et al, pp. 31-34, "Increase in thebaine content of *Papaver bracteatum* Lindl. after colchicine treatment of seeds".; Planta Medica, vol. 46(4), 1983, Nielsen B. et al, pp. 205-206, "Oripavine-A New Alkaloid".Hereditas, vol. 93(1), 1980, Nyman U, pp. 121-124, "Selection for high thebaine/low morphine content in *Papaver somniferum* L". Hereditas, vol. 89(1), 1978, Nyman U, pp. 43-50, "Selection for high thebaine/low morphine content (cpv. Morph: The) in *Papaver somniferum* L".

MORPHINE

Discovery and Chemical Properties

by Lyndon F. Small and Robert E. Lutz

In 1803 Derosne (1), by extraction of opium with water and precipitation of the extract with potassium carbonate, obtained a crystalline substance which he named "salt of opium." He observed its solubility in acids and precipitation by bases, but failed to recognize its basic character. Sertümer (2) believed that Derosne's salt of opium was morphine acid meconate; Pelletier (3) and Robiquet (4) (5) considered it to have been narcotine.

In a little-noticed paper (6) (7) (8) the pharmacist Sertümer, of Einbeck in Hannover, described the isolation of the pure base in 1805. In later papers (2) (9) (10) (11) (1817) he again called attention to his discovery of a vegetable base which was capable of neutralizing acids and forming salts. The publications aroused immediate interest, and Sertümer's results were verified by Robiquet (12) (13) within the same year.

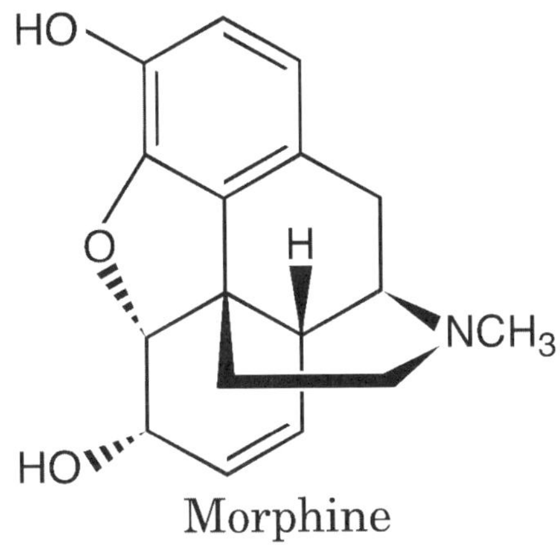

Morphine

Pelletier (3) points out that his compatriot Séguin, in a report before the Academy of Sciences in 1804 described the isolation and properties of morphine and even suggested its basic nature. This paper was first published in 1818 (14).

Further researches by Robiquet (15) (16), Pelletier (3) (17), Couerbe (18), Dublanc (19) (20), Duflos (21), and Robinet (22) resulted in improvement in the methods of separation, as well as the isolation, of new substances (narcotine, narceine, meconin, etc.).

Pelletier (3) investigated the colored material formed in the reaction between ferric chloride and morphine. He isolated a colored crystalline substance which he called iron morphite. He also studied the action of iodine and chlorine on morphine (23). Determinations of the hydrate water and acid equivalent of morphine were carried out by Robiquet (15) (16). Choulant (24) (25) prepared and analyzed a number of salts; Serullas (26) investigated the action of iodic acid, and determined its sensitivity as a reagent for morphine. Robinet (22) noted the solubility of morphine in lime water, but did not realize its phenolic nature.

The first elementary analyses by Liebig (27) (1831) gave morphine the formula $C_{34}H_{36}O_6N_2$. Regnault (28) (29) found values for $C_{35}H_{40}O_6N_2$. (*Cf.* Dumas (35), Pelletier (36).) In 1847 Laurent (30) published the formula $C_{34}H_{38}O_6N_2$, corresponding to the now accepted formula $C_{17}H_{19}O_3N$. Raoult (31) found a molecular weight in acetic acid corresponding to $(C_{17}H_{19}O_3N)_2$. Later determinations by Eykman (32) and Von Klobukow (33) showed the simple formula to be the correct one. (See also Bertrand and Meyer (34).)

Table of solubilities

[Grams of morphine base in 100 g. solvent]

Solvent	Solubility	Observer
Water	0.01 (10°), 0.04 (40°), 0.08 (60°), 0.125 (80°), 0.165 (90°), 0.217 (100°).	Chastaing (74).
Do	0.1 (cold), 0.25 (boiling)	Duflos (21).
Do	0.028	Müller (76).
Do	0.019 (20°)	Guild (77).
Water saturated with ether	0.044	Müller (76).
Ether saturated with water	0.009	Do. (76).
Ether	0.016 (boiling)	Prescott (75).
Do	0.013	Müller (76).
Ether (absol.)	0.023 (10°)	Florio (78).
Alcohol 75%	0.223 (10.8°), 1.95 (78°)	Do. (78).
Alcohol 90%	0.377 (10.6°), 2.991 (78°)	Do. (78).
Alcohol (absol.)	1.132 (10.6°), 8.623 (78°)	Do. (78).
Methyl alcohol	1.675 (10.8°), 8.466 (56°)	Do. (78).
Amyl alcohol	0.26 (cold), 1.1 (boiling)	Kubly (79), Prescott (75).
Benzyl alcohol	50 (boiling), 21.5 (20°)	Fabre (80).
Ethyl acetate	0.213	Kubly (79).
Do	0.18	Müller (76).
Chloroform	0.1 (cold)	Burg (81).
Do	0.023 (boiling)	Prescott (75).
Do	0.040 (9. 4°), 1.235 (56°)	Florio (78).
Do	0.065	Müller (76).
Chloroform+10% alcohol	0.9 (cold)	Burg (81).
Carbon tetrachloride	0.032 (17°)	Schindelmeiser (82).
Do	0.015	Müller (76).
Benzene	0.020 (9.4°)	Florio (78).
Do	0.011 (boiling)	Prescott (75).
Do	0.062	Müller (76).
Anisole	0.00 (9°), 0.95 (100°), 4.90 (150°)	Fouquet (72).
Nitrobenzene	0.51 (20°), 10.5 (boiling)	Fabre (80).
Petroleum ether	0.086	Müller (76).
Olive oil	0.00	Pettenkofer (83).
Ammonia 0.1 *N*	0.095 (25°)	Heiduschka (84).
Ammonia 0.2 *N*	0.123 (25°)	Do. (84).
Ammonia *N*	0.32 (25°)	Do. (84).
Ammonia, sp. gr. 0.97	0.85	Duflos (21).

Morphine is obtained from opium, the dried juices which exude from the scratched unripe seed-capsules of the opium poppy, *Papaver somniferum*. The amount of morphine present in opium varies between wide limits; in a good grade of opium it averages 10%, although samples containing over 20% have been reported. (For a full discussion see Jermstad (37).) Poppy seeds are alkaloid-free; morphine is first detectable in the plant 36 days after sprouting of the seeds (38).

Morphine crystallizes from dilute alcohol in small rhombic prisms (48), often having the appearance of needles (49); crystal measurements have been published by Brooke (50), Schabus (51), Rammelsberg (52), Lang (53), Decharme (54), and Wherry (55). The hydrated crystals have the specific gravity 1.317 to 1.326 (56), (1.32 (55)). The refractive indices were found by Kley (57) (58) to be 1.63 and 1.62; Keenan (59) gives n/D= 1.580; Wright (60) and Wherry and Yanovski (55) find n/D: α=1.580, β= 1.625, γ= 1.650 (1.645). The base usually crystallizes with one molecule of hydrate water, which is lost at about 100° (61) (62). The anhydrous substance melts at 247° to 248° (253° to 254° corr.) (63) with decomposition.

Morphine sublimes crystalline at temperatures between 150° and 200° (64) (65). Vacuum micro-sublimation methods for identification of the alkaloid are described by Tunmann (66) and Heiduschka and Meisner (67). Krafft and Weilandt (68) observed smooth sublimation in high vacuum at 191° to 193°. (*Cf.* Kempf (63).) Morphine has been shown present in the smoke from the opium pipe (69).

Methyl alcohol (55) (70) or amyl alcohol (71) are recommended for recrystallization; from anisole the base crystallizes in anhydrous prisms (72). It is very slightly soluble in alkali carbonates, readily soluble in alkali hydroxides (73), sparingly in alkaline-earth hydroxides (74). Ammonia precipitates the base crystalline from solutions of its salts with acids; it is somewhat more soluble in ammonia than in water. The solubilities of morphine in various media are tabulated below. It should be noted that the state of aggregation influences the solubility of the alkaloid markedly; amorphous or freshly precipitated it is said to be many times more soluble than when crystalline (75).

Morphine is levorotatory, [α]23/D = -130.9°, in methyl alcoholic solution (C=2.292) (70); [α]D = -131.7° (methyl alcohol, p =1) (55); in aqueous solution as the sodium salt, [α]22.5 = -70.23° (p=2) (85) (*cf.* Bouchardat (86)). For morphine hydrochloride (hydrated) Hesse (85) found [α]15/D = -99.54° (p=1), and for the hydrated sulphate, the same value. The rotatory power decreases with increasing concentration of the solution. Tykociner (87) reported values for a large number of salts, all in the neighborhood of [α]D = -128°; for the base he gave [α]D=-140.5° (absolute alcohol, p = 0.25 to 0.45).

The absorption spectrum has been studied by Hartley (88) and Kitasato (89), that in the ultra-violet by Brustier (90), and Steiner (91).

Gompel and Henri (92) compared the ultra-violet absorption spectra of morphine, codeine, and apomorphine with that of phenanthrene. Meyer (93) examined the absorption by the colored solution of morphine in Erdmann's reagent (sulphuric-nitric acid).

The heat of combustion of morphine hydrate is 2145.2 Cal. at constant volume, 2146.7 Cal. at constant pressure; the heat of hydration is 3.6 Cal. The heats of reaction of the base with a number of acids and with alkali have also been determined (94) (95).

Morphine is a monoacid base, whose salts react neutral to litmus or methyl orange. The free base turns litmus blue (95), and red helianthin to yellow; in aqueous solution it does not affect phenolphthalein, but when water is added to an alcoholic solution of morphine containing

Color and precipitation reactions

Reagent	Reaction	Observer
Robiquet's test, Ferric chloride	Deep blue, disappearing on warming or with excess of acid.	Pelletier (17).
Nitric acid, (sp. gr. 1.42)	With solid base or salts, intense orange-red color, destroyed by sodium thiosulphate.	Duflos (21).
Iodic acid	Iodine liberated; sensitivity increased by addition of ammonia (114); *cf.* Fulton (115).	Serullas (26).
Ferric chloride and pot. ferricyanide.	Berlin-blue; sensitive 1:100,000. *Cf.* Hesse (62), Armitage (116).	Schaer (117).
Sugar and conc. H_2SO_4	Base mixed with 6 parts of sugar, a drop of conc. H_2SO_4 added; purple-red turning blue-green then yellow; sensitive to 0.01 mg. A drop of bromine water increases sensitivity (118).	Schneider (119).
40% formaldehyde (2 drops) in conc. H_2SO_4 (3 c. c.).	Violet-red, becoming blue; *cf.* Kobert (120), Elias (121). Modified by addition of conc. HNO_3, Fulton (115).	Marquis (122).
Sodium nitrite	In acid solution, yellow, becoming orange with alkali. *Cf.* Riegel and Williams (123).	Wieland and Kappelmeier (124).
Diazotized sulphanilic acid	2% solution of the reagent is added to a solution of morphine salt, and made alkaline with sodium carbonate; red color. Action of other diazonium salts is also described.	Lautenschläger (125).
Nitric acid or sodium hypochlorite	Reagent added to a warm solution of the base in conc. sulphuric acid; carmine.	Erdmann (126), Husemann (127). *Cf.* Couerbe (128).
Perchloric acid	On heating, violet, becoming brown	Fraude (129).
Potassium perchlorate free from chlorate.	Reagent added to base in conc. H_2SO_4; brown. *Cf.* Rosenthaler (130).	Grove (131), Siebold (132).
Iodine in potassium iodide solution (Wagner's reagent).	Brown cryst. precip	Jörgensen (133), Wagner (134).
Bromine water	Boil solution of morphine salt with an excess of reagent, neutralize with $CaCO_3$, and boil; bright red, sensitive 1:1,200.	Eiloart (135).
Chlorine water	Green-yellow color; addition of NH_4OH turns it brown-yellow. Not given by codeine.	Marmé (136), Flückiger (137).
Iodine chloride	Iodine separates in the cold	Dittmar (138).
Conc. HCl-conc. H_2SO_4 mixture	Heated to 100° to 120°, purple	Pellagri (139), *cf.* Fulton (115).
Molybdic acid in conc. H_2SO_4	Violet turning blue then dirty green, finally colorless.	Fröhde (140).
Ammon. molybdate (0.1 g.) in conc. H_2SO_4 (1 c. c.) (Fröhde-Buckingham).	Cold, lilac; on heating, green. With KNO_3 becomes red, then yellow.	Bruylants (141).
Sat. sol. titanic oxide in conc. H_2SO_4.	Shaken with a solution of base in conc. H_2SO_4, blood-red; color fades with water.	Reichard (142).
Trisodium phosphate in conc. H_2SO_4.	On warming, violet, turning red with water, from which chloroform extracts a blue color.	Vulpius (143). *Cf.* Ekkert (144).
Potassium arsenate in conc. H_2SO_4.	On heating, blue-violet, turning brown; diluted, green, chloroform extracts a violet color. *Cf.* Reichard (145).	Donath (146), Tattersall (147).
Potassium chlorate in conc. H_2SO_4	Grass green, rose color at edges	Donath (146).
Ammonium sulphouranate in conc. H_2SO_4.	Dirty green color on warming	Bronciner (148).

Color and precipitation reactions—Continued

Reagent	Reaction	Observer
Vanillin or piperonal	Evap. an alcoholic sol. of base and reagent with a few drops of 0.5 *N* H_2SO_4 on steam; red-violet color.	Van Itallie and Steenhauer (149).
Uranyl acetate or ferric acetate with formaldehyde.	Reagent added to base in conc. H_2SO_4. *Cf.* Aloy (150) (151).	Aloy (152).
Benzidine	0.01 g. base added to a few c. c. conc. H_2SO_4 containing 0.01 g. reagent; yellow, becoming brown, then dark green; add to water, violet, extracted by chloroform. Test given also by codeine, dionin, heroin, apomorphine.	Ekkert (153).
Hydroferrocyanic acid, hydroferricyanic acid.	Microchemical examination of precipitate. *Cf.* Pluggo (151).	Cumming and Brown (155).
Silicoduodecitungstic acid	Buff-colored precip.; mod. sol. in alcohol or dil. acids. Sensitive 1:16,000.	North and Beal (156), Heiduschka and Wolf (157), Bertrand (158).
Potassium chromate, potassium dichromate.	Precip. of chromate and free base. Brown precip., composition uncertain.	Plugge (159).
Reinecke's salt	Characteristic crystals on microscope slide	Rosenthaler (160).
Sodium vanadate and copper sulphate in dil. acetic acid.	Precip. in solutions stronger than 0.1%	Jaworoski (161).
0.1% solution of sodium tungstate	Shake with alkaloid dissolved in a few c. c. conc. H_2SO_4; impermanent blue-violet.	Reichard (142).
0.1% solution of ammonium metavanadate, H_2SO_4 added until yellow color disappears.	Add morphine salt to reagent and warm; permanent bright green; very dilute, blue-green.	Do. (142).
Ferrous sulphate, ammonia	Base warmed with conc. H_2SO_4, a crystal of $FeSO_4$ added, poured into conc. ammonia; red-violet between layers; on shaking, blue. Not given by codeine.	Jorissen (162).
3% hydrogen peroxide	Reagent layered onto a solution of base in 2 c. c. conc. H_2SO_4; yellow-brown to emerald ring; on rotating, yellow layer over emerald.	Ekkert (163).
Lead peroxide	Base in 5% sulphuric acid shaken with PbO_2; pink solution, brown with ammonia.	Fleury (164).
Silver nitrate	Silver precip. in 30 to 60 min	Hager (165).
Formaldehyde-stannous chloride	Base in excess formaldehyde, with a drop of $SnCl_2$ sol., evap. dry; permanent blue-violet.	Reichard (166).
Ammoniacal copper sulphate	Blue solution becomes green on boiling	Duflos (21), Nadler (167), Lindo (168).
H_2O_2, ammonia, and copper	The liquids are added to morphine salt, stirred with copper wire; deep port-wine color, gas-evolution, sensitive 0.02 mg. Apomorphine gives orange color; other common alkaloids, no color.	Oliver (169).
Magnol (basic magnesium hypochlorite) in acetic acid.	Base dissolved in reagent, layered onto conc. H_2SO_4; yellow-brown ring; in 3 hours color of Hessian Purple-B; in 24 hours, yellow layer over Rhodulin Red-G layer, over pale dark blue layer.	David (170).

phenolphthalein, a rose color appears. The phenolic hydroxyl of morphine is sufficiently acidic to turn Poirrier's Blue (C4B) reddened by alkali to violet (94). The pH value for morphine salts averages 4.68; methyl red should be used for titrations involving morphine (96) (97) (98). The isoelectric point for morphine lies at pH 8.96 (Kolthoff (99) (100), but the base shows its minimum solubility in the range pH 8.4-9.4 (101). For titration methods and use of indicators see further refs. 102-113 (not a complete bibliography of the subject).

A large number of color and precipitation tests for morphine have been described; in the table are given the most important, and those having especial historic interest.

A sensitive biological test is described by Hermann (171), wherein as little as 0.01 mg. of morphine injected subcutaneously on the back of a white mouse causes the mouse to lay its tail up over the back. (Straub test.)

Quantitative determinations of morphine in opium, as well as for forensic purposes have been described in great number. These depend mostly upon isolation of the morphine itself (Dieterich (172), Pape (173), upon its precipitation quantitatively by some reagent as Mayer's (see Heikel (174), Ionesco-Matiu (175), or Wagner's (Prescott and Gordin (176)), and upon its reducing action, as in Kieffer's (177) ferricyanide method, or in the iodic acid method. Colorimetric determinations using iodic acid or Marquis' reagent are described by Heiduschka (178), Miller (179), Stein (180), and Van Itallie (181). For a critical discussion of methods of estimation see Taylor (182) or Schmidt (183).

MORPHINE SALTS

MORPHINE: ($B=C_{17}H_{19}O_3N$).

—HYDROCHLORIDE: $B \bullet HCl \bullet 3H_2O$, silky needles from water (29); cryst. anhydrous from alcohol; m. p. 200°. $[\alpha]^{25}_D=-111.5°$ (C=2.240) (70), *cf.* Hesse (85) (263). Sol. in 17.5 parts water 25°, 0.5 parts at 100°; 41.5 parts alcohol 25°, 37 parts at 60°; (anhydrous) in 51 parts methanol at 15°; sol. in 19 parts glycerine, insol. in ether or chloroform. The hydrated salt loses its crystal-water in vacuum or on drying at 100° (264) (265).

—HYDROBROMIDE: $B \bullet HBr \bullet 2H_2O$, tufts of long white needles from water; loses its crystal-water at 100° (271). Crystallizes anhydrous from alcohol. $[\alpha]^{15}_D=-100.4°$ (C=2.49) (70). Soluble in hot water, sparingly in cold.

—SULPHATE: $B_2H_2SO_4+5H_2O$, white needles (radiating tufts of flat-ended prisms, illustration (49)) sol. in 23 parts cold water, 15.5 parts at 25°, 0.7 parts at 80°; soluble in 452 parts alcohol at 25°, 192 parts at 60°; insol. in chloroform, ether (29) (36) (282). At 110° it loses $3H_2O$, the remaining $2H_2O$ at 130° with partial decomp. Thermochemistry, Leroy (94). $n_D=1.545$ (59).

Bibliography (Morphine)

(1) Derosne, Ann. chim. **45**, 257 (1803).
(2) Sertürner, Ann. chim. phys. (2) **5**, 21 (1817).
(3) Pelletier, Ann. chim. phys. (2) **50**,240 (1832).

(4) Robiquet, J. Pharm. (1) **17**, 637 (1831).
(5) Robiquet, Ann. **2**, 267 (1832).
(6) Sertürner, Trommsdorff's Journal der Pharmazie **13**, (1) 234 (1805)
(7) Sertürner, Trommsdorff's Journal der Pharmazie **14**, (1) 47 (1806).
(8) Sertürner, Trommsdorff's Journal der Pharmazie **20**, (1) 99 (1811).
(9) Sertürner, Gilbert's Ann. der Phvsik **55**, 56 (1817).
(10) Sertürner, Gilbert's Ann. der Physik **57**,192 (1817).
(11) Sertürner, Gilbert's Ann. der Physik **59**, 50 (1818).
(12) Robiquet, Ann. chim. phys. (2) **5**, 275 (1817).
(13) Robiquet, Gilbert's Ann. der Physik **57**, 163 (1817).
(14) Séguin, Ann. chim. **92**, 225 (1814).
(15) Robiquet, Ann. chim. phys. (2) **51**,225 (1832).
(16) Robiquet, Ann. **5**, 82 (1833).
(17) Pelletier, Ann. **5**, 150 (1833).
(18) Couerbe, Ann. chim. phys. (2) **49**, 45 (1832).
(19) Dublanc, Ann. **3**, 121 (1832).
(20) Dublanc, Ann. **4**, 232 (1832).
(21) Duflos, J. Chem. Phys. (Schweigger-Seidel) **61**, 105 (1831).
(22) Robinet, J. Pharm. (2) **13**, 24 (1827).
(23) Pelletier, Ann. chim. phys. (2) **63**, 164 (1836).
(24) Choulant, Ann. der Physik (Gilbert) **59**, 412 (1818).
(25) Choulant, Ann. der Physik (Gilbert) **56**, 342 (1817).
(26) Serullas, Jahresber. Fortschr. phys. Wiss. (Berzelius) **11**, 238 (1831).
(27) Liebig Ann. der Physik (Poggendorff) **21**, 1 (1831); Ann. chim. phys. (2) **47**, 147 (1831).
(28) Regnault, Ann. chim. phys. (2) **68**, 113 (1838).
(29) Regnault, Ann. **26**, 10 (1838).
(30) Laurent, Ann. chim. phys. (3) **19**, 359 (1847).
(31) Raoult, Ann. chim. phys. (6) **2**, 66 (1884).
(32) Eykman, Z. phys. Chem. **2**, 964 (1888).
(33) Von Klobukow, Z. phys. Chem. **3**, 476 (1889).
(34) Bertrand and Meyer, Ann. chim. phys. (8) **17**, 501 (1909).
(35) Dumas and Pelletier, Ann. chim. phys. (2) **24**, 163 (1823).
(36) Pelletier and Caventou, Ann. chim. phys. (2) **12**, 113 (1819).
(37) Jermstad, Das Opium (Verlag Hartleben, Wien, 1921).
(38) Kerbosch, Arch. Pharm. **248**, 536 (1910).
(39) Charbonnier, J. pharm. chim. (4) **7**, 348 (1868).
(40) Dragendorff, Die Heilpflanzen, p. 249 (Enke, Stuttgart, 1898).
(41) Baudet and Adrian, Pharm. Ztg. **34**, 23 (1889).
(42) Ladenburg, Ber. **19**, 783 (1886).
(43) Williamson, Chem. Ztg. **10**, 20, 38, 147, 238, 491 (1886).
(44) Dieterich, Pharm. Zeit. Russ. **27**, 269 (1888).
(45) Hesse, Arch. Pharm. **228**, 7 (1890).
(46) Hesse, Ann. suppl. **4**, 50 (1865-66).
(47) Hesse, Ann. **140**, 145 (1866).

(48) Schabus, Jahresber. Fortschr. Chem. **1854**, 503.
(49) Deane and Brady, J. Chem. Soc. **18**, 34 (1865).
(50) Brooke, Ann. Phil. (N. S. **6**) **22**, 118 (1823).
(51) Schabus, Bestimmung der Krystallgestalten in chem. Laboratorien erzeugten Produkte, Wien, 1855.
(52) Rammelsberg, Handb. Kryst.-phys. Chem. II 358 (1882).
(53) Lang, Sitzber. Akad. Wiss. Wien, **31**, 115 (1858).
(54) Decharme, Ann. chim. phys. (3) **68**,160 (1863).
(55) Wherry and Yanovsky, J. Wash. Acad. Sci. **9**, 505 (1919).
(56) Schroder, Ber. **13**,1075 (1888).
(57) Kley, Rec. trav. chim. **22**, 367 (1903).
(58) Kley, Zeit. anal. Chem. **43**, 164 (1904).
(59) Keenan, J. Am. Pharm. Assoc. **16**, 837 (1916).
(60) Wright, J. Am. Chem. Soc. **38**, 1655 (1916).
(61) Dott, Pharm. J. Trans. (3) **18**, 701 (1888).
(62) Hesse, Pharm. J. Trans. (3) **18**, 801 (1888).
(63) Kempf, J. prakt. Chem. (2) **78**, 201 (1908).
(64) Blyth, J. Chem. Soc. **33**, 313 (1878).
(65) Guy, Pharm. J. Trans. (2) **8**, 718 (1866-1867).
(66) Tunmann, Apoth. Ztg. **31**, 148 (1916).
(67) Heiduschka and Meisner, Arch. Pharm. **261**,102 (1923).
(68) Krafit and Weilandt, Ber. **29**, 2240 (1896).
(69) Nakajima and Kubota, Ber. ges. Physiol. exp. Pharmakol. **40**, 850 (1927).
(70) Schryver and Lees, J. Chem. Soc. **77**, 1024 (1900).
(71) Schachtrupp, irch. Pharm. (2) **132**, 1 (1867).
(72) Fouquet, Bull. soc. chim. (3) **17**, 464 (1897); J. pharm. chim. (6) **5**, 49 (1897).
(73) Chastaing, J. pharm. (5) **4**, 19 (1881).
(74) Chastaing, Bull. soc. chim. **37**, 477 (1882); Cornpt. rend. **94**, 44 (1882); Rdp. Pharm. J. chim. med. n. s. **9**, 219 (1881).
(75) Prescott, Pharm. J. Trans. (3) **6**, 404 (1875).
(76) AJuller, Apoth. Zeit. **18**, 257 (1903).
(77) Guild, Pharm. J. Trans. (4) **78**, 357 (1907).
(78) Florio, Gazz. chim. ital. **13**, 496 (1883); Jahresber. Fortschr. Chem. **1883**, 1343.
(79) Kubly, Jahresber. Fortschr. Chem. **1866**, 823.
(80) Fabre, Bull. soc. pharm. Bordeaux **62**, 68 (1924).
(81) Burg, Z. anal. Chem. **19**, 222 (1880).
(82) Schindelmeiser, Chem. Ztg. **25**, 129 (1901).
(83) Pettenkofer, Jahresber. Fortschr. Chem. **1858**, 363.
(84) Heiduschka and Faul, Arch. Pharm. **255**, 441 (1917).
(85) Hesse, Ann. **176**, 189 (1875).
(86) Bouchardat, Ann. chim. phys. (3) **9**, 213 (1843).
(87) Tykociner, Rec. trav. chim. **1**, 144 (1882).
(88) Hartley, Phil. Trans. Royal Soc. London **176**, 471 (1885).
(89) Kitasato, Acta Phytochim. **3**, 175-258 (1927); Chem. Abstr. **22**, 1779 (1928).
(90) Brustier, Bull. soc. chim. (4) **39**, 1527 (1926).

(91) Steiner, Bull. soc. chim. biol. **6**, 231 (1924).
(92) Gompel and Henri, Compt. rend. **157**, 1422 (1913).
(93) Meyer, Arch. Pharm. **213**, 413 (1878).
(94) Leroy, Ann. chim. phys. (7) **21**, 87 (1900).
(95) Leroy, Compt. rend. **128**, 1107 (1899).
(96) Wales, J. Ind. Eng. Chem. **18**, 390 (1926).
(97) Rasmussen and Schou, Pharm. Zentralhalle **65**, 729 (1924).
(98) Rasmussen and Schou, Z. Elektrochem. **31**, 189 (1925).
(99) Kolthoff, Biochem. Z. **162**, 338 (1925).
(100) Kolthoff, Pharm. Weekblad **62**, 106 (1925).
(101) Kolthoff, Pharm. Weekblad **62**, 190 (1925).
(102) Kebler, J. Am. Chem. Soc. **17**, 822 (1895).
(103) Kippenberger, Z. anal. Chem. **39**, 201 (1900).
(104) Evers, Pharm. J. **106**, 470 (1921).
(105) Kebler, Dohme and Caspari, Z. anal. Chem. **38**, 200 (1899).
(106) Schär, Z. anal. Chern. **40**, 432 (1901).
(107) McGill, J. Am. Chem. Soc. **44**, 2156 (1922).
(108) Wagener and McGill, J. Am. Pharm. Assoc. **14**, 288 (1925).
(109) Masucci and Moflat, J. Am. Pharm. Assoc. **12**, 609 (1923).
(110) Kolthoff, Z. anorg. Chem. **112**, 196 (1920).
(111) Pinkhof, Dissertation, Amsterdam, (1919)
(112) Müller, Z. Elektrochem. **30**, 587 (1924).
(113) Treadwell and Janett, Helv. Chim. Acta **6**, 734 (1923).
(114) Lefort, J. Pharm. (3) **40**, 97 (1861).
(115) Fulton, J. Lab. Clin. Med. **13**, 750 (1928).
(116) Armitage, Pharm. J. Trans. (3) **18**, 761 (1888).
(117) Schaer, Arch. Pharm. **234**, 348 (1896).
(118) Weppen, Arch. Pharm. **205**, 112 (1871).
(119) Schneider, Ann. der Physik (Poggendorff) (5) **27**, 128 (1872);
J. prakt. Chem. (2) **6**, 455 (1873).
(120) Kobert, Chem. Zentr. **1899**, II, 149.
(121) Elias, Pharm. Ztg. **46**, 394 (1901).
(122) Marquis, Z. anal. Chem. **38**, 467 (1899); Pharm. Zentralhalle **37**, 844 (1896).
(123) Riegel and Williams, J. Am. Chem. Soc. **48**, 2871 (1926).
(124) Wieland and Kappelmeier, Ann. **382**, 306 (1911) .
(125) Lautenschlager, Arch. Pharm. **257**, 13 (1919).
(126) Erdmann, Ann. **120**, 188 (1861)
(127) Husemann, Ann. **128**, 305 (1863).
(128) Couerbe, Ann. chim. phys. (2) **59**, 136 (1835).
(129) Fraude, Ber. **12**, 1558 (1879).
(130) Rosenthaler, Schweiz. Apoth. Ztg. **61**, 117 (1923).
(131) Grove, Z. anal. Chem. **13**, 236 (1874).
(132) Siebold, Am. J. Pharm. (4) **3**, 544 (1873).
(133) Jörgensen, J. prakt. Chem. (2) **2**, 433 (1870).
(134) Wagner, Z. anal. Chem. **1**, 102 (1862).

(135) Eiloart, Chem. News **50**, 102 (1884).
(136) Marmé, Z. anal. Chem. **24**, 643 (1885).
(137) Flückiger, Arch. Pharm. (3) **1**, 111 (1872).
(138) Dittmar, Ber. **18**, 1612 (1885).
(139) Pellagri, Gazz. chim. ital. **7**, 297 (1877).
(140) Fröhde, Z. anal. Chem. **5**, 214 (1866).
(141) Bruylants, Z. anal. Chem. **37**, 62 (1898).
(142) Reichard, Z. anal. Chem. **42**, 95 (1903).
(143) Vulpius, Arch. Pharm. **225**, 256 (1887).
(144) Ekkert, Pharm. Zentralhalle **69**, 1, 19 (1928).
(145) Reichard, Chem. Ztg. **28**, 1102 (1904).
(146) Donath, J. prakt. Chem. (2) **33**, 563 (1886).
(147) Tattersall, Chem. News **41**, 63 (1880).
(148) Bronciner, Z. anal. Chem. **37**, 62 (1898).
(149) Van Itallie and Steenhauer, Arch. Pharm. **265**, 696 (1928).
(150) Aloy, Bull. soc. chim. (3) **29**, 610 (1903).
(151) Aloy and Rabaut, Bull. soc. chim. (4) **15**, 680 (1914).
(152) Aloy, Valdiguié and Aloy, Bull. soc. chim. (4) **39**, 792 (1926).
(153) Ekkert, Pharm. Zentralhalle **67**, 498 (1926).
(154) Plugge, Arch. Pharm. (3) **25**, 793 (1887).
(155) Cumming and Brown, J. Soc. Chem. Ind. **47**, 84 T (1928).
(156) North and Beal, J. Am. Pharm. Assoc. **13**, 889 (1924).
(157) Heiduschka and Wolf, Schweiz. Apoth. Ztg. **58**, 213, 229 (1920).
(158) Bertrand, Compt. rend. **128**, 743 (1899).
(159) Plugge, Rec. trav. chim. **6**, 209 (1887).
(160) Rosenthaler, Arch. Pharm. **265**, 319 (1927).
(161) Jaworoski, Chem. Zentr. **1896**, II, 321.
(162) Jorissen, Z. anal. Chem. **20**, 422 (1881).
(163) Ekkert, Pharm. Zentralhalle **69**, 198 (1928).
(164) Fleury, Ann. chim. anal. **6**, 417 (1901).
(165) Hager, Pharm. Zentralhalle n. f. **6**, 105 (1885).
(166) Reichard, Pharm. Zentralhalle **47**, 247 (1906).
(167) Nadler, Z. anal. Chem. **13**, 235 (1874); Bull. soc. chim. (2) **21**, 326 (1874).
(168) Lindo, Z. anal. Chem. 19, 359 (1880).
(169) Oliver, J. Am. Med. Assoc. **63**, 513; Chemist and Druggist **85**, 45 (1914).
(170) David, Pharm. Ztg. **70**, 969 (1925).
(171) Hermann, Biochem. Z. **39**, 216 (1912).
(172) Dieterich, Z. anal. Chem. **29**, 484 (1890).
(173) Pape, Apoth. Ztg. **24**, 70 (1909).
(174) Heikel, Chem. Ztg. **32**, 1149, 1162, 1212 (1908).
(175) Ionesco and Matiu, J. pharm. chim. (8) **4**, 533 (1926).
(176) Prescott and Gordin, J. Am. Chem. Soc. **20**, 706 (1898).
(177) Kieffer, Ann. **103**, 274 (1857).
(178) Heiduschka and Faul, Arch. Pharm. **255**, 172 (1917).
(179) Miller, Pharm. J. Trans. (3) **2**, 465 (1871).

(180) Stein, Arch. Pharm. (2) **148**, 150 (1871).
(181) Van Itallie and Harmsma, Chem. Zentr. **1926**, I 2612: Chem. Abstr. **21**, 3703 (192).
(182) Taylor, Allen's Comm'l Organ. Anal. VI **383** (1912).
(183) Schmidt, Abderhalden's Handb. biol. Arbeitsmethoden **9**, 449 (1920).
(263) Hesse, Ann. **202**, 151 (1880).
(264) Tausch, Arch. Pharm. **216**, 287 (1880).
(265) Göhlich, Arch. Pharm. **233**, 631 (1895).
(271) Schmidt, Ber. **10**, 194 (1877).
(282) Merck's Index, Merck and Co. **1930**, 4th ed.

Morphine Extraction from Opium Preparations of Morphia. (1800's)

MORPHIA: U.S. Morphia.

"Take of Opium, sliced, twelve troyounces; Water of Ammonia six fluid ounces; Animal Charcoal, in fine powder, Alcohol, Distilled Water, each, a sufficient quantity. Macerate the Opium with four pints of Distilled Water for twenty-four hours, and, having worked it with the hand, again macerate; for twenty-four hours, and strain. In like manner, macerate the residue twice successively with the same quantity of Distilled Water, and strain. Mix the infusions, evaporate to six pints, and filter; then add five pints of alcohol, and afterwards three fluid ounces of the Water of Ammonia, previously mixed with half a pint of Alcohol. After twenty-four hours, pour in the remainder of the Water of Ammonia, mixed, as before, with half a pint of Alcohol; and set the liquid aside for twenty-four hours that crystals may form. To purify these, boil them with two pints of Alcohol until they are dissolved, filter the solution, while hot through animal charcoal, and set it aside to crystallize." U.S.

Sertürner the discoverer of morphia, made an infusion of opium in distilled water, precipitated the morphia by ammonia in excess, dissolved the precipitate in dilute sulphuric acid, precipitated a new by ammonia, and purified by solution in boiling alcohol, and crystallization.

The process of the French Codex is a modification of that of Sertürner. It is as follows. "Take of opium 1000 parts, solution of ammonia a sufficient quantity. Exhaust the opium, by means of cold water, of all its parts soluble in that menstruum. For that purpose, it is sufficient to treat the opium, four times consecutively, with ten parts of water to one of the drug provided care be taken to macerate the opium for some hours, and to work it with the hands. Filter the liquors, and evaporate them to a quarter of their volume. Then add sufficient ammonia to render the liquor very sensibly alkaline. Boil for some minutes, always maintaining a slight excess of ammonia. Upon cooling, the morphia, impure and much coloured, will be precipitated in granular crystals, which are to be washed with cold water. Reduce this colored morphia to powder, macerate it for twelve hours in alcohol of 24° Cartier [sp. gr. about 0.900]; then decant the alcoholic liquid; dissolve the residual morphia, already in great measure deprived of colour by the cold alcohol, in boiling alcohol of 33° Cartier [sp. gr. about 0. 850]; add to the solution a little animal charcoal and filter. Upon cooling the morphia crystallizes in colourless needles. In this state the morphia always retains some narcotina, to free it from which, boil it with sulphuric ether in a matrass with a long neck surmounted by a refrigator."

Morphine Extraction 1920

by M. Barrowcliff, M.B.E., F.I.C. and Francis H. Carr, C.B.E., F.I.C.

NOT WITH STANDING the many rivals to morphine which organic chemistry has provided of late, none has supplanted it. For its value in allaying pain, morphine is probably still to be regarded as superior to every other drug. However, the danger of inducing the habit of taking morphine and the other disadvantages of its use are serious drawbacks, and with the advance of knowledge of pharmacology it must be regarded as probable that by the combined use of antipyretic and narcotic synthetic drugs, morphine and its analogues will ultimately be replaced.

The isolation of alkaloids from plant materials follows to a certain extent the same lines whatever the nature of the alkaloid, but some being more prone to hydrolysis than others require expensive low-boiling solvents for their extraction; while many, as for instance strychnine and quinine, may be boiled with water with relative impunity, so that they are extracted by less expensive methods.

Speaking generally, the procedure is to remove by means of a solvent the bases present in the plant, leaving the sugar, starch, protein, and pectenous matter unextracted. Fats, if present, accompany the bases; chlorophyll may or may not do so, according to the solvent. The solvents employed are very numerous; alcohol, fusel oil, benzene, solvent naphtha, ether, and petroleum being variously employed according to the circumstances. If benzene, solvent naphtha, or petroleum is used it is necessary to set free the bases in the plant by treatment with lime or alkali, since the alkaloids are present in combination with weak acids and are as a rule insoluble in this condition in these solvents. Many suitable extraction plants for use with volatile solvents have been designed. That illustrated, by the Standard Chemical Engineering Co., is economical as regards heat consumption and solvent losses. It is constructed on the principle of the well-known Soxhlet extraction, the solvent refluxing from the condenser into the material packed in the upper part of the lower vessel. The extract percolates through into the lower half of this vessel, from which it is vaporised to the condenser, leaving the extract.

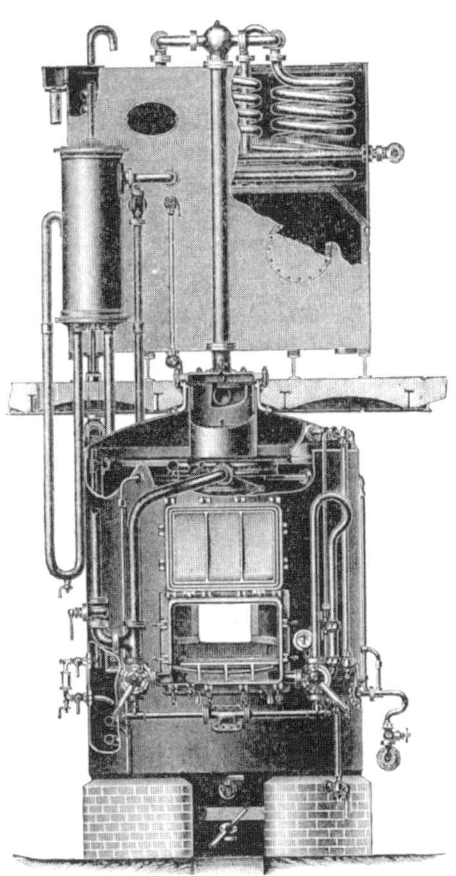

Fig.8.-Extraction plant-Fischer type

The solvent is next extracted with dilute acid; in some cases it is unnecessary first to distil away any of the solvent, but usually the greater part is first removed. The weak acid extract is frequently concentrated *in vacuo* before neutralization, and thus is obtained in very crude form the total alkaloid of the plant, admixed with a certain amount of sugar and so forth. Fat is removed at this stage by extraction with benzene or petroleum, in which the salts of the alkaloid are not soluble. The further treatment and the long and tedious separation and purification of the alkaloids must be varied not only with each kind of material, but with every batch, and requires great skill and experience and extremely careful workers.

For the extraction of an aqueous liquid with ether, petrol or other light immiscible solvent the apparatus shown in Fig. 9 is suitable. The liquid to be extracted is placed in A, which is fitted with an efficient cooling coil. The solvent enters at B either as a liquid or vapor and overflows into the still C, from which the extract is finally removed

Morphine $C_{17}H_{19}O_3N$. 285.—By the assiduous work of many chemists the constitution of morphine has been in the main elucidated;

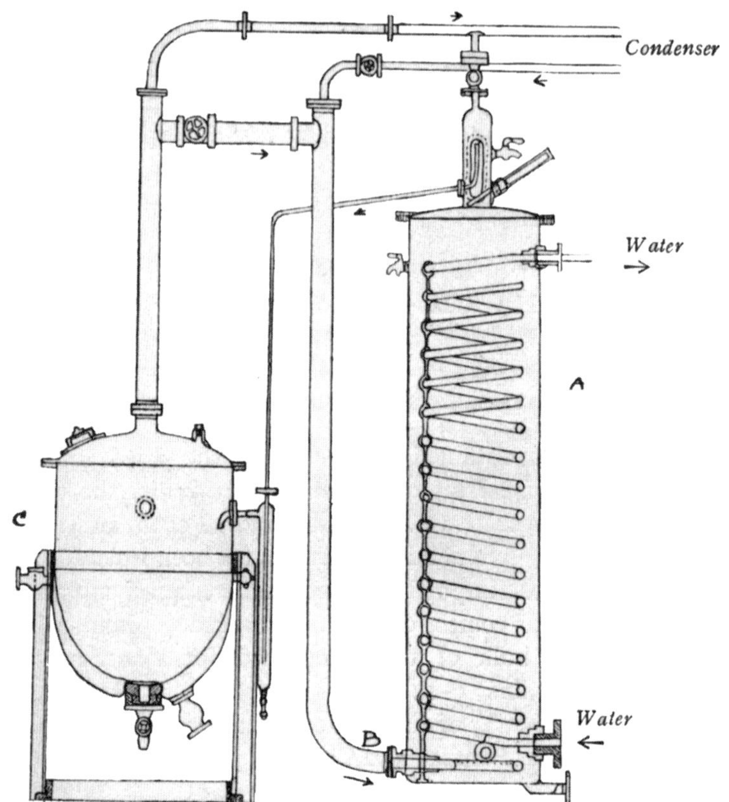

Fig.9-Extraction of aqueous liquids with light solvents.

there remains, however, a choice to be made between several formulae which explain satisfactorily its known reactions. Of those formulae, the two following are of chief importance:

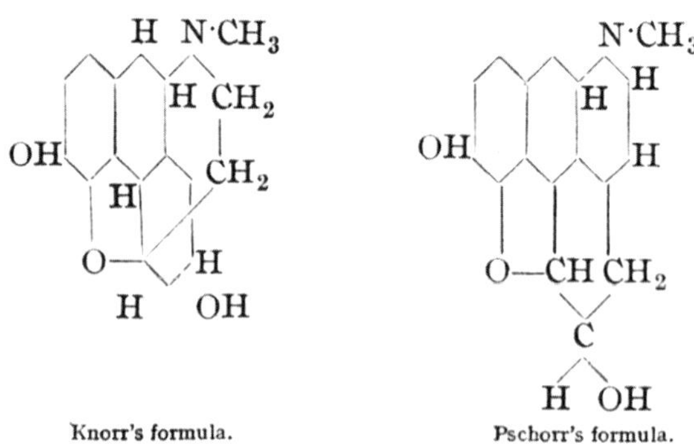

Knorr's formula.

Pschorr's formula.

Morphine is obtained from opium, the dried latex or sap of the unripe fruit of *Papaver somniferum*, the opium poppy, which is cultivated in Asia Minor, Persia, India, and China. Twenty-five alkaloids have so far been isolated from opium, the most important, medicinally, being morphine, next to which comes codeine. Smyrna opium, which comprises the bulk of that employed for manufacturing purposes, contains 9-12% of morphine, 0.3-1.0% of codeine, and 4-6% of narcotine. The recorded alkaloidal content of India, Persian, and Chinese opium is as follows:—

Opium.	Per cent. morphine.	Per cent. narcotine.
Indian	3·2–8·6	3·1–7·1
Persian	6–8	5–7
Chinese	4·3–11·2	1·6–6·6

For the extraction of the alkaloids the opium is worked down to a thin paste with calcium chloride solution and then extracted with warm water. By this treatment the morphine and other bases are converted into their respective hydrochlorides, whilst the acids with which they were combined in the drug, such as meconic acid, are precipitated as insoluble calcium salts. The insoluble matter is separated by means of a filter press or suction filter, and to prevent oxidation sodium sulphite is added to the filtrate, which is then concentrated, preferably *in vacuo*, to the consistency of a thin syrup. Addition is then made of a concentrated sodium acetate solution, which precipitates narcotine and papaverine. These are filtered off, a small proportion of alcohol is added and the morphine is precipitated from the warmed filtrate by the careful addition of lime in presence of ammonium chloride or by the addition of caustic soda. It is allowed to stand and is removed by filtration. The filtrate is extracted, after cooling, with benzene or chloroform, whereby codeine is removed. It is isolated by extraction with acid and regenerating and crystallizing as base from water.

The crude morphine is freed from traces of codeine by washing it with benzene. It is then mixed with thrice its weight of boiling water and treated with the exact quantity of 25% hydrochloric acid required for naturalization. To prevent atmospheric oxidation the solution is covered with a layer of petroleum. Morphine hydrochloride crystallizes out on cooling, is filtered off, recrystallized from water till pure, and dried at atmospheric temperature. From an aqueous solution of the pure hydrochloride, pure morphine may be obtained by precipitation with ammonia.

Anhydrous morphine melts at 230°. It is soluble in 5000 parts of water at 15°, in 500 parts at 100°, in 300 parts of cold 90% alcohol, and in 30 parts of boiling alcohol. It dissolves in 200 parts of chloroform and is only very slightly soluble in ether, ethyl acetate, or benzene.

0.2 gram of morphine should form a clear solution in 4 c.c. of caustic potash solution (5% w/w). A solution of 0.1 gram morphine in 10 c.c. of 10% hydrochloric acid should afford no red coloration with ferric chloride solution (absence of meconates).

Treated with concentrated sulphuric acid morphine should dissolve to a colorless solution.

Salts of Morphine

Morphine hydrochloride $C_{17}H_{19}O_3NHCl + 3H_2O$. 375.4—White, lustrous, silky needles. Dissolves in 24 parts of water, giving a neutral solution. It should contain 75.5% of anhydrous morphine. It may best be crystallized from water or dilute alcohol; the presence of ammonium sulphite is of assistance in preventing coloration.

Morphine Acetate $C_{17}H_{19}O_3N, CH_3COOH + 3H_2O$. 399. —For the preparation of this salt 10 parts of pure powdered morphine are mixed with 30 parts of hot water and 7 parts of 30% acetic acid. The solution is filtered hot and evaporated in vacuo at 50° to 20 parts. It is cooled, seeded with a crystal of morphine acetate and kept in a cold place. Access of air should be prevented, by a layer of petroleum or by other means. Morphine acetate crystallizes out and is dried at atmospheric temperature.

A light, white, crystalline powder. Dissolves in 3 parts of water to a solution which becomes perfectly clear on addition of a small quantity of acetic acid. To obtain the salt completely soluble in water it is necessary to crystallize it from a slight excess of acetic acid and to dry with great caution.

Morphine Acetate should contain at least 71% of morphine.

Morphine Sulphate $(C_{17}H_{19}O_3N)_2, H_2SO_4 + 5H_2O$. 758. —Forms colourless acicular crystals, soluble in 21 parts of water. It is prepared in the same way as morphine hydrochloride and is crystallised from water in the presence of ammonium sulphite.

Morphine Tartrate $(C_{17}H_{19}O_3N)_2, C_4H_6O_6 + 3H_2O$. 774, is prepared by dissolving morphine in the theoretical quantity of tartaric acid in water, from which it separates on cooling as a white crystalline powder, soluble in 10 parts of water. Excess of tartaric acid must be avoided because the acid tartrate which is then produced is sparingly soluble and separates with the neutral tartrate on cooling.

Morphine possesses the power simultaneously to exercise a depressant, narcotic action on the brain and a stimulating action on the spinal cord. It is also analgesic, slows the respiration, but has little effect on the circulation.

It is widely employed as an hypnotic, being usually administered by hypodermic injection of one of its salts. Morphine acts more quickly than opium, and is less likely to disturb the digestion or to cause headache and nausea.

Codeine $C_{18}H_{21}O_3N$. 299.—

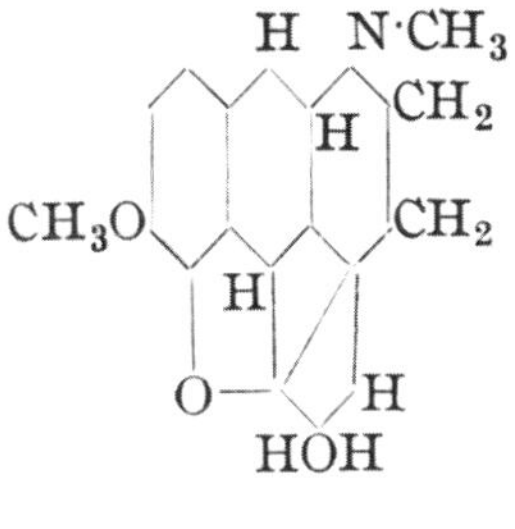

Knorr's formula. or Pschorr's formula.

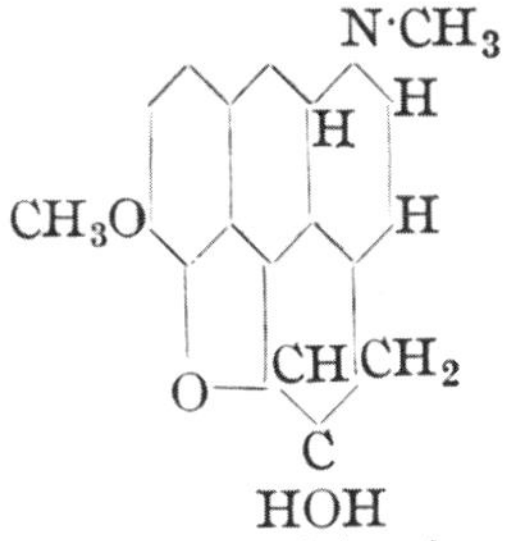

Codeine is a methyl ether of morphine. It occurs in opium in amounts varying from 0.1% to 3.0% and is isolated therefrom in the way already described (see Morphine).

Much of the codeine of commerce, however, is prepared synthetically by the methylation of morphine.

The following methylating agents have been proposed:

Methyl iodide (Compt. Rend. **92**, 1140, 1228; **93**, 67, 217, 591).
Salts of methyl sulphuric acid (D.R.P. 39887).
Nitrosomethyl urethane, or diazomethane, (D.R.PP. 92789, 95644, 96145).
Dimethyl Sulphate (D.RP. 102634).
Methyl phosphate (D.R.P. 107225).
Methyl nitrate (D.R.P. 108075).
p-toluene sulphon nitrosomethyl amide (D.R.P. 224388).
Methyl sulphite (D.R.P. 214783).
Methyl benzene (or toluene), sulphonate (D.R.P. 131980)

Source: Industrial Chemistry: Being a Series of Volumes Giving a Comprehensive Survey of the Chemical Insustry;
by M. Barrowcliff and Francis H. Carr;
pub. by D. Van Nosrand Company, NY (1920)

Pharmacology of Morphine

by Horatio C. Wood, Charles H. LaWall, Heber W. Youngken, John F. Anderson, Ivor Griffith

Uses.— There canbe no doubt that morphine is the chief narcotic principle of opium, from which, however, it differs somewhat in its mode of action. The effects of morphine are so protean that they can best be considered by taking the different functions of the body seriatim.

Nervous System.— Morphine is a cerebral depressant but a spinal stimulant. The relative predominance of one or the other of these actions depends upon the relative degree of development of the brain or spinal cord; thus in the frog it produces violent convulsions of the strychnine type, but in man the spinal symptoms are usually imperceptible and for medical purposes we may regard it as a general depressant as far as the nervous system is concerned. The primary action upon the cerebrum seems to be a diminution in the powers of perception especially of pain, although there is often an evident lowering in the acuity of the special senses. With somewhat larger doses intellection becomes depressed and a tendeney to drowsiness is manifest, and after toxic doses a deep comatose sleep may follow. When locally applied in sufficient concentration morphine lowers the functional activity of the peripheral nerve endings both motor and sensory. In this way it may, under certain conditions as shown by Wiki (J. de P. P., 1913, xv, p. 848), exercise a local anesthetic action. It is, however, less active in this regard than some of the other allied alkaloids, notably ethyl-morphine or methyl-morphine (codeine). Among the other actions of morphine which are to be attributed to its influence on nerve centers is the contraction of the pupil, due to stimulation of the oculo-motor center, slowing of the pulse from stimulation of the cardio-inhibitory center, slowing of the respiration from depression of the respiratory center, and overcoming the action of nauseants from its action on the emetic center.

Cushny and Lieb (J. P. Ex. T., 1915, iv, p. 450) have found that in the period of respiratory depression produced by morphine there is not the same sort of insensibility to carbon dioxide that is caused by some other respiratory depressants, and according to Macht (J. P. Ex. T. 1915, vii, 339) small doses of morphine may lessen the sensitiveness of the respiratory center to carbon dioxide without reducing the normal volume of air breathed. Cohen and MeGuigan (J. P. Ex. T., 1924, xxxiii, 145) believe that the diminution of respiration is not due to a true depression of the respiratory center but simply to a blockage of the afferent impulses which ordinarily excite this center. These observations are obviously of considerable importance in connection with the clinical use of this remedy in dyspneic states.

The influence upon the unstriped muscles, especially upon the intestines, is so complex that its accurate analysis is still somewhat doubtful Macht (J. P. Ex. T., 1918, xi, p. 389) has shown that morphinehas an exciting action upon unstriped muscle. On the other hand, it is well known that morphine, in the human being at least, lessens intestinal peristalsis—a fact which Macht in an earlier communication admitted and attributed to an action upon the central nervous system. In dogs defecation is a very frequent sequela after the administration of morphine. This, however, is probably due to the difference in dosage employed in dogs and man; Uhlmann and Abelin (Zeit. E. P. T., 1920, xxi, 75) from experimental studies have found that while small doses of opium diminish intestinal peristalsis, larger quantities increase. Morphine causes, certainly in the lower animals and probably also in humans, a spasmodic contraction of the pylorus, which may perhaps explain the nausea that often follows its use.

Circulation.— The action of morphine upon the circulation is quite subsidiary to its effects upon the nervous system. In therapeutic doses the only manifestation of its effects on the part of the circulatory apparatus is slowing of the pulse, due, as mentioned above, to stimulation of the inhibitory center, and flushing of the skin which appears to be the result of a special action on the cutaneous blood vessels. After large doses the blood pressure is generally somewhat lowered, probably from the combined weakening of the heart and vasomotor system.

Nutrition.— Morphine affects the nutrition both through its action upon the digestive processes and through a direct influence on the bodily chemistry. It appears to lessen all the digestive secretions including salivary, gastric, and enteric, also to diminish the peristaltic movements. The direct influence of morphine upon metabolism is not clearly understood, but there is reason to believe that it has some such action.

Elimination.— A large part of the morphine is detoxicated in the body passing out as a dioxymorphine. Some of it, however, is eliminated unchanged, more through the intestinal glands than the kidneys.

Clinical Uses.— Morphine may be used in medicine to fulfil any of seven indications:

(1) In its power to relieve pain morphine is without rival. Because, however, of its unpleasant action upon the digestive organs and the everpresent danger of formation of the habit, it should be reserved for the more severe degrees of suffering, such as in gall-stone or renal colic, or when other analgesics have failed. In this connection it should be noted that the analgesic action of morphine is greatly enhanced by combining it with even relatively feeble synergists, such as the coal tar series or scopolamine, and by recourse to this principle of combination the physician is often able to assuage the suffering with comparatively small doses of the alkaloid.

(2) As a hypnotic morphine is useful, especially when the insomnia is due to suffering. In the purely nervous types of sleeplessness it is less valuable than the aliphatic narcotics, but is often of service as an adjuvant.

(3) As a sedative to the respiratory center it is a remedy of much value in asthma and certain types of cough, such as whooping cough. In true bronchitis, however, it must be used with circumspection. In the acute stage or where the mucous membranes are dry, it often does great harm by a further checking of the bronchial secretions; on the other hand, when the secretions are very profuse it may so benumb the respiratory center as to stop their expectoration and thereby lead to a dangerous retention of fluid in the chest.

(4) In intestinal conditions it is used for its influence both on secretion and peristalsis. For the latter action it is of much service in serous diarrheas but when the diarrhea is due to irritation of the intestinal tract it is generally to be avoided, as it defeats nature's purpose to get rid of the irritant. For its influence upon the muscular movements of the bowel it is useful in various forms of intestinal spasm, such as lead colic, and also to keep the bowels at rest in certain types of peritonitis and other inflammatory conditions. Whole opium is usually preferred to morphine when an action upon the intestines is desired.

(5) For the purpose of aiding in the production of diaphoresis it is used, especially in the form of Dovert's powder, in the early stages of colds, in rheumatism, influenza, etc.

(6) To allay vomiting, especially of reflex origin.

(7) By its calmative effect it protects the system against exhaustion in debilitated conditions, as certain forms of typhoid fever. For the same purpose it is also a very valuable drug in the treatment of internal hemorrhage.

In cases where it is desired to make a profound impression uponthe general system, morphine should be given hypodermically. The dose varies enormously, according to the susceptibility of the patient and the purpose for which it is used. In a general way the dose of the morphine salts, by mouth, may be given as from one-eighth to one-half grain (0.008-.032 Gm.), and one-twelfth to one-fourth grain (0.005-0.016 Gm.) hypodermically.

In consequence of its insolubility in water, morphine in its pure state is less convenient than its salts, which are therefore always preferred. The acetate, sulphate, and hydrochloride, which have been employed, act precisely alike therapeutically, and differ from opium chiefly in being less disposed to constipate the bowels. They are also somewhat less likely to cause disagreeable after-effects than is opium, but the deodorized tincture is certainly preferable to them for many purposes. They are further adapted for hypodermic use. Oleic acid has also been proposed as a vehicle for morphine externally used, as it dissolves both the alkaloid and its salts perfectly in considerable proportion. A liniment of oleate of morphine has been proposed, consisting of 300 parts of oleic acid and 1 part of morphine scented with a little oil of bergamot. As the proportion of acid necessary to neutralize morphine is very small, the dose of the alkaloid is practically the same as that of its salts.

Dose, one-fifth of a grain (0.012 Gm.), equivalent to a grain of powdered opium.

Source: The Dispensatory of the United States of America 21st ed; by Horatio C. Wood, Charles H. LaWall, Heber W. Youngken, John F. Anderson, Ivor Griffith, pub. by J.B. Lippencott Company (1926)

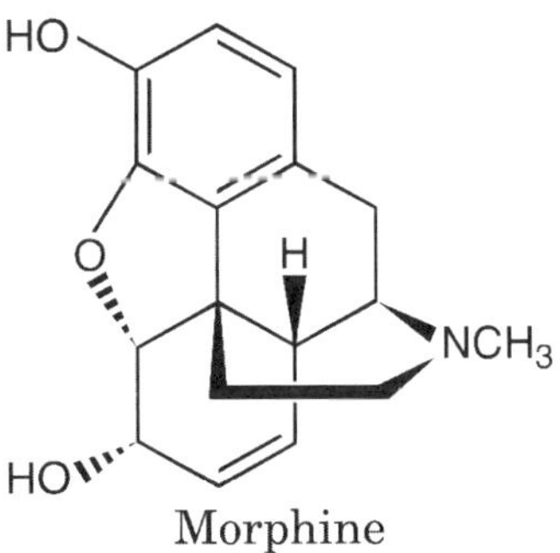

Morphine

A Process for the Extraction of Alkaloids from Poppy Straw and/or Capsules

By T. and H. Smith Limited, Blandfield Chemical Works,
J.F. MacFarlan and Company Limited and Geroge William Walker
Aug. 18, 1954 GB 713,689

This invention relates to a process of extracting alkaloids from poppies and particularly to a process of extracting morphine from poppies. A number of methods have been proposed for extracting morphine from poppies, but hitherto all these proposals have entailed the manipulation of large quantities of liquors. It is known to extract the vegetable matter of the poppy with organic solvents, but such methods result in an extract containing many substances other than morphine and its accompanying alkaloids and render purification troublesome and expensive.

It is also known to subject the vegetable matter of the poppies to the action of chemicals capable of forming water-soluble salts of morphine such as mineral acids or slaked lime. Morphine, an amphoteric substance, is capable of forming salts with acids and strong bases. These methods have the disadvantage of requiring dilute extractants and hence large volumes of solution. The morphine is liberated from the salts by neutalization and extracted with organic water immisable solvents such as fusel oil or methylene chloride.

The present invention now provides a process for extracting morphine from poppy straw and capsules in which the whole of the materials are kept in substantially solid form during extraction with aqueous liquids.

The process of the present invention comprises mixing dry, finely ground poppy straw and/or capsules with lime and just sufficient water to wet the mass, separating the aqueous extract by pressing the mass, adjusting the pH of the extract to between 4 and 5.5 by means of sulphuric acid, evaporating the thus acidified extract under reduced pressure until it has a firm conistency when cold but is fluent when hot, making the evaporated extract alkaline with an alkaline substance other than a caustic alkali and then extracting the alkaloids therefrom by means of a water immiscible organic solvent.

It is preferred, during the acidification stage of the process, to keep the pH at 4-5. When the acidified extract is being made alkaline before it is extracted with organic solvent the degree of alkalinity is not critical, but the presence of free caustic alkalis must be avoided and we therefore prefer to employ sodium carbonate. Alternatively, however, the evaporated, acidified extract may be adjusted to a pH between 6 and 7 with caustic soda and then made alkaline with a weaker alkali, such as sodium carbonate. Any organic solvent which is immiscible with water and which will dissolve the alkaloids will serve for the solvent extraction, but we prefer to use a mixture of equal proportion of xylene and fusel oil and to carry out the extraction at 100° C.

The morphine may be recovered from the solvent by extraction with a suitable quantity of hydrochloric acid and precipitation of the thus obtained solution with ammonia.

A prefered form of the process comprises mixing dry, finely ground poppy straw and/or capsules with 5% of its weight of calcium hydroxide and a quantity of water equal to substantially four times the weight of the poppy straw and/or capsules used, allowing the mass to stand for a period of 2 hours, separating the aqueous extract by pressing the mass, adjusting the pH of the extract to 5 ± 0.5 with sulphuric acid, evaporating the thus acidified extract under reduced pressure until it has a firm consistency when cold but is fluent when hot, making the evaporated extract alkaline with sodium carbonate, extracting the morphine therefrom by means of a mixture of equal proportions of fusel oil and xylene at a temperature of 100° C. extracting the morphine from the fusel oil-xylene mixture by means of sufficient hydrochloric acid to combine with substantially all of the morphine and precipitating the morphine from the thus obtained solution by means of ammonia.

During the extraction process, substantially the whole of the morphine estimated to be contained within the poppy straw and/or capsules is dissolved, and the recovery up to the liquid stage is limited only by the efficiency of the pressing, in practice, 80-85%; of the estimated morphine being obtained. The overall yield is however limited by mechanical and solubility losses and is usually about 60%.

The process, according to the invention, has a number of advantages over processes heretofore employed. Principal amongst these is the advantage that the bulk of liquid to be manipulated is kept to a minimum. It is not necessary to remove the calcium sulphate formed in acidification from the liquor as its presence does not interfere with the subsequent evaporation and extraction.

The evaporation of the extract down to a firm consistency has the further advantage that it reduces solvent losses and elliminates the formation of emulsions.

The following example will serve to illustrate more fully the manner in which the process of the invention may be carried out. In this example, the relationship of parts by weight to parts by volume is that of grams to cubic centimetres.

EXAMPLE

330 parts by weight of poppy capsule (the ripe head of *Papaver somniferum*), from which seed has been removed, are ground to pass a 1/16" mesh, mixed with 16 parts by weight of lime, and the mass moistened with 1,320 parts by volume of water. The well mixed mass is left for two hours at a temperature in the neighborhood of 15° C. The mass is then pressed, for example in a hydraulic press, and the expressed liquid collected. 1,000 parts by volume of liquor are obtained. Dilute sulphuric acid is added until the pH has been reduced to 5.0 The liquor is concentrated under a vacuum of about 20° of mercury until it has been reduced to 125 parts by volume. 20 parts by weight of anhydrous sodium carbonate are added and 150 parts by volume of a mixture of equal volume of fusel oil and xylene are added. The mixture is stirred at the boil for one hour. The upper layer of solvent separated, and the alkaloids removed by treatment with 1 parts by volume of 10% sulphuric acid followed by washing twice with 12 parts by volume of water. The oil from which the alkaloids have been removed is again added to the mass to be extracted and stirred at the boil for a further hour. The separation, extraction with acid, and washing with water are repeated. The acid and aqueous extracts are reduced to 25 parts by volume by evaporation in in vacuo, ammonia liquor is added until a slight excess is present, and crude morphine allowed to precipitate on standing in the cold. The weight of crude morphine obtained is 0.508 parts by weight of purity 85%, calculated as morphine alkaloid. The yield of pure morphine isolated is therefore 62.5% of the morphine estimated to be present in the poppycapsule.

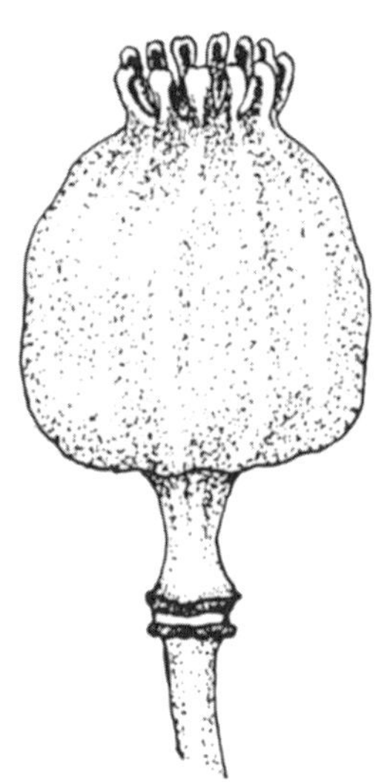

HYDROCODONE (Dihydrocodeinone; Dicodid)

Pharmacology of Hydrocodone

by Hugo Krueger, Nathan B. Eddy and Margaret Sumwalt

Nervous System Man: A narcotic or depressant effect was seen (Schelenz, 1927; Mayer, 1927); with 10 mg. T, o (Meyer and Pfaffenholz, 1932); with 15 mg. T (Römmelt, 1927); with 100 and 500 mg. T, suicidal attemps with recovery after prolonged daily use of 10-20 mg. T (Sametinger, 1935). An analgesic effect was seen (Mayer, 1927; Grünthal and Hoefer, 6836); with 15 mg. T (Kleinschmidt, 1923); with 15 mg. T, sc or o (Seifert, 1924); with 5-10 mg. T (Heinroth, 1926). Excitement and convulsions were seen in some cases with excessive doses (Sametinger, 1935).

Respiration Man: The respiration was depressed (Mayer, 1927); was relatively not much affected with toxic doses (Sametinger, 1935). Cough relief was obtained with 20 mg. T, per day (Hecht, 1923); with 15 mg. T, sc or o (Seifert, 1924).

H_3CO ... NCH_3 ... O

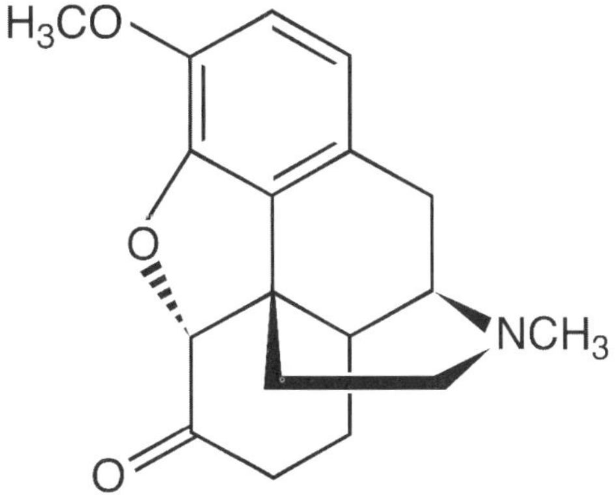

Hydrocodone

Circulation Man: Circulatory changes were insignificant (Mayer, 1927).

Blood Man: In one case of addiction to dicodide, the rate of sedimentation was normal, until after withdrawal when it became less then normal; in another case, the rate was faster than normal during addiction and became normal after cure (Schottky, 1931).

Digestion Man: The tone of smooth muscle in the gastrointestinal tract increased (Mayer, 1927). Consitipation did not develope with 15 mg. T, sc (Römmelt, 1927).

Emesis Man: Nausea and vomiting occurred (Schelenz, 1927); with 15 mg. T, sc (Römmelt, 1927); with 100-120 mg. T, sc (Sametinger, 1935); but seemed to be less frequent than with morphine (Kleinschmidt, 1923).

Other Smooth Muscle Man: Urinary retention was seen and the tone of smooth muscle in general increased (Mayer, 1927).

Toxicity Man: Two individuals accustomed to 20 mg. T, daily, survived 100 and 200 mg.; 6 accustomed individuals taking single doses of 80-200 mg. showed no symptoms; a child of 14 months and another of 7 years survived 20 mg. T; the only fatal case was that of 2-year old child after 5 mg. T (Sametinger, 1935).

Tolerance and Addiction Man: Cases of addiction to dicodide have been reported (Wolff, 1928); Hoefer, 1929; Richtzenhain, 1930; Menninger-Lerchenthal, 1931; Dansauer and Rieth, 1931; Langelüddeke, 1932; Meyer, 1935; Pilcz, 1937). Neither tolerance nor euphoria accompanied the use of dicodide (Herz, 1924; Römmelt, 1927); tolerance and euphoria were striking 20 mg. per day (Hecht, 1923); euphoria was felt with 10 mg. T, o, but with 20-40 mg. T, o, the sensations were not pleasant (Meyer and Pfaffenholz, 1932). No abstinence symptoms followed the use of 15 mg. of dicodide per day for 9 days (Römmelt, 1927). Tolerance developed for the depression by dicodide of sensitivity to pain, but not for the depression of sensitivity to pressure (Grünthal and Hoefer, 1929).

References

Dansauer, Friedtich and Rieth, Adolf. (1931). Uber Morphinismus bein Kriegsbeschädigten. Nach amtlichen Unterlagen bearbeitet. Arbeit und Gesundheit Schriftenreihe zum Reichsarbeitsblatt. Issued under the auspices of the Reichsarbeitsministerium. Berlin.

Gaupp, R. (1932) Deutsche med. Wchnschr., **58**, 1574.

Grünthal, E. and Hoefer, P. (1929) Untersuchungen über akute und chronische Morphinwirkungen. Klin. Wchnschr., **8**, 104-107.

Hecht, Paul. (1923) Uber Klinische Prufüng von Hustenmitteln. aus der Morphingruppe. Klin. Wchnschr., **2**, 1069.

Heinroth, Hans. (1926) Uber die Wirkung verschiedener Arzneimittel auf die Schmerzempfindlichkeit der Zahnpulpa. Arch. f. exper. Path u.. Pharmakol., **116**, 245.

Herz, Ernst. (1924) Erfahrungen mit Dicodid in der Psychiatrie und Neurologie. Deutsche med. Wchnschr., **50**, 431.

Hoefer, Paul .(1929) Uber die Beeinflussung der Hautsinnesqualitäten durch Morphin und ähnliche Präparate, zugleich ein Beitrag zur Kenntnis des Morphinismus. Ztschr. f. Biol., **89**, 21.

Kleinschmidt, K. (1923) Uber clie schmerzstillende Wirkung eines morphinartig wirkenden Kodeinderivats "Dicodid." München. med. Wchnschr., **70**, 391.

Mayer, Richard F. (1927) Vergleichende Beobachtungen über die Wirkung der wichtigsten Narcotica der Opiumgruppe. München. rned.Wchnschr., **74**, 1657.

Menninger-Lerchenthal, E. (1931) Rauschgiftgesetz und Suchtkrankheit (Dicodidismus). Wien. med. Wchnschr.. **81**, 431.

Meyer, F. and Pfaffenholz, W. (1932) Die psychischen Wirkungen des Dicodids und ihre Bekäimpfung. Ztschr. f. klin. Med., **120**, 634.

Meyer, Fritz M. (1935) Uber einige seltener vorkommende Formen von Rauschgiftsucht. München. med. Wchnschr., **82**, 617.

Pilcz, Alexander. Arztliches über Rauschgifte. (1937) Wien. med. Wchnschr., **87**, 998.

Richtzenhain. Erfahrungen (1930) mit Dilaudid und Dicodid in der Nervenpraxis. Therap. d. Gegenw., **71**, 431-32.

Römmelt, W. (1927) Uber die Beeinflussung des Seelenlebens durch Dicodid und Dilaudid. Psychol. Arb., **9**, 435.

Sametinger, E. Dicodidvergiftung. (1935) Deutsche med. Wchnschr., **61**, 2009.

Schelenz. (1927) Nebenwirkungen durch Dicodid. München. med. Wchnschr., **74**, 244

Schottky, Johannes. (1931) Die Blutkörperchensenkung bei Geistes- und Nervenkranken. Ztschr. f. d. ges. Neurol. u. Psychiat., **133**, 631.

Seifert, Otto. (1924) Nebenwirkungen der modernen arzneimittel. Würzb. Abhandl. a. d. ges. d. Med., **21**, 195.

Wolff, P. (1928) Zur Behandlung und Bekämpfung der Alkaloidsuchten (Morphinismus, Kokainismus usw.). Deutsche med. Wchnschr., **54**, **7**, 51, 134, 224. 266. 349, 387.

CODEINE

Discovery and Chemical Properties

By Lyndon F. Small and Robert E. Lutz

Codeine, $C_{18}H_{21}O_3N$, the methyl ether of morphine, was first isolated in 1832 by Robiquet (1) (2), who found it as an impurity accompanying morphine which had been extracted from opium by the Gregory process. Analyses by Regnault (3) (4), Liebig (5), and others (6) (7) (8) resulted in the proposal of various empirical formulas; Gerhardt (9) (10) (1842) first obtained values corresponding to $C_{18}H_{21}O_3N + H_2O$. Gerhardt's analyses were confirmed by Anderson (11). Wright (12) believed that this formula should be doubled; his view has not been accepted.

Codeine is found in opium in far smaller amounts than morphine, usually between the limits 0.2% to 0.8% (13). It has not been reported as occurring in any plant other than the poppy. Codeine is the second alkaloid to appear in the young plant, being first detectable about 30 days after the seed has sprouted; poppy seeds contain no codeine (14). Its character as the methyl ether of morphine was first established by Grimaux (15) in 1881, although speculations to this effect (16) (17) had appeared previous to this time. Since the development of practicable alkylation methods, it has been obtained largely from the more abundant morphine by methylation.

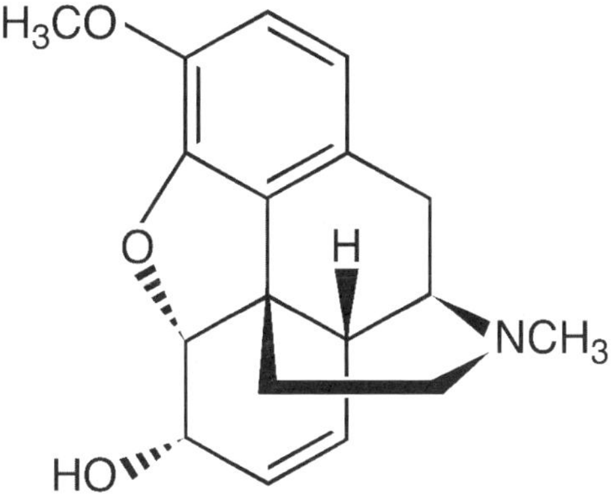

Codeine

Of the numerous separation procedures, those based on the Gregory (18) method have probably found the most application. The concentrated aqueous extract from finely powdered opium is treated with strong calcium chloride solution, which removes as calcium salts the meconic acid, lactic acid, and sulphuric acid. From the mother liquor the so-called Gregory-salt, a mixture of the hydrochlorides of morphine and codeine, crystallizes. Ammonia precipitates the morphine from a solution of the purified Gregory-salt, while the codeine remains in solution from which it may be separated by extracting with benzene or by concentrating to the point where a mixture of ammonium chloride and codeine hydrochloride crystallizes.

Source: Chemistry of the Opium Alkaloids (1932)

Other methods ,which have been proposed for the separation of codeine are those of Merck (19) (20), Mohr (21), Hesse (22) (23), and Plugge (24) (25). A recent paper by Kanewskaja (26) reviews these procedures and describes a newly developed process which permits the isolation of 87% of the codeine present in opium.

The preparation of codeine by methylation of morphine wasaccomplished independently by Grimaux (15) (27) (1881) and Hesse (28) by the action of methyl iodide on morphine in the presence of alkali. Since the morphine and codeine are converted in large part to the methiodides, the yield of codeine base is very small. A number of more advantageous methods have been developed in factory practice, and are reported in the patent literature as follows :

Methylation of morphine or morphine alkali salts with salts of methyl sulphuric acid, A. Knoll (29) (30) .

Methylation in the presence of sodium methylate or sodium ethylate using dimethyl sulphate (31), trimethyl phosphate (32), or methyl nitrate (33), E. Merck.

Methylation of morphine alkali salts with dimethyl sulplite, Gerber (34). Methylation of morphine-N-oxide with dimethyl sulphate and alkali, and reduction of the resulting codeine-N-oxide to codeine, E. Merck (35) .

The use of diazomethane was covered in 1896 by patents of Farbenfabr. vorm. Friedr. Bayer & Co. (36) (37) (38), which included modifications using nitrosomonomethylurea (39), p-toluenesulphonitrosomethylamide or nitroso-methylbenzamide (40).

Methylation with esters of sulphonic acids, as methyl benzene sulphonate, E. Merck (41).

The most advantageous methylation process has proved to be that using phenyltrimethylammonium hydroxide (Boehringer Sohn (42)) as methylating agent:

$$HO(C_{17}H_{17}ON)OH + C_6H_5N(CH_3)_3OH \rightarrow$$

Morphine

$$CH_3O(C_{17}H_{17}ON)OH + C_6H_5N(CH_3)_2 + H_2O$$

Codeine

There is no loss of morphine or codeine through formation of quaternary N-alkyl compounds, and the dimethyl aniline formed during the reaction is readily removed by steam distillation. A modification of this method, due to Rodionov (43), may be operated conveniently and economically on a laboratory scale.

Codeine crystallizes from dry ether or benzene in small anhydrous prisms of m.p. 155°. From water or dilute alcohol large clear rhombic prisms (44) holding one molecule of crystal-water are obtained; the hydrated base sometimes shows a melting point below that of the anhydrous (6), depending upon the mode of heating. Transparent rhombic octahedra separate from :rnoist ether. Deane and Brady (45) describe the crystals from alcohol or water as octahedra running to four-sided prisms (crystal drawings given). The base crystallizes from carbon disulphide in anhydrous rhombohedra (46). Crystal measurements have been published by Keferstein (47), Senarmont (48), Arzruni (46), Wherry and Yanovsky (49), and Heydrich (50). Hydrated codeine crystals effloresce somewhat on exposure to air, and lose their crystal-water completely at 100°. The hydrated base also becomes anhydrous in boiling water, melting to an oily liquid.

Gaubert (51) states that codeine crystallized above 60° forms rhombic hemihedral crystals, the stable (α) form. At lower temperatures it exists in four kinds of spherulites, viz, a β-form at ordinary temperatures, a γ-form at about 40° and two other spherulite forms between 45° and 60°. These modifications differ in their power to rotate the plane of polarization. Kremann and Schniderschitz (52) could find no evidence in the cooling curve of codeine for the existence of Gaubert's spherulites.

Codeine is sparingly soluble in water; it in much more soluble than morphine in most organic solvents. One gram of codeine dissolves, in 120 g. of water, 1.6 g. of alcohol, 0.75 g. chloroform or 13 g. of ether, at 25°; in 0.96 g. of alcohol at 60° (53). Other values for the solubility are given in the accompanying table.

Table of solubilities

[Grams of codeine in 100 g. of solvent]

Solvent	Solubility	Observer
Water	0.9 (20°), 1.1 (40°), 3.2 (100°)	Rakshit (54).
Do	1.28 (15°), 3.77 (43°), 5.88 (100°)	Robiquet (2).
Do	1.17 (cold), 5.9 (hot)	Knoll (30).
Do	0.85 (15°)	Tambach and Henke (55).
Ammonia 10% w/v	0.9 (20°), 1.5 (40), 3.2 (80°)	Rakshit (54).
Alcohol 90%	27.0 (20°), 61.0 (40°), 89.5 (90°)	Do. (54).
Amyl alcohol	15.68 (temperature not given)	Kubly (56).
Ether	3.4 (20°)	Rakshit (54).
Acetone	20.4 (20°), 26.4 (40°), 36.3 (50°)	Do. (54).
Chloroform	22.8 (20°), 35.4 (40°), 47.4 (50°)	Do. (54).
Carbon tetrachloride	1.328 (17°)	Schindelmeiser (57).
Benzene	8.3 (20°), 17.6 (40°), 72.5 (80°)	Rakshit (54).
Do	9.6 (temperature not given)	Kubly (56).
Anisole	7.8 (9°), 15.28 (16°), 164.0 (100°)	Fouquet (58).

Codeine which has been crystallized once from anisole becomes more soluble in this medium, dissolving to the extent of 10.7 g. per 100 at 0° (58).

For the density of codeine crystals (hydrate), Schröder (59) found the values 1.323 and 1.311; Wherry (49) gives the specific gravity of anhydrous or hydrated crystals as 1.31 The refractive indices (Kley (60)) are 1.66 and 1.56; Wherry and Yanovsky (49) give for anhydrous codeine crystals n/D: $\alpha = 1.62$, $\beta = 1.63$, $\gamma = 1.65$; for the monohydrate, n/D: α=1.54, β=1.64, γ=1.69. (Cl. Wright (61).) In a cathode-light vacuum codeine boils and distills at 179° (62), Kempf (63) sublimed codeine at 1.5 mm. pressure at 140° to 145°; the sublimed product showed the melting point 157°. Eder (64) accomplished the sublimation at 10 mm., 100° to 130°. Microsublimation methods are described by Heiduschka (65).

Codeine precipitation and color reactions

Reagent	Reaction	Observer
Conc. H_2SO_4 containing $FeCl_3$	Blue, becoming dirty-green at about 150°. *Cf.* ref. 53.	Hesse (84) (85) (86).
Conc. H_2SO_4 and sugar	Base moistened with moderately conc. sol. of sugar, and a drop of H_2SO_4 added: purple-red color, changing after ½ hour.	Schneider (87).
Tattersall test: Sodium arsenate and conc. H_2SO_4.	Green or blue; dilute and add NaOH, yellow	Tattersall (88), Vitali (89).
H_2SO_4 containing HNO_3	Pale green, becoming violet-green	Couerbe (6).
HNO^3, followed by alcoholic KOH.	Brick-red	Vitali (90).
Boil with PbO_2 and acetic acid; filter and add H_2SO_4.	Filtrate pale yellow, becomes intense blue-violet with H_2SO_4.	Deér (91).
Silicotungstic acid	Buff ppt. slightly sol. in alcohol or dilute acids.	Bertrand (92), North and Beal (93), Heiduschka and Wolf (94).
Phosphotungstic acid	Precipitate	Heiduschka and Wolf (94).
Vanillin, or piperonal, with a few drops of 0.5 *N* H_2SO_4.	Evap. dry on steam bath: blue-violet	V. Itallie and Steenhauer (95) (96).
Ammonium uranate $+H_2SO_4$	Blue color	Brociner (97).
Uranium salts, solarized	Intense blue. Unsolarized solutions give no color.	Aloy (98) (99).
Ammonium selenite in conc. H_2SO_4.	Brilliant green; given also by morphine	Lafon (100), da Silva (101).
Marquis' Reagent: 3cc. conc. H_2SO_4+3 drops 30% HCHO sol.	Red-violet, becoming blue-violet	Kobert (102), Linke (103) Elias (104).
Magnol (basic magnesium hypochlorite).	5 mg. alkaloid in 3 cc. of acetic acid cont. 2% Magnol, layered onto 3 cc. conc. H_2SO_4: pale green stripe over lilac layer over green-brown (Resoflavin color)	David (105).
Sodium hypochlorite solution +conc. H_2SO_4.	Sky-blue	Raby (106).
Antimony trichloride	Pale green color	Smith (107).
Zinc chloriodide	Precip. of hairlike light brown crystals	Tunmann (108).
Iodine chloride	Precipitate	Dittmar (109).
Benzidine	0.02 g. base dissolved in 2 cc. conc. H_2SO_4 with 0.01 g. benzidine: yellow, becoming brown, then dark green; added to water, gives a violet solution, from which $CHCl_3$ extracts color. Test given also by morphine, dionin, heroin and apomorphine.	Ekkert (110).
Chlorine-water	No color	Marmé (111).
Potassium iodate or iodic acid	Not reduced. *Cf.* Rosenthaler, (112) formation of clumps of crystals.	Do. (111).
Pellagri-Vulpius reaction		Ekkert (113).

Codeine solutions are levorotatory. Hesse (66) found the values $[\alpha]15D$=—135.91° (97% alcohol, p=2) and $[\alpha]15D$=137. 75° (80% alcohol, p=2), the degree of rotation being practically independent of the concentration. In chloroform, $[\alpha]15D$=-111.5° (p = 2) (66). The earlier determination of Bouchardat and Boudet (67) gave $[\alpha]$=—118.2° (alcohol); in a later determination Grimaux (68) found $[\alpha]D$=—130.34°

(codeine prepared from morphine) and $[\alpha]_D$=—133.18° (C=1.43) for natural codeine. Tykociner (69) reported values for numerous codeine salts, all in the neighborhood $[\alpha]_D$=—134°. The absorption spectrum of codeine solutions was studied by Hartley (70), and Kitasato (71), that in the ultra-violet by Brustier (72) and Steiner (73). Gompel and Henri (74) compared the ultra-violet absorption spectrum with that of other phenanthrene alkaloids and of phenanthrene itself.

Codeine is a strong mono acid base; in aqueous solution it turns litmus blue, colors phenolphthalein and turns red helianthin yellow (75). It is precipitated (often in crystalline form) from solutions of its salts only incompletely by ammonia. Electrometric titration of codeine hydrochloride shows the neutral point to lie at pH 4.93 (76) (77), whence methyl red is recommended as indicator for codeine titrations. See also Kolthoff (78), Müller (79), Kebler (80), Kippenberger (81), Masucci and Moffat (82).

Thermochemical studies on codeine were carried out by Leroy (75) (83). The heat of combustion at constant volume is 2325.8 Cal., at constant pressure 2327.7 Cal.; heats of hydration, solution, and neutralization were also measured.

The more important color and precipitation tests which have been proposed for codeine are outlined in the following table.

Wagenaar (114) describes numerous microchemical precipitation reactions for codeine; Kerbosch (14) gives the action of a large number of precipitants. Tunmann (115) describes the use of codeine triiodide as a means of identification.

The estimation of codeine in the presence of morphine and in opium preparations is discussed by Taylor (116) ; see also Rakshit (54).

Bibliography (Codeine)

(1) Robiquet, Ann. chim. phys. (2) **51**, 225 (1832).
(2) Robiquet, Ann. **5**, 82 (1833).
(3) Regnault, Ann. chim. phys. (2) **68**, 113 (1838).
(4) Regnault, Ann. **26**, 10 (1838).
(5) Liebig, Ann. **26**, 41 (1838).
(6) Couerbe, Ann. chim. phys. (2) **59**, 136 (1835).
(7) Couerbe, Ann. **17**, 166 (1836).
(8) Dollfus, Ann. **65**, 214 (1848).
(9) Gerhardt, Ann. **44**, 280 (1842).
(10) Gerhardt, Ann. chim. phys. (3) **7**, 251 (1843).
(11) Anderson, Ann. **77**, 341 (1851).
(12) Wright, J. Chem. Soc. **25**, 150, 652 (1872).

(13) Dragendorff, Die Heilpflanzen, p. 249 (Enke, Stuttgart 1898).
(14) Kerbosch, Arch. Pharm. **248**, 536 (1910).
(15) Grimaux, Compt. rend. **92**, 1140, 1228 (1881); **93**, 67, 217, 591 (1881).
(16) Matthiessen and Wright, Ann. suppl. **7**, 177 (1870).
(17) Wright, Pharm. J. Trans. (3) **2**, 884 (1872).
(18) Gregory, Ann. **7**, 261 (1833).
(19) Merck, Ann. **11**, 279 (1834).
(20) Merck, Ann. **18**, 79 (1836).
(21) Mohr, Ann. **35**, 119 (1840).
(22) Hesse, Ann. **153**, 47 (1870).
(23) Hesse, Ann. suppl. **8**, 261 (1872).
(24) Plugge, Rec. trav. chim. **6**, 157 (1887).
(25) Plugge, Arch. Pharm. (3) **25**, 343 (1887).
(26) Kanewskaja, J. prakt. Chem. (2) **108**, 247 (1924).
(27) Grimaux, Phil. J. Trans. (3) **12**, 48 (1881).
(28) Hesse, Ann. **222**, 203 (1883).
(29) Knoll, D. R-P. 39887 (1886); Frdl. **1**, 582; Houben **1**, 63.
(30) Knoll, Arch. Pharm. **227**, 229 (1889).
(31) Merck, D. R-P. 102634 (1898); Frdl. **5**, 807; Houben **1**, 711.
(32) E. Merck, D. R-P. 107225 (1898); Frdl. **5**, 808; Houben **1**, 776.
(33) E. Merck, D. R-P. 108075 (1898); Frdl. **5**, 808; Houben **1**, 787.
(34) Gerber, D. R-P. 214783; Frdl. **9**, 1020; Houben **3**, 296.
(35) Merck, D. R-P. 418391 (1923); Frdl. **15**, 1515.
(36) Farbenfabrik vorm. Bayer and Co., D. R-P. 92789; Frdl. **4**, 1247; Houben **1**, 776.
(37) Farbenfabrik vorm. Bayer and Co., D. R-P. 96145 (1897); Prdl. **5**, 806; Houben **1**, 595
(38) Farbenfabrik vorm. Bayer and Co., D. R-P. 95644 (1897); Frdl. **5**, 805; Houben **1**, 585
(39) Farbenfabrik vorm. Bayer and Co., D. R-P. 189843; Frdl. **8**, 1151; Houben 2, 876
(40) Farbenfabrik vorm. Bayer and Co. D. R-P. 224388 (1909) ; Frdl. **10**, 1216
(41) E. Merek D. R-P. 131980 (1901); Frdl. **6**, 1156; Houben **2**, 177
(42) Boehringer and Sohn D. R-P. 247180 (1909); Frdl. **10**, 1215; Houben **3**, 780
(43) Rodionov, Bull. soc. chim. **39**, 305 (1926).
(44) Miller, Ann. **77**, 381 (1851).
(45) Deane and Brady, J. Chem. Soc. **18**, 34 (1865).
(46) Arzruni, Z. Kryst. **1**, 302 (1877).
(47) Keferstein, Ann. Physik (Poggendorff) **99**, 275 (1856).
(48) Senarmont, Jahresber. Fortschr. Chem. **1857**, 416.
(49) Wherry and Yanovsky, J. Wash. Acad. Sci. **9**, 505 (1919).
(50) Heydrich, Z. Kryst. Mineral. **48**, 270 (1910).
(51) Gaubert, Compt. rend. **156**, 1161 (1913).
(52) Kremann and Schniderschitz, Monatsh. **35**, 1423 (1914).
(53) U. S. Pharmaeopceia IX.
(54) Rakshit, Analyst **46**, 481 (1921).
(55) Tambach and Henke, Pharm. Zentralhalle **38**, 159 (1897).
(56) Kubly, Jahresber. Fortschr. Chem. **1866**, 823.
(57) Schindelmeiser, Chem. Ztg. **25**, 129 (1901).
(58) Fouquet, Bull. soc. chim. (3) **17**, 464 (1897); J. pharm. chim. (6) **5**, 49 (1897).

(59) Schröder, Ber. **13**, 1075 (1888).
(60) Kley, Rec. trav. chim. **22**, 367 (1903).
(61) Wright, J. Am. Chem. Soe. **38**, 1647 (1916).
(62) Krafft and Weilandt, Ber. **29**, 2240 (1896).
(63) Kempf, J. prakt. Chem. (2) **78**, 201 (1908).
(64) Eder, Schweiz. Wochschr. **51**, 228, 241, 253 (1913).
(65) Heidusehka and Meisner, Arch. Pharm. **261**, 102 (1923).
(66) Hesse, Ann. **176**, 189 (1875).
(67) Bouchardat and Boudet, J. pharm. chim. (3) **23**, 292 (1853); Ann. **88**, 213 (1853).
(68) Grimaux, Compt. rend. **92**, 1228 (1881).
(69) Tykociner, Rec, trav. chim. **1**, 144 (1882).
(70) Hartley, Phil. Trans. Roy. Soc. London **176**, 471 (1885).
(71) Kitasato, Acta Phytochim. **3**, 175-258 (1927); Chem. Abst. **22**, 1779 (1928)
(72) Brustier, Bull. soc. chim. (4) **39**, 1527 (1926).
(73) Steiner, Bull. soc. chim. biol. **6**, 231 (1924).
(74) Gompel and Henri, Compt. rend. **157**, 1422 (1913).
(75) Leroy, Ann. chim. phys. (7) **21**, 87 (1900).
(76) Rasmussen and Schou, Pharm. Zentralhalle **65**, 729 (1924).
(77) Rasmussen and Schou, Z. Electrochem. **31**, 189 (1925).
(78) Kolthoff, Z. anorg. Chem. **112**, 196 (1920).
(79) Müller, Z. Electrochem. **30**, 587 (1924).
(80) Kebler, J. Am. Chem. Soc. **17**, 822 (1895).
(81) Kippenberger, Z. anal. Chem. **39**, 201 (1900).
(82) Masucci and Moffat, J. Am. Pharm. Assoc. **12**, 609 (1923).
(83) Leroy, Compt. rend. **129**, 220 (1899).
(84) Hesse, Ber. **4**, 693 (1871).
(85) Hesse, Arch. Pharm. **212**, 330 (1878).
(86) Hesse, Arch. Pharm. **198**, 29 (1871).
(87) Schneider, Ann. der Physik (Poggendorff) (5) **27**, 128 (1872); J. prakt. Chem. (2) **6**, 455 (1873).
(88) Tattersall, Chem. News **40**, 126 (1879).
(89) Vitali, Ber. **14**, 1583 (1881).
(90) Vitali, L'Orosi **14**, 405; J. Chem. Soc. **62**, 755 (1892).
(91) Deér, Pharm. Monatsh. **6**, 117 (1925).
(92) Bertrand, Compt. rend. **128**, 743 (1899).
(93) North and Beal, J. Am. Pharm. Assoc. **13**, 889 (1924).
(94) Heiduschka and Wolf, Schweiz. Apoth. Ztg. **58**, 213, 229 (1920).
(95) Van Itallie and Steenhauer, Arch. Pharm. **265**, 696 (1928).
(96) Van Itallie and Steenhauer, Pharm. Weekblad **64**, 925 (1927).
(97) Brociner, J. Pharm. (5) **20**, 390 (1889).
(98) Aloy, Valdiguié and Aloy, Bull. soc. chim. **39**, 792 (1926).
(99) Aloy and Valdiguié, J. pharm. chim. (8) **4**, 390 (1926).
(100) Lafon, Compt. rend. **100**, 1543 (1885).
(101) da Silva, Compt. rend. **112**, 1266 (1891).
(102) Kobert, Chem. Zentr. **1899**, II 149.
(103) Linke, Ber. deut. pharm. Ges. **11**, 258 (1901).

(104) Elias, Pharm. Ztg. **46**, 394 (1901).
(105) David, Pharm. Ztg. **70**, 969 (1925).
(106) Raby, J. Pharm. (5) **9**, 402 (1884).
(107) Smith, Ber. **12**, 1420 (1879); Chem. News **40**, 26 (1879).
(108) Tunmann, Schweiz. Apoth. Ztg. **55**, 348 (1917).
(109) Dittmar, Ber. **18**, 1612 (1885).
(110) Ekkert, Pharm. Zentralhalle **67**, 498 (1926).
(111) Marmé, Z. anal. Chem. **24**, 643 (1885).
(112) Rosenthaler, Schweiz. Apoth. Ztg. **59**, 477 (1921).
(113) Ekkert, Pharm. Zentralhalle **69**, 1, 19 (1928).
(114) Wagenaar, Pharm. Weekblad **64**, 671 (1927).
(115) Tunmann, Apoth. Ztg. **31**, 148 (1916).
(116) Taylor, Allen's Comm'l Organ. Anal. VI, 383 (1912).

Pharmacology of Codeine

by Horatio C. Wood, Charles H. LaWall, Heber W. Youngken, John F. Anderson, Ivor Griffith

Uses.—Codeine resembles morphine in its general physiological action. Von Schroeder (A. E. P. P. 1883, xvii) has shown that it heightens the reflex activity of the spinal cord. It also exerts a depressant effect on the higher cerebral centers; Macht (J. P. Ex. T., 1916, viii, p: 1) has shown that it lowers the threshold of pain perception, the efficient dose being approximately 3 or 4 times as large as that of morphine. Its sedative action upon the respiratory center is similar in type to that of morphine, although it requires, according to the observations of Macht (J. P. Ex. T., 1915, viii, 339), almost ten times as much codeine as it does morphine to produce a corresponding effect. Like morphine it also tends to increase the tone of unstriped muscle tissue (Macht, J. P. Ex. T., 1918, xi, 389). Its narcotic action differs in type from that of morphine, especially in the fact that it is much less likely to give rise to habit.

It has been highly lauded in the treatment of diabetes mellitus, and cases of recovery under its use reported. In the grave form of this disorder we have seen it fail to exert any perceptible influenee, but the evidence is sufficient to demand a fair trial of the remedy in any individual case. Medical practitioners often use it to quict cough, to allay intestinal pain, and to fulfil various other of the minor narcotic indications for which opium is commonly administered. Although less efficient than morphine it has the advantage of being less constipating and less liable to habit formation. On account of its frequent contamination with morphine, care should be exercised as to the commencing dose, but no marked effect is to be expected, if the alkaloid be pure, from less than one grain (0.065 Gm.), and this dose may be rapidly increased until some symptoms are produced. It may be given in pill or in syrupy solution.

The symptoms of codeine poisoning in may differ considerably from those of morphine. There is usually narcosis, sometimes preceded by a feeling of exhilaration and followed by convulsions. In most of the reported cases nausea and vomiting have been prominent symptoms and there has also been evidence of circulatory depression. The pupils are contracted, the pulse rate usually increased. We are not familiar with any case of fatal codeine poisoning, but alarming symptoms have followed the ingestion of 4 grains (Myrtle, B. M. J., 1874), and Boissonnas (R. M. S. R., 1919, xxxix, 581) reports a case of violent poisoning in a child of 3 years from 0.04 Gm. (3/5 of a grain). The treatment of codeine poisoning should be along the same lines as that of morphine poisoning.

Dose, one-fourth to two grains (0.015-0.13 Gm.).

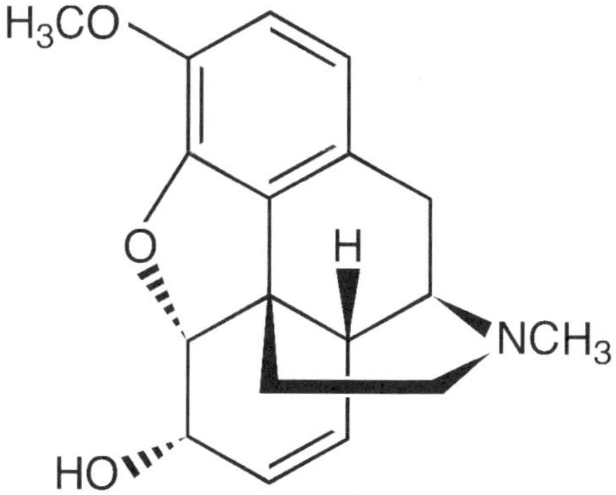

H_3CO O H NCH_3 HO

Codeine

Preparation of Morphine from Codeine

by Ali Shafiee, Iraj Lalezari and Narges Yassa
US 4,114,314
September 19, 1978

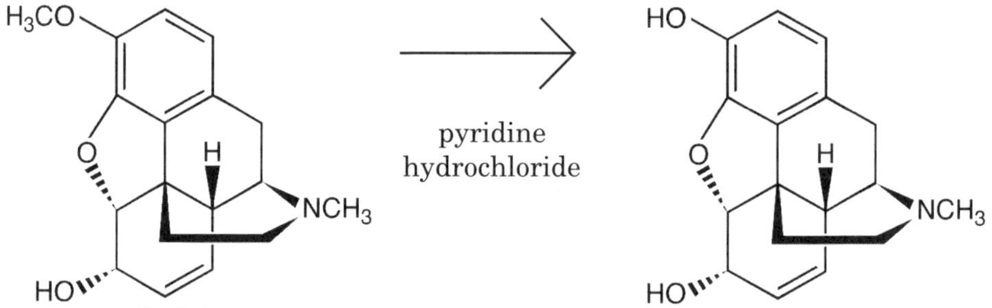

Codeine → (pyridine hydrochloride) → Morphine

Rapoport et al. (J.A.C.S. 5485 and 5900, 73, 1951) have claimed a 22% yield of morphine from codeine employing pyridine hydrochloride as the cleavage agent. 1.00g codeine was heated with pyridine hydrochloride for six minutes under nitrogen. The reaction mixture was dissolved in 20 ccm water, basified with 10ccm 4N NaOH and extracted with chloroform to yield 0.210g morphine.

THE OPIUM POPPY AND OTHER POPPIES

by Charles C. Fulton

U.S. TREASURY DEPARTMENT BUREAU OF NARCOTICS
UNITED STATES GOVERNMENT PRINTING OFFICE
WASHINGTON: 1944

PREFACE

This paper was called into being by the passage of the Opium Poppy Control Act, which made necessary a better understanding of the poppy that produces opium, and the potentialities of other poppies. It was prepared by Charles C. Fulton, chemist in charge, Alcohol Tax Unit, Bureau of Internal Revenue, St. Paul, Minn. at the direction of Mr. H.J. Anslinger, Commissioner of Narcotics. The author is greatly indebted to Dr. Rogers McVaugh, Bureau of Plant Industry, for checking the entire article to bring the usage of botanical names into conformity with that of the United States Department of Agriculture.

When first listed, the bibliographic references have been given very fully. When repeated, they have been abbreviated somewhat, and the chapter and reference number of the first citation noted in parentheses.

It is hoped that this paper will be internationally useful.

PART I THE OPIUM POPPY

I. Distinction of the opium poppy from other commonly cultivated poppies

(a) Papaver somniferum

Opium is the dried or partially dried latex of a particular species of poppy, the "sleep-bearing" poppy, *Papaver somniferum* L. The latex as it flows from the wounded plant is milky white, but it turns brown on exposure to the air, and opium has a dark brown color. Definitions usually include the statement that the latex or milky juice is obtained by incising the unripe seed-capsules. This is-quite true, as regards the opium of commerce; but opium, though it would probably be less potent, could be made of the latex from leaves, stems, or buds. Opium is frequently described as the inspissated juice, the term inspissated meaning no more than "concentrated by evaporation." The United States Pharmacopoeia officially defines opium as "the air-dried, milky exudation obtained by incising the unripe capsules of *Papaver somniferum* Linné or its variety *album* De Candolle (Fam. Papaveraceae)." (1)

Opium owes its narcotic properties principally to the alkaloid morphine. To meet the standard of the U.S. Pharmacopoeia it must yield, in its normal, moist condition, not less than 9.5 percent of anhydrous morphine. The granulated and powdered opiums of the Pharmacopoeia are dried more thoroughly, and brought to a standard of 10 to 10.5 percent of anhydrous morphine, opium of a higher percentage being reduced either by admixture with opium of a lower percentage, or with some inert diluent. (1) The morphine is actually present in the drug as sulfate and meconate salts, but its proportion is determined in terms of the anhydrous free base.

Some 20 other alkaloids are also formed by *Papaver somniferum* and are present in opium. Other poppies have milky juices, but these do not contain the same constituents as opium.

The Opium Poppy is the same as the common "garden poppy" of Europe, and is not the same as the Oriental Poppy. The latter name rightfully belongs to *Papaver orientale*, a perennial poppy often grown in this country for its showy flowers. The garden or opium poppy is an annual; but where climatic conditions are suitable is often sown in the fall, and harvested the following summer.

Papaver somniferum is extremely variable. The flowers, the color of the seeds, the shape of the pod, and so on, differ greatly. Numerous varieties are grown for the seeds, for opium, or merely for the flowers. However, the general appearance of the plant itself does not vary so much. When well-grown it is tall, generally 3 to 4 feet, and the flowers are large, 4 to 5 inches across, largest of any annual poppy. It can generally be recognized by its foliage, which is smooth and of a characteristic whitish dull green color, called "glaucous." The leaves are oblong, clasping the stem by a cordate base, 4 to 10 inches long, 2 to 4 inches wide, wavy, lobed or toothed. (2) More detailed description of the variations will be given later.

(b) Other commonly cultivated poppies

The opium poppy is quite distinct from the three other poppies of the genus Papaver most commonly grown for their flowers in the gardens of this country. These are: (2)

Papaver rhoeas, L., annual; the common - "corn poppy" or "field poppy" of Europe, where it grows wild in the grain fields and other places. Flowers commonly bright red, but there are numerous color varieties of which the most popular are the Shirley poppies. The plant is much smaller than the opium poppy, the foliage hairy and a strong green.

Papaver orientale L., the Oriental poppy, perennial; flowers quite large, commonly orange-scarlet. *Papaver bracteatum* Lindl. is a near relative. Hybridization of the two species with selection has produced flower-varieties of various colors which are becoming fairly common in flower gardens. These and these only are known to flower gardeners as Oriental poppies.

Papaver nudicaule L., the Iceland poppy, perennial; but often grown as an annual or biennial, frequently in rock-gardens. The plant and flowers are small, the flowers typically yellow but ranging in cultivated varieties from white to orange-red. A near relative or subspecies, *Papaver alpinum* L., the Alpine poppy, is similar and even smaller; flowers white.

The opium poppy of course differs still more widely from the well known poppies of other genera, such as the California poppy (*Eschscholzia californica*), the Mexican poppy (*Argemone mexicana*), etc. In Part II "Other poppies," these and such others of the Papaveraceae, as have been chemically analyzed will be discussed with reference to their production of alkaloids.

I. REFERENCES

1. The Pharmacopoeia of the United States of America. Twelfth Revision. By authority of the United States Pharmacopoeial Convention. Prepared by the Committee of Revision and Published by the Board of Trustees. Official from November 1,1942.

2. Bailey, L. H. The Standard Cyclopedia of Horticulture. New York. The Macmillan Co., 1935. Volume III, article Papaver.

II. Origin of opium poppy culture

Much confusion has arisen from the erroneous supposition that the opium poppy, *Papaver somniferum*, is a native of the Far East. It is not a native of China but of the Mediterranean region. It has been known and, it would appear, cultivated in Europe for at least some 4,000 years, since remains of poppy seed cake and poppy capsules have been found in the Swiss Lake Dwellings of Neolithic Age. This does not indicate with any certainty the place of origin of the cultivated plant, for the Neolithic

"Age" in Central Europe developed from a cultural movement up the Danube Valley, emanating from Asia Minor.

The poppy was probably first cultivated for its edible and oil producing seed, as it still is throughout Central Europe. (1) (2)

Our earliest literary references are in the Iliad of Homer (about the 9th century B. C.), and these apparently relate to the culture for seed.

- In Book VIII:

> And now he bowed his head as a garden poppy in full bloom when it is weighed down by showers in spring—even thus heavily bowed his head beneath the weight of his helmet. (3)

- In Book XIV:

> Penelos then drew his sword and smote him on the neck, so that both head and helmet came tumbling down to the ground with the spear still sticking in his eye; he then held up the head, as though it had been a poppy-head, and showed it to the Trojans, vaunting over them as he did so. (3)

This latter simile obviously relates to the large, round, and high-held fruit of the domesticated Papaver somniferum, for none other would suggest such a comparison.

In the Odyssey of Homer is the following interesting passage,

- In Book IV:

> Then Helen, daughter of Zeus, turned to new thoughts. Presently she cast a drug into the wine whereof they drank, a drug to lull all pain and anger, and bring forgetfulness of every sorrow. Whoso should drink a draught thereof, when It is mingled In the bowl, on that day he would let no tear fall down his cheeks, not though his mother and his father died, not though men slew his brother or dear son before his face, and his own eyes beheld it. (4)

Considering the familiarity of the Greeks with the opium-bearing poppy, the drug referred to can scarcely be anything other than opium, or an extract of the poppy plant, though the knowledge is poetically attributed to the Egyptians in following lines. Opium is the great reliever of pain, whether of physical or emotional origin; and an infusion of opium is a beverage of hospitality, even to this day amongst the Rajputs of India. (5)

Poppy culture was also alluded to by Hesiod (ca 8th century B. C.). If Homer may possibly have referred to something else in the Odyssey, the drug from the poppy was certainly known to Theophrastus (lived 37-287 B.C.) and other ancient Greek writers. Dioscorides in the first century A. D. gave a complete account, and drew a distinction between *meconion* (the name used by Theophrastus), made from an extract or the expressed juice of the whole plant, and *opion*, made from latex from the capsule alone, add exactly the same as our modern opium. (1) (6) (7) Doubtless "poppy tea" was used many hundreds of years before *meconion* was prepared.

Thus opium was known to the ancient Greeks some 2,000 years ago, and the opium poppy grown long before Homer's time, probably almost from the first beginning of civilization in that part of the world. In contrast, the opium poppy was apparently unknown in ancient times in either India or China, and its present widespread cultivation in those countries for opium has been a development of fairly recent historical times. Poppy culture was first introduced into the Far East about the seventh century A. D., but opium did not become the scourge of China until about 1650 A.D. Machiguchi states that, although there are no written records covering its introduction, poppy culture is believed to have first begun in Japan about 500 years ago. (1) (2) (8)

Poppy culture is no doubt at least as ancient in Asia Minor as in Europe. In Anatolia, from whence the best medicinal opium largely comes today, it goes back beyond recorded history. Our earliest literary data, from the ancient Greek writers, pertain as much to their colonies on the islands and shores of Asia Minor as to Greece proper. The native habitat of *Papaver somniferum* is usually given as "Greece and the Orient," the Orient meaning in this case (as it always did until recent times) the Near East. At any rate it was somewhere in this northeastern corner of the Mediterranean lands that the opium poppy was first reduced to cultivation, and opium first produced. (2)

Papaver somniferum today is wholly a cultivated plant. To be sure some plants are found growing wild, but they are simply escapes from cultivation, or at any rate 80 crossed with escapes and cultivated plants as to be essentially the same as the cultivated dehiscent varieties. There has been much speculation as to the original wild form. A close relative, *Papaver setigerum* DC., grows wild throughout southwestern Europe to this day, in Italy, France, and Spain; and also in Morocco and Algeria, and the islands between, and even in the Canaries. The older botanists generally considered this the "living ancestor" of the cultivated poppy, and many considered it merely a variety or subspecies of *Papaver somniferum* being the truly wild form. Recent studies by Russian investigators, however, have upheld the claim that it is a distinct species, and have shown that it can hardly be the ancestral form of the cultivated poppy. Still it is such a close relative as to show that the original wild *Papaver somniferum* was truly a European plant, extending, very likely, eastward into Asia Minor. (9) (10)

II. REFERENCES

1. Hedi, Gustav. Illustrierte Flora von Mittel-Europa. IV Band, 1 Hälfte. München, 1913.

2. Basilevskaja, Nina A. "On the Races of the Opium Poppy, Growing in Semiretchie, and the Origin of Their Culture." Trudy Prikl. Bot., Gen. i Sel. 19 (2): 95-184. (1928). (Bulletin of Applied Botany, Genetics and Plant Breeding). (Russian, with English summary pp. 170-184).

3. The Iliad of Homer, rendered into English prose for the use of those who cannot read the original. By Samuel Butler. London: A.C. Fifield, 1914.

4. The Odyssey of Homer. Done into English Prose. By S.H. Butcher and A. Lang. Macmillan and Co., London, 1912

5. The Encyclopedia Britannica, 14th edition, 1929. Article "Opium-Eating and Opium-Smoking".

6. The Encyclopedia Britannica, 11th edition, 1911. Article "Opium."

7. The Dispensatory of the United States of America. The 23rd Edition. By Horatio C. Wood, Jr., and Arthur Osol, assisted by Heber W. Younken and Louis Gershenfeld. J. B. Lippincott Company, Philadelphia, London, Montreal. 1943.

8. Machiguchi, Eizo. "Contribution to the knowledge of Japanese Opium." Journal of the Pharmaceutical Society of Japan, 529, 185-228 (1926). In Japanese. Translation made for the U. S. Narcotics Bureau.

9. Vesselovskaya, Mariia Alexandrovna. The Poppy—Its classification and its importance as an oleiferous crop. Supplement 56 to the Bulletin of Applied Botany, of Genetics and Plant Breeding. The Lenin Academy of Agricultural Sciences in U. S. S. R. Leningrad, 1933. (Russian and English.)

10. Kuzmina, N. E. "Cytology of the Cultivated Poppy in Connection with Its Origin and Evolution." Trudy Prikl. Bot., Gen. i Selek. Ser. II, 8: 81-82 (1935). English summary, pp. 190 -196. (Bulletin of Applied Botany, Genetics and Plant Breeding. Series II. Genetics, Plant Breeding, and Cytology.)

III. Culture for seed, flowers, opium, alkaloids

(a) Poppy seed

Throughout Central Europe *Papaver somniferum* is grown as the "garden poppy" in enormous acreages. The term "garden poppy" relates to the kitchen garden rather than the flower garden, and to the culture for seed with no production of opium. The northern limit of successful cultivation on a large scale is said to be 56° or about "the latitude of Moscow. In southern Europe the plant, as an oil producer, cannot compete with the olive.

The seed is eaten both raw and cooked, especially in pastry, and is also pressed for oil. The seed is often called "Maw" seed, a word related to or a corruption of the German *Mohn*, poppy. The seeds have a sweet, nutty flavor. They are not really a spice, though commercially handled in the United States by the spice trade. They contain some 40 to 50 percent oil. The oil is used for culinary purposes, as an artists' oil, and for other purposes. It is classed as a "drying oil," and has high value for some uses in that it does not readily turn rancid. The residue or cake from rich oil has been pressed is used for cattle feed. In Europe commercial poppy growing primarily for the seed is on a huge scale in Russia, Austria, Czechoslovakia, Hungary, Poland, Belgium, and Holland. (1) (2) (3)

Immigrants to the United States from the countries mentioned have brought their liking for poppy seed with them, and in many instances had continued to grow the poppy in this country. This is particularly true of the Czechs. It is natural that these people, whose families and ancestors have cultivated the poppy for generations without ever collecting opium, often have no realization that their "garden poppy" is the opium poppy, nor that it is *Papaver somniferum*. Such, however, is the fact.

Before the outbreak of the present war most of the poppy seed used commercially in this country was imported, chiefly from Holland and Poland. The following figures from the Bureau of Customs Statistics show the amount imported for three years, in pounds:

	1937	1938	1939
Total for all countries ----------	7,609,019	9,649,164	5,814,884
From the Netherlands ----------	4,956,136	6,719,478	3,776,218
From Poland and Danzig ------	2,641,653	2,743,486	989,559

Generally over 8,000 tons were imported annually; in 1938 over 4,800 tons.

The Czech plantings in the United States were then chiefly home gardens. After the war broke out the large importations were cut off, the price rose from about 7 cents a pound to 50 cents or more a pound, and many farmers began commercial plantings of large acreage of the opium poppy for the sake of its seed production. This culture is now forbidden in the United States, except under license.

The blue or slate-colored seed is favored for culinary purposes. Many of the Czechs in this country believe that only the white seeded poppy will produce opium, although this has no foundation whatever in fact. The United States Dispensatory under "Turkey Opium" mentions that in the exportation of the seeds of the poppies actually producing opium in Turkey, the United States importers will take only the blue seeds, although the properties of the white seeds are exactly the same. (4) It is now impossible, because of the war, to import enough of the blue or dark seeds to meet the demand, and as the white seeds are sometimes obtainable there have been instances, discovered by the U. S. Food and Drug Administration, of the white kind being dyed in imitation of the slate-blue seeds, to make them acceptable. The preference may have a basis in that the blue or dark seeds are easier to see or more attractive in appearance when dusted on a poppy-seed roll; but the idea that either the seed or the plant is essentially different has no basis.

(b) Flowers

Throughout Western Europe and in the United States varieties of *Papaver somniferum* are frequently grown as ornaments of the flower garden. In cultivation the poppy readily develops varieties with “double” flowers, that is, flowers that have a multitude of petals instead of four apiece. The petals may be plain or fringed. They show a wide range of colors from white through numerous tints and combinations to red or dark violet. The floral varieties will be more particularly described and also given by name in later chapters. They were carried by all American seedsmen prior to the enactment of the Opium Poppy Control Act, generally listed merely as “Tall Annual Poppies.” At least one English company listed them frankly as varieties of Papaver somniferum, (5), and they are so described in horticultural reference books. (6) (7) (8) Apparently only some of the single varieties are used for the commercial production of edible seed or for opium. The ability of the fancy flowering varieties to produce morphine is the same as for plainer kinds, as was found in analyses made for the Bureau of Narcotics on specimens grown by flower-seed producers in California.

(c) Opium

The opium production of the world is chiefly in Asia, especially in China, India, Iran, Asia Minor, and Afghanistan, also in French Indo-China, Semiretchie (in Asiatic Russia), Korea, and Japan., China is by far the largest producer and also the largest consumer. Various Chinese governments have attempted to suppress poppy cultivation, as well as opium smoking. In the past the efforts generally broke down at times of weakness of the central government, especially when the financial necessities of rival "war lords" caused them to encourage poppy growing. The present government of Chiang Kai-shek inaugurated a 6-year plan in 1935, for the suppression of opium. However, since 1931 the Japanese have encouraged, protected, promoted, and even forced Chinese opium production and use; and the situation in Manchukuo and the rest of occupied China is far worse than ever before.

In Europe there is considerable opium production in the Balkans, in Yugoslavia and Bulgaria. Egypt was famous for its opium from ancient times to within the present century, but now prohibits poppy culture. Our name for one of the opium alkaloids, thebaine, goes back to Egyptian Thebes. In recent years the clandestine production of opium in Mexico has become a serious problem.

Much of the legitimate (medicinal) opium for the United States has been imported indirectly, and prior to 1932 the producing country was not always known. Since then the statistics show that by far the most of it has come from Turkey and Yugoslavia, the greater proportion from Turkey. In 1933 and 1934 a very little came from Greece. From 1935 to 1939 importations from England have included some opium produced in Bulgaria, in 1936 a little produced in Persia, and in 1937, 1938, and 1939 a little produced in Afghanistan. (9)

Opium has been produced experimentally in the United States quite a number of times. There is no difficulty in obtaining it with a high morphine content. However, human labor is too large a part of opium production for any possibility of legitimate commercial success in this country. Also, in most sections there is danger that rain might come at the time the capsules are incised and wash the opium away.

(d) Alkaloids

In Europe, except in the Balkans, the production of opium is negligible. However, about 10 years ago (1932-33), the process of a Hungarian scientist, Janos von Kabay, was put into commercial operation, for the direct extraction of morphine from poppy plants, or from the dry chaff of capsules and other parts of the plant left from the separation of the seeds, without passing through the intermediate stage of opium. The poppy capsules, exclusive of the seeds, contain about 0.3 to 0.6 percent morphine. The raw material was extremely cheap, for it consisted of the chaff of the garden poppies, which was ordinarily thrown away or burnt. The process proved adequate to meet the needs of Hungary for medicinal morphine. This or a modified direct extraction process was soon taken up by Poland and then by Germany and Russia and other European countries. The use of direct extraction has doubtless been greatly expanded as a result of the war. (10) (11)

It is of interest to note that the direct extraction of alkaloids from the poppy plant or chaff was suggested in this country back in 1906, by Dr. Rodney H. True of the U. S. Department of Agriculture. (12) He made some experiments, but there was no commercial production.

In most countries selection of poppy varieties has been chiefly confined to deciding on the varieties best adapted to the climate, soil, and growing conditions. Such other selection as there has been in opium producing countries has been chiefly for an abundant flow of latex. The statement occasionally met with that the garden poppy produces very little opium apparently has reference only to the flow of milky juice from which the official opium is made by evaporation. Feldman and Klyatchkina report that the garden poppy variety grown in Russia has heads with just as high a content of opium alkaloids as the heads of poppies grown specifically for opium; and that, while the alkaloidal content of poppyheads varies to some extent with different plants or varieties, there is no apparent connection between this and the production of opium (i. e., of milky juice, or latex). (11) Of course the plants of the garden or opium poppy come under the Opium Poppy Control Act whether the flow of latex is scanty or abundant. The "garden poppy" is simply a horticultural variety of *Papaver somniferum*, and produces the same alkaloids in about the same amount in the capsules as do the varieties used primarily for opium production.

(e) General remarks as to culture

The opium poppy will grow almost anywhere and is or has been commercially grown over most of the world, from latitude 56° N. to the equator. It will grow at any altitude at which any crops can be grown, and in almost any soil. It responds well to fertilizers or a rich soil, nevertheless in some places it is found the most profitable crop for the poorer soils. Occasionally trouble with fungus disease is encountered. For opium or extraction of alkaloids from the chaff it is best to grow the poppies in a dry region where they can be irrigated, especially because rain at the wrong time will wash the opium away from incisions, or leach morphine out of the capsules after they are dry. Both the U. S. Department of Agriculture and farmers growing the poppy commercially for its seed have proved that it can be grown very successfully in many parts of the United States.

III. REFERENCES

1. Vesselovskaya, M. "The Poppy." Leningrad, 1933. (II, 9) Includes a map showing the areas of poppy culture in Europe and Asia.

2. The Encyclopedia Americana. New York, Chicago, 1927. Article "Poppy".

3. Jamieson, George S. Vegetable Fats and 0ils. The Chemical Catalog Company, New York 1932

4. The Dispensatory of the United States of America. Centennial (22nd) edition. By Horatio C. Wood, Jr., Charles H. La Wall, Heber W. Youngken, Arthur Osol, Ivor Griffith, and Louis Gershenfeld. Philadelphia and London. J. B. Lippincott Co., 1937.

5. Sutton's Amateur's Guide in Horticulture and General Garden Seed Catalogue for 1937. (An English Seed Catalog). Sutton and Sons, Ltd., Reading, England.

6. Bailey, L,. E. The Standard Cyclopedia of Horticulture. N. Y., 1935. (I, 2).

7. Foley, Daniel J. "Annuals for Our Garden." New York. The Macmillan Co. 1938

8. Sudell, Richard (editor). The New Illustrated Gardening Manual. New York, Charles Scribner's Sons. 1937.

9. Traffic in Opium and Other Dangerous Drugs. Report by the Government of the United States of America. U. S. Treasury Department, Bureau of Narcotics, Washington. Published annually, 1931-1943, covering the years 1930 to 1942.

10. Kabay, Helene von. "An Account of the Janos von Kabay Method of Determining the Morphine Content of Poppy Straw." League of Nations. O. C. 1546 (1) (h). Geneva, February 6, 1939.

11. Klyatchkina, B. A. "The Alkaloidal Content of the Poppy Plant." Feldman, J., and Klyatchkina, B. A. "Memorandum Regarding Research Work on the Poppy Plant and the Alkaloids Contained Therein." "Annex." League of Nations. O. C. 1546 (1) (e). Geneva, April 17, 1937.

12. True, Rodney H. Oil, Paint and Drug Reporter, 70, 16, p. 37. New York, October 17,1906. (Convention Extra.)

IV. The alkaloids of *Papaver somniferum*

(a) In opium

The virtues and faults of opium alike reside in its content of alkaloids. Of these morphine is the chief, both in amount and importance. In fact, opium is generally evaluated solely on its morphine content, although it is recognized that this basis is inadequate. When the opium is used as such, the other alkaloids have some effect, particularly the highly poisonous thebaine. When used as a source of alkaloids, the codeine, thebaine, and papaverine are valuable products. Codeine and papaverine are themselves used medicinally, while thebaine is used to manufacture eucodal and other drugs.

Codeine has about one-third the physiological effect of the same quantity of morphine, and of a similar nature. Thebaine has an action rather like that of strychnine. Papaverine has some narcotic effect. Narcotine and narceine are the other chief alkaloids. In fact narcotine is usually second only to morphine in amount, but its physiological effect is comparatively small. In spite of its name it has almost no narcotic action, but is a spinal stimulant and (in opposition to morphine) a respiratory stimulant. Narceine, usually sixth of the chief alkaloids seems to be almost inert. (1)

Morphine constitutes 10 percent of standardized opium or the pharmacopoeial dry, powdered opium. In the crude gum opium the percentage varies widely, with varieties of the plant, environmental factors, and methods of collection. It varies also, of course, with the moisture content, but if the moisture is determined, the morphine percentage can be calculated to the dry basis. The highest grades contain over 20 percent of morphine. In some countries the capsules are lanced repeatedly, as long as they will yield any latex. Opium from successive lancings of the same capsules was shown by Annett to be much lower in morphine and relatively (sometimes actually) higher in some of the secondary alkaloids. By collecting separately the juice from successive lancings he found the opium from first lancings to be nearly always above 10 percent, while from sixth lancings a typical value was only 1.6 percent of morphine. (2) Arima and Iwakiri give for Manchurian opium of inferior value (perhaps obtained in the same way) 3.71 percent morphine in one case and 2.65 percent in another. (3)

Each of the other alkaloids also varies, almost independently of the morphine. When the morphine content is abnormally low, that of the other alkaloids is likely to be higher than usual; but this inverse correlation is not very definite, even in the case of codeine, which, because of its close relationship (it is methyl-morphine) might be expected to take the place of morphine.

Although tens of thousands of analyses of opium have been made, most of these have been solely for the morphine content, as far as the alkaloids are concerned. Moreover, there is not yet complete agreement on the best method for determining even this, the chief alkaloid. The secondary alkaloids have been occasionally determined, by various methods, some having but little value. It is certain that the figures generally given are too low, both for average contents and for range, except perhaps for morphine itself, and possibly narcotine. Rakshit has pointed out that a determination of total alkaloids in the average Indian opium gives just about double the amount that would be expected from adding together the "average" values for the separate alkaloids, as given by Pictet and others. These "average" values were originally based on the amounts of the pure alkaloids isolated by various experimenters and so were naturally underestimates. (4)

Pictet's "average values," given in "The Vegetable Alkaloids," have been copied into a number of other reference books. Those values include codeine 0.8 percent, thebaine 0.4 percent. (5) Alternative values given by Allen's Commercial Organic Analysis show codeine 0.2-0.4 percent, thebaine 0.1-1 percent. (6) But analyses in recent years show usually about 1 to 4 percent of each, or up to about ten times as much as would be expected from these figures. Apparently something like 1.5 percent of each should be expected. Thus, Anneler reports over 1 percent of each of these alkaloids in Turkish, Russian, and Persian opium; Arima and Iwakiri show over 2 percent of each in Manchurian opium of the first class; and Chassovnikova's figures for opiums experimentally obtained from Turkish, Tianshan, Chinese, Tarbagatai and Djungar varieties of opium poppies show that even if these were reduced to the standard of 10 percent morphine (the morphine content as reported on the dry basis being quite high) all would still be above 2 percent in combined codeine and thebaine, with only the Turkish a little below 1 percent in codeine, and only the Djungar slightly below 1 percent in thebaine. (7) (3) (8) Annett found from 1.8 to 4.8 percent codeine in Indian opium. (2) Arima and Iwakiri also report 3.98 percent codeine and 4.26 percent thebaine in third class Manchurian Kirin opium, along with 9.11 percent morphine. (3) This will show how excessive the content of secondary alkaloids may sometimes be. The pharmacopoeial opium in Europe and America is generally of Turkish or Balkan origin, and possibly these kinds have a lower content of secondary alkaloids than most other kinds. However, they probably average considerably more than is generally said.

Even if the "averages" are made more nearly correct they are often meaningless because the alkaloids vary so independently of one another. Following are some broad statements of the usual range for the chief alkaloids, and the names of minor alkaloids, with comments on some:

Morphine—3 to 23 percent.
Narcotine—1 to 11 percent.
Codeine—from several tenths of 1 percent up to 4 percent.
Thebaine—from several tenths of 1 percent up to 4 percent.
Papaverine—from a few tenths of 1 percent up to 2 percent at least.
Narceine—from 0.1 percent or so, probably up to 1 percent.

The above are the six chief alkaloids, usually the only alkaloids individually accounted for in analyses. In fact, narceine is often omitted.

Cryptopine—from several hundredths up to a few tenths of 1 percent. According to most textbooks, this alkaloid is likely to accompany papaverine; but in extraction methods it is found with codeine or thebaine. Cryptopine is related to protopine, and is found (along with protopine) in several other plants besides *Papaver somniferum*.

Meconidine has been reported several times as occurring up to a few tenths of a percent, but there is considerable doubt as to its existence as a distinct alkaloid.

Porphyroxine may occur in similar amount. It was apparently isolated as a pure alkaloid by Rakshit, and its characteristics described in 1919; later it was further investigated and found to be closely related to codeine. (9) (10) Nevertheless there seems to be still some question as to its existence. The most recent investigator suggests a possibility that Rakshit's porphyroxine may have been merely impure codeine. (11)

Protopine or fumarine is a very minor alkaloid in opium but of interest in that it occurs in a great many other plants. (See chapter XVI). It is said to constitute about 0.003 percent of opium.

Other minor alkaloids of opium are: Pseudomorphine, codamine, lanthopine, laudanine, laudanidine, (1-laudanine, tritopine), laudanosine, oxynarcotine, gnoscopine (r-narcotine), hydrocotarnine, neopine (an isomer of codeine), papaveramine, and papaveraldine (xanthaline).

For information as to the constitution and relationships of the opium alkaloids the books by Small and Lutz, and Henry, should be consulted. (12) (13)

The oxidation of morphine may begin, as frequently happens with phenols, by the addition of a second phenolic hydroxyl adjacent to the first. A substance which apparently is this o-diphenol-oxymorphine has been readily produced from morphine in the laboratory; but it seems never to have been recognized as an alkaloid present in opium.

The writer has recently found choline present in opium; identified in solution by microcrystal tests after separating it from the other constituents so far as possible by simple extraction methods. It constitutes probably a few hundredths of a percent. Choline is not, strictly speaking, an alkaloid.It is one of the simpler natural bases related to the alkaloids, but is occasionally spoken of as an alkaloid. Its occurrence in opium is not especially surprising except that it has not been previously reported, for choline has a widespread distribution throughout the vegetable kingdom, and indeed in the animal kingdom also.

(b) In the plant

The alkaloids of the plant are the same as those of opium, since gum opium is simply the air-dried latex, and smoking opium a boiled-down aqueous extract thereof. There may be two or three trifling exceptions to this statement, as a few minor alkaloids which occur only in traces may be formed from the major alkaloids, generally by oxidation, in the course of evaporation. There have been scarcely any examinations of absolutely fresh latex, even for morphine alone.

Morphine, codeine, thebaine, narcotine, papaverine, and narceine have all been isolated from the dried capsules; and the first four of these even quantitatively determined in some lots, though how accurately it is difficult to say. The European factories using capsules or poppy chaff for alkaloid extraction have by now doubtless made many observations which have not been published. A new alkaloid, narcotoline, (closely related to narcotine), was isolated from the capsules by the firm of C. H. Boehringer Sohn, in Germany. It was reported on by Wrede in 1937. (14)

The writer has found choline in the capsules of the opium poppy, as well as in opium. It is a substantial constituent of the capsules of *Papaver glaucum* and *Papaver rhoeas* (Chapter XVII). In the opium poppy capsules its proportion is minute.

The quantitative analysis of the capsules, even for morphine alone, is difficult, and years ago was probably inaccurate more often than not, the results usually being much too low. Modern analyses agree fairly well as to the morphine content of the capsules (exclusive of the seeds), generally showing 0.25 to 0.5 percent though the variation may extend well beyond these limits. Wüest and Frey reported a range of 0.18 to 0.89 percent morphine, with average values of 0.37 to 0.53 percent. (15) Chemical Abstracts incorrectly stated their figures as "up to 9 percent morphine and average 3-5 percent." (16) Actually the figures were reported in "0/00", or parts per 1,000. Analysts still differ greatly in regard to the content of the stalks, some reports showing morphine 0.01-.05 percent, others about 0.1-0.15 percent. (17) (18) (19)

Probably the most thorough study so far of alkaloids in the plant is the one made by Kerbosch over 30 years ago, reported in 1910. (20) His results were not quantitative (except a few for narcotine), but they rest on the solid basis of positive and sure identification of each alkaloid in every case. In the blooming plants of a variety from Asia Minor (seed from Smyrna) he found not only morphine but also narcotine, codeine, and papaverine in all parts except the stamens, that to say in leaves, stems, roots, carpels, and petals. His method was weakest for thebaine, which he did not detect in the plants (except in some large extractions made for the quantitative narcotine determinations). The varieties studied may probably have been low in thebaine anyway. A variety yielding opium with a high thebaine content doubtless has it in all the parts that contain the other alkaloids. Narceine, generally the least in amount of the six chief alkaloids of opium, Kerbosch found in the capsules, leaves, and roots when the plants were 66 days old. The unripe seeds (at 76 days age) contained only narcotine. (20)

Some very interesting observations were made on the development and distribution of alkaloids in the plants. Narcotine was present as a mere trace in the ripe seeds, but was already present in greater amount three days after sprouting. The sprouting seeds manufacture narcotine, doubtless from their protein reserve, even when germinated in a nitrogen-free environment. Codeine, peculiarly enough, next developed. In some plants 21 days old and only 4 cm. long, narcotine, codeine, and morphine could all be detected. In another variety these three alkaloids and also papaverine could be found at 36 days age. Some conclusions such as that thebaine develops last, were probably due to the method or the particular varieties used, but the foregoing seem established. Morphine greatly exceeds narcotine and codeine in the developed plant, so should be detected first unless the others really precede it. However, it was already present in plants only 4 cm. long. (20)

In 1987 Peter Valaer, chemist for the U. S. Internal Revenue Bureau, examined seedlings pulled up three weeks after planting the seed. These tiny plants were about an inch (2.5 cm.) tall, above ground and were proved to contain morphine.

There seems to be no doubt that morphine accumulates in the heads. They have been found richest in morphine in the bud stage as well as in the later capsule stage. (21) (22) Kerbosch found that the fruits from green immaturity to ripe dryness always contained any alkaloid that could be detected elsewhere in the plant at the time. Moreover, he showed that the latex itself was different, in appearance and in morphine content, if obtained from the capsule or the lower part of the plant. (20)

Annett came to this same conclusion in a different way. He showed that opium from successive lancings of the same capsules showed a large and steady decline in morphine content, for instance from 13.9 percent from first lancings to 1.6 percent from sixth lancings. Thus latex flowing into the capsule from other parts after a lancing, or newly formed by the plant, had less and less morphine content. Annett is sometimes quoted as showing that codeine increased as morphine decreased, but actually his article denies this. Morphine always showed a marked decline while the changes in narcotine and codeine content were not regular. Codeine usually increases but in comparatively small degree. Narcotine often declines considerably but sometimes increases. (2) Machiguchi confirms the decline in morphine, stating for one example that when opium from the first lancings contains 20 percent morphine, that from the fifth lancings contains about 5 percent. (23)

Annett, Sen, and Singh make a remarkable statement in regard to this phenomenon, that "the percentage of total nitrogen in the opium of the successive scarifications remains practically constant." (24) Some other nitrogenous substance must be present in place of the morphine, but whether it is ordinarily a precursor, or is an alternative the plant may form, or is a decomposition product of morphine, remains entirely unknown. There are in fact many puzzles in connection with the alkaloids in the growing plant that still remain unsolved.

(c) In the seeds

The seeds have been examined quite a number of times by U. S. Treasury chemists, and no morphine could be found in them. They contain mere traces of basic material which could not be identified with any of the alkaloids known in opium.

Some early investigators reported traces of morphine in the seeds, but this was ascribed by Clautriau and by Kerbosch to contamination with latex. This might occur particularly with seeds from capsules incised for opium, for if a capsule is cut through it "bleeds" internally. (This is said to prevent development of the seeds, but probably it could occur to a slight degree.) The morphine content when reported at all was only 0.003-0.005 percent. Clautriau reported clean seeds alkaloid-free. Kerbosch tested washed seeds and found slight traces of narcotine and amorphous basic material. (20) As some varieties, particularly of the European garden poppy, scarcely form narcotine even in the latex, it is probably absent from most seeds. Anyway, in slight traces it could have no narcotic effect.

Müller (1914) reported the seeds as alkaloid-free. Chistoni (1931) and Fuchs (1932) found traces of basic material which could not be identified with any alkaloids of opium. Chistoni reported this isolated basic material as toxic to mice, but Fuchs denied this. Arima and Ninomiya (1938) reported the seeds of the Manchurian opium-producing poppy as practically alkaloid-free. (25) (26) (27) (28) These are the more recent investigations.

In 1935 Chemical Abstracts showed R. Bunge as reporting a toxicity to mice of poppy-seeds, and claiming to find in them morphine, codeine, and thebaine. (29) Actually this was a mistranslation. His article was about poppy-heads, not seeds (Uber die Giftigkeit reifer Mohnköpfe). (30)

IV. REFERENCES

1. The Dispensatory of the United States of America 22nd ed., 1937. (III, 4.).

2. Annett, Harold Edward. "Factors Influencing Alkaloidal Content and Yield of Latex in the Opium Poppy (*Papaver somniferum*)." Biochemical Journal 14, 5, 618-636 (1920).

3. Arima, Zyunzo, and Iwakiri, Mitsuo. "Manchurian Opium. I. Analysis of the main alkaloids." Report of the Institute of Scientific Research, Manchoukuo, 2, 221-230. (German summary 43) 1938. (Chemical Abstracts 33, 1875.) In consulting the original the writer was dependent on the German summary but found by comparison of figures a serious misprint in the tabulated values, 0.65 for 2.65% morphine in Kirin inferior quality opium. The misprint was copied in Chemical Abstracts.

4. Rakshit, Jitendra Nath. "The Determination of Total Alkaloids, Sugar, and Oily Substances in Opium." The Analyst 51, 491 (1926).

5. Pictet, Amé. "The Vegetable Alkaloids." Rendered into English, Revised and Enlarged by H. C. Biddle. 1st edition. John Wiley & Sons. New York, 1904.

6. Alien's Commercial Organic Analysis, Vol. VII. 5th edition. Philadelphia, P. Blakiston's Son & Co. 1929. "Opium Alkaloids" by Frank O. Taylor. Page 656, same values as given Pictet. Page 724, another set of "average values" for secondary alkaloids.

7. Anneler, Ernest. "Ueber die Bestimmung von Codein, Narcotin, Papaverin, und Thebain im Opium." Festschrift herrn Emil Christoph Barell. Basel, 1936.

8. Chassovnikova, K. A. "Variability of the Qualitative Composition of the Alkaloids in Subspecies of *Papaver somniferum*." (In Russian: Summary in English). Biokhimia 2, 701-704. (1937). Translation made for the U. S. Narcotics Bureau by A. Stein, Associate Structural Engineer, Federal Works Agency, Public Buildings Administration.

9. Rakshit, Jitendra Nath. "Porphyroxine." Journal of the Chemical Society (London) 115, 455 (1919) .

10. Rakshit, Jitendra Nath. "Die chemische Konstitution des Porphyroxins." Berichte der Deutschen Chemischen Gesellschaft 59, 2473 (1926).

11. Rajagopalan, S. "A Search for Porphyroxine in Bengal Opium." Current Science 12, 24 (1943). (Chemical Abstracts 37, 4860.)

12. Small, Lyndon F., and Lutz, Robert E. "Chemistry of the Opium Alkaloids." U. S. Treasury Department, Public Health Service, Supplement No. 103 to the Public Health Reports, United States Government Printing Office, Washington, 1932.

13. Henry, Thomas Anderson. "The Plant Alkaloids." 3rd edition. P. Blakiston's Son & Co., Inc. Philadelphia, 1939.

14. Wrede, Fritz. "Uber Narcotoline, ein neues Alkaloid aus Mohn (*Papaver somniferum*)." Archiv für experimentelle Pathologie und Pharmakologie. 184, 331-5. (1937)

15. Wüest, H. M., and Frey, A. J. "Opiate aus Mohnstroh." Festschrift herrn Emil Christoph Barell. Basel, 1936.

16. Chemical Abstracts 31, 2350 "Opiates from Poppy-straw." H. M. Wüest and A. J. Frey.

17. Analyses by U. S. Treasury chemists in recent years; also analyses reported to Bureau of Narcotics by manufacturing drug companies experimenting with extraction of alkaloids from poppy-straw. (Unpublished.)

18. Kabay, Helene von. "Janos von Kabay Method." L. of N., O. C. 1546 (1) (h) (1939). (III, 12).

19. Jespersen, J. C. "Analysis of Opium Poppies Grown in Denmark." League of Nations. O. C. 1546 (1) (f), Geneva, April 24th, 1937.

20. Kerbosch, M. G. J. M. "Bildung und Verbreitung einiger Alkaloide In Papaver somniferum L." Archiv der Pharmazie 248, 536-567 (1910).

21. Feldman, J., and Klyatchkina, B. A. "Memorandum regarding Research Work on the Poppy Plant and the Alkaloids Contained Therein" and "Annex." L. of N. 1546 (1) (e) (1937) (III, 13).

22. True, Rodney H., and Stockberger, W. W. "Physiological Observations on Alkaloids, Latex, and Oxidases in *Papaver somniferum*." American Journal of Botany, vol. 3, No. 1, pp. 1-11, 1916.

23. Machiguchi, Eizo. "Contribution to the Knowledge of Japanese Opium," Jour. Pharm. Soc. Japan 629, 186-228 (1926). Translation made for the U. S. Bureau of Narcotics. (II, 8).

24. Annett, Harold E., Sen, Hari Das, and Singh, Har Dayal. "Investigations on Indian Opium. No. 1 Non-environmental factors influencing the alkaloidal content and yield of latex from the opium poppy (*Papaver somniferum*)." Memoirs of the Department of Agriculture in India, Vol. VI, No. 1, pages 1-154.

25. Müller, A. "Die Bedeutung der Alkaloide von *Papaver somniferum* für das Leben der Pflanze." Archiv der Pharmazie 252, 280-92 (1914).

26. Chistoni, A. "The oil and alkaloid content of the seeds of *Papaver somniferum*." Arch. farmacol. sper. 52, 29-32. 1931. Chemical Abstracts 25, 4084.

27. Fuchs, Leopold. "Untersuchungen an *Fructus papaveris* in verschiedenen Reifestadien." Pharmazeutische Monatshefte 13, 223-5. (1932.)

28. Arima, Zyunzo, and Ninomiya, Mamoru. "Use of Poppy seeds in Manchoukuo. I." Rept. Inst. Sci. Research Manchoukuo 2, 237-43 (in German, 45-6). 1938. Chemical Abstracts 33,1875.

29. Chemical Abstracts 30, 3080. "The toxicity of ripe poppy seeds." R. Bunge

30. Bunge, R. "Uber die Giftigkeit reifer Mohnköpfe." Archiv für experimentelle Pathologie und Pharmakologie, 179, 465-474. (1935.)

V. Poppy capsules

(d) In medicine

If the flow of latex of some variety of *Papaver somniferum* is scanty or even lacking (supposing that to be possible) it is only necessary to extract the heads with water and evaporate the extract to obtain a product that is essentially a kind of opium. The ancient Greeks were acquainted with this method also of obtaining medicine or narcotics from the poppies, they did not know, of course, our modern pure salts of alkaloids. The use of a tea of poppy capsules has always continued in folk-medicine; and the use of a syrup or tincture of poppy capsules was continued in official medicine in the United States until recent years. A syrup of poppy capsules, and also the poppy capsules themselves (Papaveris Fructus) were official in the National Formulary IV (1916-1926). The dose of the dried capsules was 16 grains, equivalent probably to about one-fifteenth grain of morphine. The syrup was rather weak. (1) The National Formulary III (1906-1916) had a stronger syrup, and also a tincture of poppy capsules. A mere teaspoonful of the latter probably yielded nearly as much morphine as the present average dose of the sulfate salt of morphine (one-sixth grain); the dosage listed was 2 cc. (2)

The capsules for the official N. F. drug were directed to be picked in the unripe stage. It was formerly assumed that at the proper stage for opium production the alkaloidal content would be at its maximum. This is not quite correct; the real difficulty was that once the capsule dries out and the flow of latex to the poppy-head ceases, any rain will leach out the morphine without any chance for it to be replaced. Hence a dry climate where the poppies are watered by irrigation is desirable if the alkaloids are to be extracted from the dry chaff left from the separation of the seeds.

The capsules were probably dropped from official medicine in this country and Britain chiefly because of the variability and great uncertainty as to their content of morphine. It was formerly considered, too, that the alkaloidal content was almost negligible, and this has been proved not to be the case. For example, Merck's Index as recently as the 4th edition (1930) stated the narcotic content of poppy capsules as "opium bases (chiefly morphine) combined with meconic acid; very small quantity present, however, at all events not over 0.12 percent alkaloids or 0.03 percent (0.16-0.28 percent B. P. C.) morphine (in the seedless capsules)." The present (5th) edition of The Merck Index (1940) states the content as 0.15 0.5 percent morphine. (3) (4)

A. W. Blyth and M. W. Blyth state that "the ignorant use of poppy tea has frequently caused the death of young children" in England. (5)

(b) As a problem in antinarcotics enforcement

The present (23rd) edition of the United States Dispensatory states, "Poppy capsules contain the same active ingredients as opium but in such very minute proportion that they do not come under the anti-narcotic legislation." (6) This is copied from the preceding edition, and is now more erroneous than ever, since the Opium Poppy Control Act of 1942 covers the capsules clearly and unmistakably. The statement never was entirely correct. The morphine content of the capsules is by no means insignificant or negligible, since a single medium-sized capsule (about the size of a small hen's egg) may contain an average dose of morphine; nor were the capsules exempted from antinarcotics enforcement because of a belief that the narcotic content was too small to matter. They were exempted for a time, but have been held subject to antinarcotics laws ever since 1932.

The question of the capsules came up before the Internal Revenue Bureau (then administering the law) in 1921, and it was then decided, not upon chemical but upon legal grounds, that the poppy capsules themselves did not come under the Harrison Act. It was considered that the capsules are distinct from opium itself and are not derivatives of opium. The ruling then was, that "Poppy heads in their natural state do not come within the purview of this act, and as long as they remain in such condition are not taxable thereunder." However, if a compound, preparation or remedy is made from poppy heads, or, as an extract thereof, which contains opium or a salt or derivative thereof in a sufficient quantity to bring it within the scope of the act, such product will be subject to all the provisions of the act and the regulations promulgated thereunder." (7) For the sake of anyone who may be puzzled over the meaning of "a salt of opium" it may be mentioned that the language follows that of the law and is probably not just as a chemist would have stated it.

It may be of interest to note here what was written at the time by one of the U. S. Internal Revenue chemists, Peter Valaer, regarding a possible use of capsules by narcotics addicts:

One of the dried poppy capsules represented by Lab. No. 79817, an egg-shaped capsule, about the size of a small hen's egg, was powdered and extracted with boiling water and the extract evaporated to the consistency of thick molasses or when it would just drop off a yen hook or opium needle, a test frequently made by illicit manufacturers of smoking opium from the crude gum. This residue showed the characteristic taste, odor and appearance of smoking opium before and after burning, the amount obtained from the capsule being about the quantity commonly sold by illicit dealers for one dollar (approximately four pills for smoking). (7)

No doubt the "smoking opium" so prepared was of an inferior quality, and could hardly have commanded the price mentioned, which was that of good opium in 1921. However, there is no doubt, either, that this capsule extract contained morphine and the other alkaloids of smoking opium in substantial proportion; in fact the morphine content of the capsules then in question was proved by analysis.

The Harrison Act exempts preparations containing no more than one-fourth of a grain of morphine in one fluid ounce, or in the case of solid preparations, one avoirdupois ounce, provided these are medicines and not for the purpose of evading the intentions and provisions of the Act. In a prosecution in Oregon in 1923, of a Hindu narcotic addict who was making a "tea" from poppy capsules by extracting them with hot water, the tea on hand was found to contain 1.8 grains morphine per fluid ounce. In another similar case in the state of Washington in the same year, the tea contained 0.44 percent morphine, or 2.0 grains per fluid ounce. (7) The tea cannot be concentrated to a very much higher percentage of morphine without further manipulation, for water dissolves considerable material from the dried capsules, and even when the extract is evaporated until fairly solid, the morphine percentage is not likely to be quite as much as three times that of the original capsules (not including the seeds). However, the teas actually made far exceeded the exemption, and certainly an addict can get plenty of morphine by drinking enough poppy tea.

In 1932 it was discovered that numerous narcotic addicts on the West coast, chiefly Hindus in British Columbia, were drinking tea of poppy capsules, which were then sold without restriction in the drug stores of Vancouver. Some Hindus were also growing fields of the poppy. Most of the capsules in question had been imported into the United States at New York, and re-exported to Canada; some were also sold in the State of Washington, and there used, in part, by narcotic addicts. Most of the addicts known to use the capsules were Hindus, with some Chinese and others, who, if they had not already known, were rapidly learning the properties of poppy tea.

This time it was ruled that the capsules come under the Narcotic Drugs Import and Export Act, and their importation into the United

States was entirely forbidden. Canada at the same time subjected them to all the controls required for other narcotics. In most countries they are still sold freely, and are used in home-made medicines.

One peculiar result of the United States ruling was the discovery that there had been a considerable importation of unbroken poppyheads by the tens and hundreds of thousands for use as decorations. The capsules were gilded and otherwise painted and used for funeral wreaths and Christmas or winter decorations. One may suspect that the use for funerals was the original one, and that it was symbolic of sleep.

In 1941 a ton of poppy-heads was sent to a leading United States importer of crude drugs by mistake for an order for a ton of dried poppy flower-petals. The poppy flower-petals used in certain herb medicines are not from the opium poppy but are the red flowers of *Papaver rhoeas*. They contain a little rhoeadine, an alkaloid, but their principal use is merely in coloring the preparation.

The Opium Poppy Control Act of 1942 now forbids any domestic production of the opium poppy, save under license in case this is necessary for medical supplies of opium or opium alkaloids.

V. REFERENCES

1. The National Formulary. Fourth Edition. Official from September 1, 1916. By authority of the American Pharmaceutical Association.

2. The National Formulary of Unofficial Preparations. Third Edition. By authority of the American Pharmaceutical Association. Baltimore, 1906.

3. Merck's Index. Fourth Edition. Merck & Co., Rahway, New Jersey, 1930.

4. The Merck Index. Fifth Edition. Merck & Co., Rahway, New Jersey, 1940.

5. Blyth, Alexander Wynter, and Blyth, Meredith Wynter. Poisons, Their Effects and Detection. 4th edition. Charles Griffin and Co., Ltd. London, 1906.

6. The Dispensatory of the United States of America. 23rd edition.1943. (II, 7).

7: Files of the United States Bureau of Narcotics.

VI. Variations in flowers, seed colors, and capsules

(a) Causes of Variation

The most widespread plants are the most variable, and *Papaver somniferum* is spread all over the world. Variations are greater in widespread than in localized plants, for (a) There are more individual plants in which variations may occur; (b) The species grows under widely different geographical and climatic conditions; (c) Widely separated and isolated areas may more readily develop local races.

In addition, cultivated plants vary more than wild ones, and *Papaver somniferum* is almost wholly a cultivated plant. The cultivated plants vary more because (a) They are living under unnatural conditions; (b) Aberrations may be preserved by the intervention of man; (c) Slight variations may be developed into distinct varieties by horticultural selection.

De Vries calls *Papaver somniferum* "many-formed" remarking that it is "so-called very variable, but in all its forms very constant." (1) However, many of the forms now considered constant were doubtless developed by selection from slight variations, as were the Shirley Poppies from *Papaver rhoeas*. (2) The Poppy flower is readily self-fertile, so that a variety may tend to perpetuate itself, but it should never be overlooked that the opium poppy is almost wholly a cultivated plant.

(b) Flowers

Under the conditions mentioned above it should not be surprising that the opium poppy has varieties so different from each other that at first glance they would hardly be thought to belong to the same species.

As previously mentioned, the flowers may be either single or double, and the petals either plain or fringed. The double fringed kinds are called "carnation flowered," the double plain "paeony flowered." There are also double kinds with the inner petals fringed, the outer plain; and there are single kinds with fringed petals. Most reference books giving information relative to opium or seed production describe only the commonly grown single varieties. Botanies generally describe the form that may be found growing wild in the territory covered. The best idea of the floral varieties can, therefore, be gained from horticultural reference books, such as The Standard Cyclopedia of Horticulture by Bailey. (2)

The petals may be white, pink, lavender, red, purple, or violet, or various combinations of these. The single varieties, at least, generally have either a white or a violet spot at the base of each petal. Two colored plates given by Vesselovskaya show fourteen of these variations, including the pure white petal. (3) The very common single variety, white with large violet spots, is well illustrated by a colored plate in Hegi's "Illustrierte Flora von Mittel-Europa." (4) The red double fringed variety is beautifully illustrated by a colored plate in "Atlas des Plantes de Jardins" by D. Bois, and the same plate is also used in "Favorite Flowers of Garden and Greenhouse" by Edward Step. (5) (6)

Bailey states in one place that the flowers are not yellow or blue (2), but this statement requires some modification. The white flowers of a certain kind may have a yellowish-greenish tint (3); and Bailey admits that a yellow variety has been advertised, though of doubtful authenticity. Moreover, Fedde remarks that the color of the petals may even be orange. (7) Thus the opium poppy flower colors do not include a pure, bright yellow, but the color may approach some kind of yellow. On the other side of the color range the violet flowers may approach blue quite closely, so much so that the flowers of a certain shade would without doubt be called "blue" by most people. A colored illustration of this variety will be found in "Familiar Garden Flowers" by Hulme and Hibberd. (8)

However, the common garden variety known as the "Blue Poppy" ("Dutch Blue," "Holland Blue," or "Moravian Blue Poppy," etc.) seems to be so named only from its seed color and not from the color of its flowers. It is also, and more accurately, known as the "Blueseeded Poppy." The most common flower variety of the garden poppy is probably the single kind having large white petals each with a violet spot at the base.

(c) Seed colors

Other kinds of variation usually noticed or used as the basis for classification do not affect the production of opium or alkaloids anymore than the color of the flowers, and that is not at all.

The seeds, according to various authors who state their colors, may be white, yellow, pink or red, gray or slate-colored, pale or dark blue, glaucous, greyish purple, brown,, or black. According to Melville the grey, blue, and brown seeds contain only brown pigment. "The blueness is due to an optical effect caused by the scattering of light from a multitude of small crystals of calcium oxalate present in the subepidermal cells of the seed coat. This phenomenon is comparable with that responsible for blue eyes, and the blueness of pools containing finely suspended matter, such as are found in limestone districts." (9) At any rate, sometimes the seeds of the blue kind certainly look quite blue.

There is little connection between the color of the seeds and the general color of the flowers; possibly more between the color of the seeds and the color of the spots at the base of the petals (as to whether light or dark).

A varietal classification frequently used divides the poppies actually used for opium production into just two kinds: the white poppy, variety *album* DC., with white seeds and generally white flowers, and the black poppy, variety *nigrum* DC., with dark seeds and generally violet or red flowers. (Used, for example, by the United States Dispensatory.) (10) The people of Central Europe also generally divide the poppies into just two kinds, the "white poppy" and the "blue poppy," these being distinguished by seed color chiefly if not entirely. However, there are any number of intermediate forms and also those with pink or red seeds; and this kind of classification has no significance for opium, morphine, or seed production, save by reason of human preference. The white-seeded kind seems to be often preferred for opium production; or, at least, those who grow the "garden poppy" think it ought to be. The dark-seeded kind is nearly always preferred for seed production. Statements of the kind preferred for oil (from the seeds) are contradictory.

The United States Pharmacopoeia XII includes mention of variety *album* in the official definition for opium, as follows: "Opium is the air-dried milky exudation obtained by incising the unripe capsules of *Papaver somniferum* Linné or its variety *album* De Candolle (Fam. Papaveraceae)." (11) Mention of the variety is superfluous—as was pointed out by Rusby, Bliss, and Ballard in "The Properties and Uses of Drugs" (12)—since a species includes its varieties, unless they are specifically excluded from use for the official drug. Possibly the definition was intended to give official recognition to the fact that - "Papaver album" is variety *album*, of *Papaver somniferum*.

In former years some United States seed companies frankly listed the white poppy in their catalogues as the opium poppy, *Papaver somniferum*. At the same time they would list half a dozen floral varieties of "tall annual poppies" without anything to indicate that these belonged to exactly the same species. There seems to be a strong feeling that the pure white poppy—white in flowers and seed—is the "true" opium poppy. It is difficult even to guess at the origin of the unfounded idea, for the countries actually producing opium grow poppies with seeds and flowers of nearly all the colors that have been mentioned.

Basilevskaja lists for the seed colors of opium-producing poppies in Semiretchie (in Asiatic Russia) the following: white, pink, yellow, grey, glaucous and dark blue. (13) Zhukovsky and collaborators include in La Turquie Agricole a colored plate showing the seed colors of the opium poppies of Anatolia (Planche II). This shows the following six colors: white, brownish yellow or ochre, pink-red, light blue, dark blue, and black or extremely dark blue. (14)

(d) Capsules

The capsules may be of different shapes; elongate, egg-shaped, globular, oblate-depressed, etc. Three very different shapes are illustrated in the National Standard Dispensatory. (15) Pieper gives a diagrammatic classification of the capsules into six types (Abb. 10) and a picture of each type (Abb. 12). (16) Vesselovskaya illustrates numerous shapes in her monograph, "The Poppy," both by photographs and by a "Schema of the shapes shown by the capsules of the poppy" (Fig. 12), which gives diagrammatic differentiation of twelve types. (3)

Aside from providing varietal distinctions the shape of the capsules means nothing, save possibly that some shapes may make more attractive decorations and some may be a little easier than others to incise for opium.

A very interesting monstrosity has been grown, and probably still is in some parts of Europe. n this variety, a number of secondary pistils develop around the main capsule, springing from its base at just about the same place the stamens are attached. Earlier writers stated that the inner stamens were converted into pistils, but Roelofs (1937) describes it thus: "In this variety there occur in the flower between the stamens and the pistil little organs which as to position and number much resemble the former, but in a morphological respect are to be entirely regarded as pistils." The number of these secondary pistils varies from one to one hundred or more, it being impossible to count them exactly in the latter case as they are grown together, forming a crown around the main capsule. Roelofs illustrates six degrees of polycephaly. (Pl. V.) (17)

This variety was described, probably for the first time, by Prof. Goeppert of Breslau in 1851— "on a constant variety of poppy in which the anthers are transformed into carpels." It was designated as *Papaver officinale* Gmel. (a synonym for *Papaver somniferum*) variety *monstrosum* Goepp. The article includes an illustration. (18)

The illustrations of course show the capsule, with the cluster of little capsules around it, after the petals have fallen. Bailey incorrectly states that there are no petals. (2) This aberration has also been illustrated by de Vries and by the Revue Horticole. (1) (19) It is known as variety *Monstrosum*, *Monstruosum*, *Polycephalum* or *Proliferum*.

VI. REFERENCES

1. Vries, Hugo de. Die Mutationstheorie (pp. 97-100). Leipzig, 1901.

2. Bailey, L .H. The Standard Cyclopedia of Horticulture. New York, 1936. (I, 2).

3. Vesselovskaya, M. The Poppy. Leningrad, 1933. (II, 9).

4. Hegi, Gustav. Illustrierte Flora von Mittel-Europa. München, 1913. (II, 1).

5. Bois, D. Atlas des Plantes de Jardins. Librairie des Sciences Naturelles. Paris, 1896. (Plate 20) .

6. Step, Edward. Favorite Flowers of Garden and Greenhouse. London, 1896. (Plate 18).

7. Fedde, Friedrich. "Papaveraceae"; in Die natürliche Pflanzenfamilien, 2nd ed., vol. 17 b. A. Engler und K. Prantl. Verlag von Wilhelm Engelmann. Leipzig, 1836. (*Papaver somniferum*).

8. Hulme, F. Edward, and Hibberd, Shirley. Familiar Garden Flowers. Casell & Co., Ltd., London, Paris, and Melbourne, 1879-87.

9. Melville, Ronald. (Museums of Economic Botany, Royal Botanic Gardens, Kew). "Cultivation and Food Value of the Oil Poppy." Garden Chronicle, vol. 109 (3rd series), p. 54. Feb. 8, 1941. (No. 5224).

10. The Dispensatory of the United States of America, 23rd ed., 1943 (II,7).

11. The Pharmacopoeia of the United States of America. Twelfth Revision. Official from November 1, 1942. (I, 1),

12. Rusby, Henry H.; Bliss, A. Richard (Jr.); and Ballard, Charles W. The Properties and Uses of Drugs. P. Blakiston's Son & Co. Philadelphia, 1930

13. Basilevskaja, N. A., "On the Races of the Opium Poppy Growing in Semiretchie." Trudy Prikl. Bot. 19 (2), 95-184 (1928). (II, 2).

14. Zhukovsky, P., and collaborators. La Turquie Agricole. (Partie AsiatiqueAnatolie). Moscow, Leningrad, 1933. In Russian (titles also in French). (Opium Poppies pp. 476-507).

15. The National Standard Dispensatory. By Hobart Amory Hare, Charles Caspari, Henry H. Rusby, Joseph F. Geisler, Edward Kremers, and Daniel Base. Lee Brothers & Co. Philadelphia and New York, 1905.

16. Pieper, Hilde. "Vergleichende Untersuchungen von Varietaten des Kultur Mohns." Landwirtschaftll Jahrbucher. 89: 333-392. (1939).

17. Roelofs, E. T. "Phenotypical and Genotypical Eversporting Varieties. II. Papaver somniferum polycephalum." (In English) Genetica (Nederlandsch Tijdscrift voor Erfelijheids=en Afstammingsleer). 19, 481-517. (1937).

18. Goeppert. "Sur une variété constante de Pavot dont les authères se transforment en carpelles." Flore des Serres et des Jardins de L'Europe. VI (1850-51) pp. 241-42 and 245-46. (Communication from M. le Prof. Goeppert of Breslau and note by L. VH.)

19. Revue Horticole 65, 348-351. (1893) "Les Pavots Annuels."

VII. Agricultural varieties

(a) Dehiscent and indehiscent varieties

A differentiation of greater practical importance is that between dehiscent and indehiscent varieties. In the dehiscent varieties (scattering their seed at maturity) pores open at the top of the capsule, underneath the margin of the stigma, and between its rays, when the seed is ripe. Then by inverting the capsule and shaking, the seeds come out like salt from a shaker. In the indehiscent varieties the pores do not open, at least not on the majority of the capsules. There are intermediate forms in which the pores may or may not open depending on weather conditions and other factors; or the pores may only half-open. Perhaps no varieties are absolutely indehiscent under all conditions.

The indehiscent varieties, which do not lose any seed until the capsule is broken, are naturally best for seed production. They are the largest and most highly cultivated forms, and have the largest capsules. Some varieties mainly dehiscent are also known chiefly as cultivated forms, generally for opium rather than seed. The half-wild kinds that, when cultivated, readily escape, and now grow wild more or less throughout Europe and other parts of the world, are naturally fully dehiscent. Their capsules are comparatively small. They show, however, the same wide range in color of the flowers, etc., as the highly cultivated kinds. There is every reason to believe that the indehiscent varieties have been developed from the dehiscent forms. Both kinds produce morphine or opium. (1)

(b) Ecological varieties; geographical races

There are also ecological varieties. The poppies grown for hundreds of years in a certain region become adapted to it, to the length of growing season, length of day, rainfall, etc. The adaptation is reflected in the appearance of the plant, the vegetative characters, period of growth, etc., so that the different ecotypes or climatypes can be distinguished, at least for some years, when all are grown in the same region. Moreover, from the accident of the first introduction of a particular type into a region, a certain geographical area may have poppies showing a certain combination of characteristics, including those that are not at all dependent upon climate. Natural selection, and still more, human selection will also operate differently in different regions, even on those characteristics independent of climate, and upon those that are really unessential, but which may catch the fancy of the cultivator. It seems reasonable, therefore, that the classification into subspecies should be largely geographical, as Vesselovskaya contends.

Perhaps "geographical races" would be a better term than "subspecies," but Vesselovskaya uses "race" for the smallest subdivision. She classifies the cultivated varieties on the ecological basis into seven groups: northern, Central Asiatic, Mongolian, Tian-Shanian, Asia Minor, southern, and subtropical. The "half-wild" dehiscent varieties are allowed three groups: northern (European), intermediate (Asia Minor), and southern (Indian). Taking stated characteristics into consideration she then divides the species-Papaver somniferum into seven subspecies, agreeing in the main with the ecological groups. Her subspecies are: *eurasiaticum*, *centroasiaticum*, *mongolicum*, *tianshanicum*, *anatalicum*, *indicum*, and *subspontaneum*. The southern and sub-tropical ecotypes are both included in the sixth subspecies, while the seventh (*subspontaneum*) comprises the semi-wild completely dehiscent forms. The subspecies are then divided into varieties according to the colors of flowers and seeds. These in turn, if desired, may be divided into "types" by other characteristics. "Race" is used for a smallest or homogeneous subdivision. (1)

The subspecies differ markedly in various respects. The difference in height or size of the plants is sometimes quite striking. Basilevskaja gives two pictures showing the low character of the opium poppies of the Tian-Shan race, cultivated in Semiretchie. The plants hardly come above the knees of the cultivators. She also illustrates the taller condition of the Djungarian poppy race. (2) Vesselovskaya gives measurements and photographs for typical plants of the various subspecies. (1) However, there is hardly a better picture of the tall large type of opium poppy plant (though not labelled *Papaver somniferum*, and in fact over a misleading line) than the full page photograph in The World Book Encyclopedia, article "Poppy." (3)

The ecotypes are naturally of great importance to the commercial grower. If the seed he uses comes from a region too dissimilar, especially in length of growing season, the poppies will not do well. However, all the ecotypes produce morphine or opium.

VII. REFERENCES

1. Vesselovskaya, M. The Poppy. Leningrad, 1933. (II, 9).

2. Basilevskaja, N. A. "On the Races of the Opium Poppy Growing in Semiretchie". Trudy Prikl. Bot. 19 (2), 95-184 (1928). (II, 2).

3. The World Book Encyclopedia. The Quarrie Corporation. Chicago, 1940. Article "Poppy".

VIII. Chemical variations

(a) In regard to opium and morphine

It is doubtless apparent from the discussion to this point that the different kinds of variation in *Papaver somniferum* are, in general, so independent of each other, that only the particular kind of variation we are really interested in has significance. If we are primarily interested in floriculture then the floral variations are significant; otherwise not. If the poppies are grown for edible seed and oil then the only variations of significance are the quantity of seeds produced, their oil content, and possibly their color. If grown for opium then the yield of latex and its content of morphine are the significant characteristics. Likewise if opium poppies are ever grown in this country for direct extraction of alkaloids it will be the chemical variations that count. Unfortunately almost nothing is known about them except that they do occur.

In considering chemical varieties, we must make allowance for environmental factors, particularly the soil and fertilizer. Light and well-drained but fertile soil is most desirable, but the plants will grow in almost any type of soil. They respond well to fertilizers, especially nitrates, and then produce more opium.

Annett considered the total morphine production proportional to the growth of the plant. He also showed that opium from successive lancings of the same capsules declined steadily in morphine content. Some, at least, of the secondary alkaloids increased in relation to the morphine, or even, in many cases, in actual percentage in the opium. Moreover, the opium from the main or terminal capsules was somewhat higher in morphine than that from the lateral capsules. (1)

Making all allowances necessary for such factors, there are still hereditary chemical variations. They are not closely connected with any distinction between seed-producing poppies and the varieties grown primarily for opium. Varieties are known with a high yield of both opium and seed. Moreover the yield of opium does not indicate the percentage of morphine in the capsule. Some varieties of the “garden poppy” (that is, varieties of *Papaver somniferum*, grown exclusively for seed) have a high morphine content, others comparatively low.

No variety is known in which morphine is absent. Possibly such a variety could be produced by selective breeding. This would take a number of years if it could be done at all. The variety might be subject to “relapse” and the strain would have to be kept pure, necessitating rechecking every year or so. Consequently it is not intended here that any hope be held out to farmers who want to grow their own poppy seed, that any variety of *Papaver somniferum* can be found or developed within any reasonable number of years, that could be grown under the Opium Poppy Control Act.

Varieties have been segregated and established, in Turkey at least, that yield opium with 20 percent morphine, as long as the strain is kept pure. Also there are varieties with a low morphine content in the opium; but generally selections have been made with a view to increasing the yield of opium and morphine.

The morphine content of the opium does not give us a great deal of information about the actual production by the plant. First, the yield of latex has to be taken into consideration, for abundant latex, with a low morphine content, may be equivalent to scanty latex with a high morphine content.

Moreover, Vorozhtsov and Troshchenko reported (1935) that a considerable part of the morphine present in the fresh latex is decomposed during the usual evaporation of the juice on the capsule. They attribute this to the air (oxygen) and enzyme (oxidase) in the latex. The Tianshan race of opium poppy was used, ordinarily yielding opium of 11-13 percent morphine. The fresh juice when analyzed within 2 hours and calculated to the dry basis contained about 20 percent morphine, but the opium contained only 11.6 percent. By collecting the latex in a vessel with a little potassium fluoride, which inactivated the enzyme, 22 percent morphine was found (calculated to the dry basis), and the latex remained stable at this content for several months. (2) (Further reported by Nilov, Nilova, and Troshchenko.) (3)

If this is all correct, varieties yielding opium with a high morphine content may merely lack oxidase in the latex (or have something present that inactivates the oxidase) instead of really producing more morphine than other kinds. They would still be chemical varieties, at any rate. The question of the alkaloids in the really fresh plant and latex badly needs more investigation. True and Stockberger back in 1916 even concluded that alkaloids are not present as such in the fresh latex, but are formed from something else by oxidase action! (4) This conclusion seems most doubtful.

It is very possible that the ancient and orthodox method of collecting opium should be greatly modified. Two thousand years ago it was the only way known of obtaining a concentrate of high morphine content. Today, especially for legitimate use, the opium is usually just an intermediate step in manufacturing the pure alkaloids.

(b) In regard to secondary alkaloids

The chemical variations that have actually become established—by accident—as distinct varieties, pertain to the secondary alkaloids. A fact that stands out is that papaverine, which is often the fourth alkaloid in amount, or even the third, is sometimes found completely absent in some kinds of opium, while the same methods show its presence in other kinds.

Thus, van Itallie and Kerbosch examined qualitatively 19 samples of opium from 7 different regions of the world, for the 6 principal alkaloids. They found all 6 in all of them except that 4 of the 5 samples from India contained no papaverine. (5)

Chassovnikova found that opium from a Chinese variety of *Papaver somniferum* contained neither papaverine nor even narcotine, whereas both were present in the opium from four other subspecies investigated. In fact, narcotine was the second alkaloid for the other subspecies, and the same method of analysis which showed none at all in the Chinese subspecies yielded 4.8 to 7.6 percent in the other kinds. (6)

Manchurian opium, while containing both narcotine and papaverine, is low in the latter and exceptionally high in both codeine and thebaine, as shown by the analyses of Arima and Iwakiri. (7) The same is true of Tianshan opium, which in Chassovoikova's analyses showed over 3 percent of codeine and over 4 percent of thebaine. (6) A very different variety is grown in India, for Rakshit remarks that thebaine is only nominally present in Indian opium. (8)

Feldman and Klyatchkina, from analyses of the capsules, remark that "all kinds of poppies" (that is, all varieties of the species *Papaver somniferum*) contain morphine and codeine, but that "the presence of narcotine and papaverine depends on the kind of poppy." They also state that the "garden poppies" are low in narcotine as compared with the "opium poppies." (9). Kerbosch found similarly that poppies from European seed produced much less narcotine than those from Smyrna seed. (10)

On the other hand Küssner's report on the alkaloid content of the capsules of a variety grown in Germany shows almost as much papaverine as morphine, with high narcotine, scarcely any codeine, and no thebaine. (11)

In the summer of 1943 the writer examined capsules of a garden poppy grown in Minnesota, with the extraordinary result of finding narceine (usually sixth) as the second alkaloid, along with no papaverine at all. Moreover, an alkaloid was separated, which, within the limits of the method, had the solubilities of papaverine, but gave the color reactions of narceine. This may possibly have been methyl-narcotine. Currently, methyl-narcotine is not supposed to exist in opium, although it was reported by two early investigators. (12) No doubt it is usually absent, but it is in just such plants as these, with abnormally high narceine, that it might be present. Lack of material and lack of time prevented any extensive investigation.

It is evident that in growing poppies either for opium or for the direct extraction of alkaloids a great deal more attention should be paid to the variations from the chemical standpoint, and to the established chemical varieties.

VIII. REFERENCES

1. Annett, Harold Edward. "Factors Influencing Alkaloidal Content and Yield of Latex in the Opium Poppy (*Papaver somniferum*)." Biochemical Journal 14, 618-36 (1920). (IV, 2).

2. Vorozhtsov, N. N., and Troshchenko, A. T. "Der Morphingehalt im Milchsafte des Opium Mohns." Comptes Rendus de L'Acadamie des Sciences de L'Union des Republique Sovietiques Socialistes, 1935 (2), 555-558 (In Russian; German Summary 558).

3. Nilov, V. I., Nilova, W. P., and Troshchenko, A. T. "Fermentative Oxidation of Morphine in the Latex of the Opium Poppy." Biokhimiya 1, 165-82 (1936). Chemical Abstracts 30, 7779.

4. True, Rodney H., and Stockberger, W. W. "Physiological Observations on Alkaloids, Latex, and Oxidases in *Papaver somniferum*." Am. J. Botany 3, 1-11 (1916) (IV, 22.)

5. Itallie, L. van, and Kerbosch, M. "Beiträge zur Zusammensetzung des Opiums." Archiv der Pharmazie 248, 609-613 (1910).

6. Chassovnikova, K. A. "Variability of the Qualitative Composition of the Alkaloids in Subspecies of *Papaver somniferum*." Biokhimia 2, 701-704. (1937.) (Chemical Abstracts 32, 1861.) Translation made for the U. S. Bureau of Narcotics by A. Stein. (IV, 8.)

7. Arima, Zyunzo and Iwakiri, Mitsuo. "Manchurian Opium. I. Analysis of the Main Alkaloids." Rept. Inst. Sci. Research, Manchoukuo 2, 221-30. (In German 43) (1938). Chemical Abstracts 38,1875. (IV, 3.)

8. Rakshit, Jitendra Nath. "Morphine, Codeine, and Narcotine in Indian Opium." The Analyst 46, 481-8 (1921).

9. Feldman, V., and Klyatchkina, B. A. "Memorandum Regarding Research Work on the Poppy Plant and the Alkaloids Contained Therein." L. of N.O.C. 1548 (1) (e) (1937). (III, 13.)

10. Kerbosch, M. G. J. M. "Bildung und Verbreitung einiger Alkaloide in Papaver somniferum L." Arch. Pharm. 248, 536-567 (1910). (IV, 20.)

11. Küssner, W. "Alkaloid Content of Poppy Capsules." E. Merck's Jahresbericht. 54, 29-40 (1940). Chemical Abstracts 35, 8203.

12. Small, Lyndon F., and Lutz, Robert E. Chemistry of the Opium Alkaloids. (page 46.) Washington, 1932. (IV, 12.)

IX. Names for varieties

(a) Geographical, national, and provincial names

Although the geographical races or subspecies of *Papaver somniferum* may correspond to major geographical areas, the use of the names of minor units, as countries, states, and provinces, to designate varieties, has never been anything but a source of confusion. If seed is obtained from Macedonia or Persia, then the plant is called "The Macedonian Poppy" or "The Persian Poppy." Yet, according to the Encyclopaedia Britannica, there are four varieties grown in Macedonia, and six "forms"—all attributed to variety *album,* but differing in color of flower and quality of opium—in Persia. (1)

On the other hand, exactly the same variety of the northern ecotype may be grown in Holland, Moravia, Hungary, and elsewhere. When seed is obtained from these places and grown in the United States, the same poppy is variously known as "The Dutch Poppy," "The Moravian Poppy," "The Hungarian Poppy," etc. Still worse, if the plant has been grown in Oregon for a time, then seed sent from there to California, it becomes "The Oregon Poppy" in California. This has already occurred.

There are two totally different poppies of other genera rightfully known as the California Poppy and the Mexican Poppy, since their scientific names are *Eschscholzia californica* and *Argemone mexicana*, respectively; yet already we have opium poppies known as "California Poppies" and "Mexican Poppies" merely because they have been grown in those places.

The poppy immortalized by the First World War and the poem "In Flanders Fields" is the red corn poppy, *Papaver rhoeas*, which grows wild in Flanders. However, the opium poppy is cultivated there, and the name "Flanders Poppy" has already caused some confusion. The article "Poppy" in The World Book, an encyclopedia, states correctly that "the common red poppy, a species that grows wild in the grain fields and grassy meadows of Great Britain and the continent of Europe, is the one referred to in the popular wartime poem, In Flanders Fields, by John McCrae"; nevertheless the accompanying full page illustration, over the line, "In Flanders Fields the Poppies Blow," shows an unquestionable field of opium (garden) poppies, with an old peasant woman cultivator. (2)

The name "Flanders Field poppy" is not objectionable as is "Flanders poppy," since it both relates the kind of poppy more specifically to the poem, and also indicates the distinction of the "field poppy," *Papaver rhoeas*, which grows wild in Europe, from the "garden poppy" which is *Papaver somniferum*.

It is hoped that the naming of varieties of *Papaver somniferum* for minor geographical or political areas, such as countries, states, and provinces, will be entirely abandoned.

The name "Oriental Poppy" as intended to distinguish the Chinese or Far-Eastern variety of opium poppy has been a source of extreme confusion for years. First, the name already rightfully belonged to *Papaver orientale*, an entirely different species native to the Near East. Secondly, there is often doubt as to whether "The Orient" signifies the Far or the Near East. Thirdly, the name was generally used on the erroneous supposition that the opium poppy is a native of the Far East. Fourthly, in extending the term to all opium-producing poppies it was commonly opposed to "The Domestic Poppy," although whether this last name was intended for *Papaver rhoeas* or the European "garden poppy" is by no means clear. If by "The Domestic Poppy" was meant *Papaver rhoeas*, it was not sufficiently distinguished from the opium poppy; while if the term meant the European garden poppy there was made an apparent distinction, in fact an opposition, without any real difference.

Let us hope that in the future the term "Oriental Poppy" will be reserved for the use flower-gardeners always give it; that is, that it be applied only to *Papaver orientale* and its near-relative *Papaver bracteatum* and their hybrids.

(b) Botanical names

The following specific names of the genus *Papaver* are listed in the Index Kewensis as equivalent to *Papaver somniferum*. (3) They apply to varieties or subspecies, or even, in many cases, the typical form, being then mere synonyms for *somniferum*. The only exception appears to be *setigerum*, which is listed in the Index as equivalent to *somniferum*. It was considered by many botanists to be the truly wild subspecies, but others considered it a distinct species, and recent work indicates that the latter view is correct. The names are given with reference to their author and the publication in which first described.

album Mill. Gard. Dict. ed. 8, n. 9. 1768.
album & nigrum Crantz, Stirp. Austr. ed. 1, fasc. 2: 129. 1763.
amoemum Lindl. Bot. Reg. Misc. 56. 1839.
amplexicaule Stokes, Bot. Mat. Med. 3:181. 1812.
glabrum Gilib. Fl. Lituan. 213. 1781.

(The name *Papaver glabrum* has also been applied to a variety of *Papaver dubium*.)

hortense Hussen. Chard. Nanc. Fl. 39. 1835.

indehiscens Dum. Fl. Belg. Prod. 130. 1827.

officinale Gmel. Fl. Bad. 2: 479. 1806.

opiiferum Forsk. Fl. Aegypt-Arab. p. 113, n. 336. 1775.

nigrum, Bub. Fl. Pyren. 3:267. 1897-1901.

nigrum Garsault, Fig. Pl. Anim. Med. t. 440. 1764.

polycephalum Hort. ex Vilm. Fl. Pl. Terre, ed. 1: 594. 1863.

(Vilmorin merely gave *Papaver polycephalum* Hort. as a synonym for *Papaver somniferum* var. *monstruosum* & Hort. (4) See Chapter VI, d.)

setigerum DC. Fl. Fr. 5 (suppl.), 585 1815

(Now held to be a distinct species.) and finally,

somniferum L. Sp. Pl. 508. 1753.

The Index Londinensis, with its supplement, lists 161 sources of illustrations of *Papaver somniferum*, including many colored plates showing the flowers with stalk, leaves, etc. (5). Some of the illustrations, however, show only the fruits (capsules) or other parts. In addition there are seventeen sources for illustrations of the following varieties:

var. *album* DC. (the "White Poppy").

var. *glabrum* Boiss.

var. *laciniatum* Reichb.

var. *leptocaulotum* Fedde.

var. *nanum*, Hort. (double fringed; "Chamois-rose" color).

var. *nigrum* DC. (the "Black Poppy").

var. *polycephalum* Hort. (The name probably should be var. *monstrosum* Goepp. See chapter VI, d).

(c) Horticultural names

The following are some of the names applied to floral varieties of the opium poppy. Sometimes Latin names are used in the style of botanical names. These are occasionally stated, rather carelessly, as if they were specific names, as for instance "*Papaver murselli*"; or they may be given more fully and correctly, as for example "*Papaver somniferum* var. *murselli*, Hort." The English language names are the ones that were found in most seed catalogs, prior to the passage of the Opium Poppy Control Act. In the seed catalogs the floral varieties of *Papaver somniferum* were generally listed merely as "Tall Annual poppies."

Latin names:
- Giganteum.
- Magnificum.
- Paeoniflorum (peony-flowered, or double plain).

Strains of double fringed kinds:
- Cardinale (Scarlet. A salmon-pink of the "Cardinal" strain was also offered).
- Fimbriatum.
- Murselli ("Mikado" is a representative of this strain).
- Nanum (originally "chamois-rose" color).

Various names for the aberration with supernumerary carpels:
- Monstrosum (apparently this was the name first used. See chapter VI, d).
- Monstruosum (Vilmorin's spelling) (4)
- Polycephalum (apparently botanists most often use this name).
- Prolifère (P. prolifère Hort., Revue Horticole 65: 348.1893) .
- Proliferum (name used by Fedde, Das Pflanzenreich 40).

English Language names:

Single kinds:
- Admiral (white, banded scarlet).
- Charles Darwin (dark purple with black spots).
- Dainty Lady (rosy-mauve with darker spots).
- Danebrog or Danish Flag (bright red with white spots at the base of the petals forming a cross).
- Flag of Truce (pure white).
- King Edward (scarlet red).
- Maid of the Mist (white, fringed petals).
- Mephisto (scarlet, spotted black).
- The Bride (pure white).
- Victoria Cross (same as Danebrog).

Chinese poppies (dwarf kinds).

Double Plain kinds:
- Paeony-flowered (mixed, or in separate color strains as):
  - Scarlet.
  - Chamois-rose.
  - Raspberry-rose.
  - White.
  - Mauve.
- Mauve Queen.
- Black (double and semi-double; probably an extremely dark violet).

Double Fringed kinds:
- Carnation-flowered.
- Cardinal (scarlet; also salmon-pink of the same strain).
- Mikado (white, crimson striped or tipped)
- Pink Gem.
- White Swan.

References: (6) (7) (8) (9).

The reference book, Standardized Plant Names, has apparently confused the Opium Poppy with the Oriental Poppy and mingled the names of the two together. Most of the names given above are marked in it as "Or." for Oriental (10)

IX. REFERENCES

1. The Encyclopaedia Britannica, 14th edition, 1929. Article "Opium."

2. The World Book Encyclopedia. The Quarrie Corporation. Chicago, 1940. Article "Poppy" (VII, 3)

3. Index Kewensis. An Enumeration of the Genera and Species of Flowering Plants. From the time of Linnaeus to the year 1885, inclusive, together with their authors' names, the works in which they were first published, their native countries and their synonyms. Compiled under the direction of Joseph D. Hooker by B. Daydon Jackson. Oxford, 1895. Supplements bring up to 1935.

4. Vilmorin-Andrieux et Cie. Fleurs de Pleine Terre. Paris, 1863.

5. Index Londinensis to Illustrations of Flowering Plants, Ferns and Fern Allies. Prepared under the auspices of the Royal Horticultural Society of London at the Royal Botanic Gardens, Kew. By O. Stapf. Oxford, 1931. Supplement for the years 1921-35. By W. C. Worsdell, under the direction of Arthur W. Hill. Oxford, 1941.

6. Sutton & Sons, Reading England. Seed Catalogue, 1939. (III, 5).

7. Bailey, L. H. The Standard Cyclopedia of Horticulture. New York, 1935. (I, 2).

8. Foley, Daniel J. Annuals for your Garden. N. Y., 1938 (III, 7).

9. Sudell, Richard (editor). The New Illustrated Gardening Manual. N. Y., 1937 (III, 8).

10. Kelsey, Harlan P., and Dayton, William A. Standardized Plant Names, 2nd edition. J. Horace McFarland Company, Harrisburg, Pennsylvania, 1942

X. The closest relatives of *Papaver somniferum*

(a) Botanical opinions on species

It often happens in regard to a widespread and variable plant, or in regard to closely related plants, that botanists disagree as to whether there is only one variable species, or several which should be regarded as distinct. In the case of the cultivated poppy the question seems to be well settled. Although several other specific names have been bestowed and were often used in the past, such as *Papaver officinale*, *P. hortense*, and *P. opiiferum*, botanists now seem well agreed that there is only one poppy cultivated for either opium or edible seed, and that is *Papaver somniferum*.

There are, of course, poppies cultivated for their flowers which belong to quite distinct species and even to other genera. It is also true that the seeds of some other species may be eaten, and possibly such a poppy may have been grown for that purpose at one time or another. However, the only poppy grown commercially anywhere or known to have been grown in the United States for edible seed, is *Papaver somniferum*, the Opium Poppy.

The numerous strains or races of poppies actually used for opium production all belong to the one species, *Papaver somniferum*. It is probable enough, however, that among its closest relatives there may be found at least one (*Papaver setigerum*) that produces morphine or perhaps even yields a true opium of similar composition to that from *Papaver somniferum*.

It is in regard to these closest relatives that there have been differences of botanical opinion. Some botanists have lumped together five more or less different poppies, considering the other four of them as merely subspecies of *Papaver somniferum*. Many have considered at least one of them, *Papaver setigerum*, as no more than a subspecies. Others, however, have considered *P. setigerum*, as well as *P. glaucum*, *P. gracile*, and *P. decaisnei*, as distinct species, belonging, along with *P. somniferum*, to the section Mecones of the genus *Papaver*. Recent work indicates that these species are quite distinct. In fact, it seems possible now that one or more of them ought not to be assigned to the section Mecones.

(b) The species *setigerum*, *glaucum*, *gracile*, and *decaisnei*

Fedde in his monograph on the Papaveraceae in Das Pflanzenreich distinguishes five species which he assigns to the section Mecones of the genus *Papaver*. These are *somniferum*, *setigerum*, *glaucum*, *gracile*, and *decaisnei*. (1)

Papaver setigerum DC. Fl. Franc. 5 (Suppl.): 585. 1815

Of the species named above, *P. setigerum* is most closely related to *P. somniferum* and has been frequently considered a subspecies. Even those botanists who considered it distinct usually, in the past, regarded it as a species ancestral to the cultivated poppy. Vesselovskaya decided that it is distinct, although she found that it will cross quite readily with *P. somniferum*. (2) Kuzmina pointed out that the chromosome numbers indicate not only that *Papaver setigerum* is distinct but also that it can hardly be regarded as the ancestor of *Papaver somniferum*.

The haploid number of chromosomes in *Papaver somniferum* is 11 (Tahara, 1915) and in Papaver setigerum is 22 (Ljungdahl, 1922). These numbers were verified by Kuzmina (1935). The fact that one number is a multiple of the other shows a close genetic relationship between the two species, but if *P. setigerum* were the ancestor the numerical relation should be the other way around. "It has been proved experimentally that the evolution of polyploid relations proceeds from lower to higher numbers. Reversion would only mean return to the initial form with few chromosomes." (Kuzmina). (3)

Papaver setigerum grows wild in the Mediterranean region, chiefly in the western part, and more in southern Europe than in North Africa. Isolated specimens have been found in Greece and Cyprus. It has been sometimes grown in gardens for its flowers, but apparently has not been carried nor advertised by American seedsmen within recent years.

The flower is generally described as violet, but the colored plates purporting to illustrate it do not show this. Thompson illustrates a red poppy, Bonnier a purple-red with violet spots, and Sweet a flower chiefly white, with very dark violet spots surrounded by light lavender. The plant is of smaller size than Papaver somniferum and more hairy, the leaves greener and more deeply incised, the capsules much smaller and, of course, completely dehiscent. (4) (5) (6) (7)

Of some twenty-eight species of *Papaver* that have been examined for chromosome numbers, only *P. somniferum* and *P. setigerum* have the number 11 or a multiple. (8) Perhaps these are the only opium poppies. It seems fairly certain that *Papaver setigerum* is a true opium poppy; and yet there do not seem to be any reports of actual chemical analyses.

Papaver glaucum Boiss. & Hausskn.
in Boiss. Fl. Orient 7:116.1867. The Red Tulip Poppy

This plant, though it has been considered to be a very close relative of *Papaver somniferum*, or even a subspecies, has now been found not to be an opium poppy.

Papaver glaucum is a native of the Near East, the region of Syria, Assyria, Persia. It is cultivated in the United States for its flowers, and has been listed by a number of seed companies. The flowers are scarlet, the two inner petals spotted black or purple-black inside at the base. The inner petals stand up in cup form, so that the flowers strongly resemble red-tulips. The foliage much resembles that of *Papaver somniferum*, but the habit of growth is different. The plant branches just above the tap root into a number, sometimes a large number, of nearly equal stalks. (*P. somniferum* produces a main stalk and capsule, with side branches bearing smaller capsules.) The capsules of

P. glaucum are completely dehiscent and are small, only about the size of *Papaver rhoeas*, though the plant is considerably larger and taller than *P. rhoeas*. Descriptions and illustrations of the flowers and plant as introduced into horticulture will be found in the following references: (9) (10) (11).

Bailey's referring to Papaver glaucum as "the plant sold under this name" (4) seems to imply a question in his mind of the identification of *Papaver glaucum* of the seed catalogs with *Papaver glaucum* of the botanists, but no one else seems to have questioned this.

This "Tulip Poppy" should not be confused with the "Mexican Tulip Poppy" or "Giant Yellow Tulip Poppy," *Hunnemannia fumariaefolia* Sweet.

In the summer of 1943 the writer was supplied with a few plants of the cultivated *Papaver glaucum* of floriculture, for chemical examination. These were kindly supplied the Bureau of Narcotics by the Waller-Franklin Seed Company, Guadalupe, California. No morphine whatever could be detected in these plants. In fact, no evidence was observed of any opium alkaloid. Instead, the chemical analysis revealed the principal alkaloid as similar to rhoeadine, and indicated a much closer relationship of this plant to Papaver rhoeas than to *Papaver somniferum*. Consequently the analysis will be more fully dealt with in Part II, "Other Poppies"

When first introduced into floriculture *Papaver glaucum* was described as resembling a cross between *P. rhoeas* and *P. somniferum*. Morphologically, it is much like the latter. However, from the fact that an attempted cross between *P. glaucum* and *P. somniferum* did not succeed, Basilevskaja in 1928 concluded that the likeness is only exterior. (12) Kuzmina in 1935 pointed out that the chromosome number of *P. glaucum* is 7 (Sugiura 1931), while that of *P. somniferum* is 11 (Tahara 1915), and that "these data exclude *P. glaucum* from the ancestors of *P. somniferum* and even raise the question as to the appurtenance of this species to the section Mecones." Only *P. somniferum* in the genus *Papaver* has so far been found with the chromosome number 11, but *P. setigerum*, its closest relative, has a multiple of this, 22. The two other poppies assigned to the Mecones, *P. gracile* and *P. decaisnei*, have not been examined. On the other hand numerous poppies of other sections of the genus have the number 7 or a multiple, including *P. rhoeas* with the number 7.

Adding the chemical evidence to the other points to be considered, it would seem that *Papaver glaucum* does not even belong in the same section of the genus *Papaver* (Mecones) with *Papaver somniferum*.

Papaver gracile Auch.
in Boiss. Pl. Aucher ex Ann. Sc. Nat. 2, 16:372. 1841.
Papaver decaisnei Hochst. & Steud.
in Schimp. Pl. Arab, exs. (1835) n. 125 ex. Boiss. Fl

These can be dismissed briefly as little is known about them and they do not seem to have been grown in the United States. *Papaver gracile* is found in the Anatolian peninsula and Cyprus. *Papaver decaisnei* is found in Egypt, Armenia, and Persia. They are small plants as compared to *Papaver somniferum.* Their relationship to the latter does not seem to have been further studied in recent years. *Papaver decaisnei* has been considered least closely related to *P. somniferum* of the poppies of section Mecones. Apparently nothing whatever is known of the chemical composition of *P. gracile* and *P. decaisnei*, and their chromosome numbers are also unknown.

Basilevskaja gives a map of the distribution of the close relatives of *Papaver somniferum.* (12) Fedde should be consulted for the botanical descriptions. He also illustrates the capsules and buds, both in Das Pflanzenreich and in Die natürliche Pflanzenfamilien. (1) (13).

(c) Hybrids of *Papaver somniferum* with quite different species

Some remarkable crosses have been made between species within the same genus but not of particularly close relationship. When the species differ considerably, the plants of the first hybrid generation (F1) are often sterile, so that the cross cannot be propagated further, at any rate not by seed. However, in some cases the F2 generation has been raised, and a hybrid race can be obtained.

One of the most successful crosses between quite different species seems to have been that of *Papaver somniferum* an annual, with *Papaver bracteatum*, a perennial. This was first accomplished by Henry de Vilmorin in 1890. He used pollen from a double garden variety of *Papaver somniferum*, obtaining the seed from *Papaver bracteatum.* The first hybrids were sterile, but later some hybrid races were obtained, both annual and perennial. (14) Whether any of them took any permanent place in floriculture seems rather doubtful.

The cross was repeatedly made at Verrières for the firm of Vilmorin-Andrieux et Compagnie. The hybrids were further reported on by Philippe L. Vilmorin in 1906. He said that best results had been obtained with pollen from a horticultural variety Double Mauve of Chinese Poppy (*Papaver somniferum*). (15)

Rather recently (1930) Kasseyeva failed to obtain the hybrid by pollination of *Papaver bracteatum*, as the resultant seed did not germinate; but obtained quite fertile seeds from the pollination of *Papaver somniferum* with pollen of *Papaver bracteatum*, and reared a second hybrid generation. This cross showed a marked patrocliny (dominance and prevalence of paternal characters); that is, the hybrid plants resembled *Papaver bracteatum* rather than *Papaver somniferum*. (16)

Somewhat earlier the crossing of these two species was studied by Pirovano (1926), who gives illustrations of some of the hybrids. (17)

Apparently nothing whatever is known as to the inheritance of the capacity to produce opium alkaloids in such crosses.

Papaver rhoeas is reported to have been crossed with *Papaver somniferum,* and also (variety *pinnatifidum*) with *Papaver setigerum*. (12) Hybrids of *Papaver somniferum* have also been obtained with *Papaver orientale* (Yasui 1921; Ljungdahl 1922), and with *Papaver nudicaule* (Yasui, 1927). (3)

To what extent such hybrids may be introduced into floriculture is speculative. It is quite likely that eventually some hybrid of marked floral value may be obtained. It will be most interesting to learn whether such hybrids form the alkaloids of *Papaver somniferum*, if only this is determined. They are mentioned here chiefly to call attention to them. They are not a present problem; neither is anything known of their chemical or narcotic properties.

X. REFERENCES

1. Fedde, Friedrich. "Papaveraceae," in Das Pflanzenreich by A. Engler. 40 Heft, Papaver, pp. 288-387. (Mecones, 338-344). Leipzig, 1909.

2. Vesselovskaya, M. "The Poppy." Leningrad, 1933. (II, 9).

3. Kuzmina, N. E. "Cytology of the Cultivated Poppy in Connection with Its Origin and Evolution" Trudy Prikl. Bot. (Ser. II) 8, 81-92, 190-195, (1935). (II, 10).

4. Bailey, L. H. The Standard Cyclopedia of Horticulture, New York, 1935, (I, 2).

5. Thompson, H. Stuart. "Flowering Plants of the Riviera." Longmans, Green & Company, 1914. (Plate 1).

6. Bonnier, Gaston. Flore complète illustrée en conleurs de France, Suisse et Belgique. Neuchatel (Suisse), Paris, Bruxelles. 1911. (Plate 24, *Papaver setigerum*; also *Papaver somniferum* and other poppies).

7. Sweet, Robert. "The British Flower Garden." London, 1825-27. Vol. II, Plate 172.

8. Tischler, Georg. "Pflanzlicher Chromosomenzahlen." Tabulae Biologicae, 4, 24, (1927); 12, 65, (1936); 16, 172-173, (1938).

9. Revue Horticole (Paris) 64, 463-464 (1892), "Pavot-Tulipe"; 65, 350 (1893), "Les Pavots Annuels."

10. La Semaine Horticole, 2, 467 (1898) "Le Pavot Tulipe."

11. Gartenflora, 40, 608 (1891). "Neue und empfehlenswerte Pflanzen, Nenheiten für 1891/92 von Ernst Benary, Erfurt." (*Papaver glaucum*).

12. Basilevskaja, N. A. "On the Races of the Opium Poppy Growing in Semiretchie, and the Origin of their Culture." Trudy Prikl. Bot. 19 (2), 95-184 (1928) (II, 2).

13. Fedde, Friedrich. "Papaveraceae," in Die Natürliche Pflanzenfamilien, von Engler und Prantl. 2d ed., 1936. Vol. 17b. (VI, 7).

14. Vilmorin, Henry de. "On Some Hybrid Poppies." Journal of the Royal Horticultural Society, 24, 203-04 (1900).

15. Vilmorin, Philippe L. Hortus Vilmorinianus. Catalogue des Plants Lignenses et Herbacées existant en 1905. Verrières-Le-Buisson, 1906

16. Kassayeva, M. A. "Hybridization experiments between *Papaver somniferum* L. and *Papaver bracteatum* Lindl." Trudy Vsesoluz. S'ezd. Gen., Selek, Semenov., Plemenn, Zhivotnov. (Proceedings of the U. S. S. R. Congress of Genetics. Plant and Animal Breeding). 2, 295-306 (1930) (Russian: with English summary pp. 305-306

17. Pirovano, A. "Risultati di ibridazioni fra Papaver somniferum e Papaver bracteatum." Annali di Botanica 17,171-194 (1926).

XI. Determination of opium poppies

It is expected that the determination of opium poppies, under the law, will be primarily chemical. The Opium Poppy Control Act provides that the term "opium poppy" "includes the plant *Papaver somniferum*, any other plant which is the source of opium or opium products, and any part of any such plant." (1) Botanical proof that a plant is *Papaver somniferum*, would be satisfactory, but it is thought that by using a chemical proof, the definition will forestall arguments as to whether a particular kind of poppy found growing in a certain field does or does not belong to the species *Papaver somniferum*. If it is proved to contain morphine, the most essential narcotic component of opium, that is sufficient to bring it under the Opium Poppy Control Act.

With the fresh plant the chemical identification of the true Opium Poppy is quite easy. A few drops of fresh latex shaken up with several mils of water or dilute acid and filtered will yield a clear and colorless solution containing the alkaloidal salts, from which morphine can be isolated in a high degree of purity. In fact, the writer has found it possible to identify morphine with certainty by tests on a single drop of latex from a capsule, without even the necessity of making any extractions. The drop was smeared on a microscope slide and on several spots of a spot-plate. Iodine Reagent M-2 gave unmistakable morphine-iodine crystals, and Fröhde's, Marquis' and Mecke's reagents yielded their characteristic color reactions. (2) (3) Such experiments show in a remarkable way how the true Opium Poppy bleeds morphine from every wound.

When the plants, as received by the chemist, are not fresh enough for the latex to flow, or when dried material is submitted, it is necessary to make an extraction. When quantitative results are not needed, the following rapid procedure can be used for a small quantity of either green or dried parts of the poppy plant, such as capsules, leave, or petals.

METHOD FOR THE ISOLATION OF MORPHINE FROM PARTS OF THE TRUE OPIUM POPPY FOR IDENTIFICATION

Break or tear up the material and digest it three times successively with enough alcohol to cover it, warming on the steam bath. Filter the extracts into an evaporating dish and evaporate off the alcohol. Treat the residue with ether and pour off the solvent through a filter and discard it. This will remove chlorophyll, as well as the plant resins, etc., that are soluble in organic solvents. Treat the residue with 5 to 15 mils water slightly acidified with acetic acid. and filter this extract into a separatory funnel. Make the solution slightly ammoniacal, using litmus paper indicator, and extract with an equal volume of (2+1) chloroform and isopropyl alcohol solution, filtering into another separatory funnel. Extract twice more with (3+1) chloroform and isopropanol, and discard the aqueous solution. Extract the chloroform-isopropanol solution with a total of 8 to 15 mils sodium hydroxide solution (about 2%), in three portions. Combine the first two alkaline extracts in separatory funnel A, leaving the third in separatory funnel B. Discard the chloroform-isopropanol solution or use it for examination as to the presence of other alkaloids. Wash the alkaline solution in funnel A free of nonphenolic alkaloids by shaking it with an equal volume of chloroform, twice; and each time shake the chloroform with the alkaline solution in funnel B, then discard it. Acidify both alkaline solutions, using litmus paper indicator. While acid, they can be again washed with chloroform, if it is thought that this will help purify the morphine extract. Make the solution in funnel B slightly ammoniacal, pour it into funnel A, and replace it with 2 mils water. Make the solution in funnel A slightly ammoniacal and extract once with (2+1) and twice with (3+1) chloroform-isopropanol. Wash each extract by shaking with the slightly ammoniacal water in funnel B, filter into an evaporating dish, and evaporate off the solvent on the steam bath. The residue is sufficiently pure morphine for easy identification. Scrape up a very little and test on the microscope slide with Iodine Reagent M-2. (2) Test other scrapings on the spot plate with Fröhde's, Marquis', and Mecke's reagents; and make other color tests if desired. (3) Dissolve the remaining residue in a little dilute acid and test with Marme's reagent (K_2CdI_4) for other crystals. Bouchardat's reagent (aqueous iodine in KI solution, also known as Wagner's reagent) can also be used. (3) (4)

The whole procedure can be carried out within two hours, and has been used for the certain identification of morphine in a single green leaf of no great size, in half a gram of the dried flower petals, etc.

This method requires numerous minor modifications to be made strictly quantitative, but can be made at least semiquantitative by making the extraction of the original material fairly exhaustive (in some type of continuous extractor), and following through with care not to lose any appreciable part of the morphine in the residue or solutions discarded, increasing the quantities of reagents when necessary. As some neutral substances may be carried along, the quantitative determination is probably most accurate when the morphine is titrated, using methyl red indicator, and on a small scale, hundredth-normal acid. While a quantitative or semiquantitative determination is not needed for the purpose of identifying opium poppies, it serves to show that some substantial proportion of morphine is present, not just a mere trace. If examination of the other alkaloids is desired, petroleum ether instead of ethyl ether should be used to remove the chlorophyll, resin, etc.; and it may even be best to recover traces of alkaloids from it by shaking with dilute acetic acid. Moreover, in taking up the alkaloids in water, sufficiently strong acid must be used to dissolve the narcotine.

The Iodine Reagent M-2 is applied to a very little of the dry alkaloid, and gives the most characteristic and sensitive micro-crystal test known for morphine, and also the readiest crystallization. Four kinds of crystals are produced and usually all can be found in the same test drop at different concentrations of morphine. Under the microscope they appear as black needles; brown threads; minute brown or orange-brown rod-plates; and moderately large red, red-brown, or red-black square-cut or irregular plates. The last-mentioned crystals are generally considered the characteristic morphine-iodine crystals, and regarded as one of the best micro-crystal tests for any alkaloid. They require the highest concentration, but still only about a microgram of morphine. The black needles require the least concentration, and afford a limiting sensitivity for the test of 0.1 microgram (one ten-millionth of a gram), when this minute amount of morphine can be concentrated in one spot.

(2) The reagent will keep for at least two or three months in a rubber-bulb dropping flask.

For doubtful poppies and to establish negative results with complete certainty, the chemist must have sufficient plant material, perhaps 50 or 100 grams, or more. He should then use a quantitative method for morphine that seems the best available for the material et hand. With a quantitative method substantially all the morphine will be obtained, if any is present, separated from nearly all the other alkaloids. The analyst will then be sure of its absence, if the residue gives no morphine reaction; and he will have enough to be sure of it if it is present, utilizing further methods of purification if necessary.

A quantitative method devised by Mallory and Valaer has been published. (5) It was recommended for poppy capsules, although this does not sufficiently appear from the title. The "acid hydrolysis" treatment was considered necessary to get all the morphine out. It is too drastic for some of the opium alkaloids, and a less severe treatment with some kind of continuous extraction may be preferred. Another method, as used at the Washington Laboratory by Levine, chemist for the Bureau of Narcotics, has been supplied the Alcohol Tax Unit Branch Laboratories. (6) These Laboratories make the enforcement examinations for the Bureau of Narcotics throughout the United States.

The morphine must be identified beyond doubt. Many other plants contain alkaloids, and some others contain phenolic bases which may be extracted in the same way as morphine and be found in the final residue in which the analyst expects to find morphine. Such bases will give precipitates with alkaloidal reagents, and various color reactions with such reagents as Marquis', Fröhde's, and Mecke's. Therefore in identifying morphine it is essential that any reactions on which reliance is placed be exactly like those of known morphine. An inexperienced analyst should compare the reactions directly with those of known morphine. It is neither necessary nor desirable to rely wholly on any single test, even the most characteristic microcrystals, for one can use both the best crystal tests and some of the most characteristic color reactions.

Narcotic agents or others desiring a test should submit sufficient material, including at least one whole plant, preferably several, if possible with a pressed or fresh flower, in order that the chemist may see what it looks like. When a quantitative determination of morphine in the capsules of *Papaver somniferum* is desired, a sample of about four ounces (dry weight) should be submitted, if possible; and these should be picked before they become leached out by rain, following maturity.

In the case of close relatives of *Papaver somniferum* which have not been previously examined, something more than just the morphine examination may be needed. A complete examination to determine exactly what alkaloids are present, and their nature, is outside the scope of the ordinary enforcement work; but any chemist who examines different kinds of poppies will have opportunities to make some scientifically valuable observations, provided the chemical results are carefully tied to the right botanical names. The alkaloidal constituents of various poppies, so far as known, are given in Part II, Chapter XVII.

XI. REFERENCES

1. U. S. Treasury Department, Bureau of Narcotics. Regulations No. 7, relating to the Production, Manufacture, Purchase, Sale, and Giving Away of Opium Poppies and Opium and Opium Products, under the Opium Poppy Control Act of 1942. Washington: 1943. This publication includes the text of the Law.

2. Fulton, Charles C. "Crystal Tests for Minute Amounts of Morphine." The Journal of Laboratory and Clinical Medicine 23, no. 6,622-626 (1938),

3. Fulton, Charles C. "The Principal Chemical Tests for Morphine." The American Journal of Pharmacy, vol. 109, no. 6, May 1937.

4. Stephenson, Charles H. Some Microchemical Tests for Alkaloids. Including chemical tests of the alkaloids used, by C. E. Parker. J. B. Lippincott Co. Philadelphia and London, 1921.

5. Mallory, G. E., and Valaer, Peter (Jr.). "Detailed 'Acid Hydrolysis Method for Opium Analysis'." American Journal of Pharmacy 107, no. 12, 515-525 (1935).

6. Determination of Morphine Content of Poppy Capsules. (Photostat distributed to Alcohol Tax Unit Branch Laboratories by U. S. Bureau of Narcotics. Procedure written by Joseph Levine.)

PART II OTHER POPPIES

[Distinct from *Papaver somniferum*; their status under the Opium Poppy Control Act in the light of our present knowledge of their constituents]

XII. Plants coming under the Opium Poppy Control Act

The Opium Poppy Control Act of 1942 prohibits the cultivation of the opium poppy in the United States, except under license; and licenses may be issued only for production of opium or opium products to meet the medical and scientific needs of the nation.

As explained in Part I, the only plant used for actual production of opium is *Papaver somniferum*. However, it has numerous varieties and in the past has sometimes gone under several different names, even amongst botanists. Moreover, its closest relative, *Papaver setigerum*, may be capable of producing true opium, although apparently it has never been analyzed. Possibly a few other species also produce morphine.

In order to forestall arguments as to whether opium-producing poppies in a particular case do or do not belong to the species *Papaver somniferum*, as well as to include other poppies which may be capable of producing opium or its narcotic principle, morphine, the Act defines "opium poppy" and "opium products" quite broadly, as follows:

"The term 'opium poppy' includes the plant *Papaver somniferum*, any other plant which is the source of opium or opium products, and any part of any such plant."

"The term 'opium products' includes opium and all substances obtainable from opium or the opium poppy, except the seeds thereof."

Of course it is not intended to stretch this definition over the whole vegetable kingdom by reason of common substances obtainable from opium which have nothing to do with its narcotic action, such as moisture; acetic, lactic, and sulfuric acids (which are present in the form of acetates, lactates, and sulfates); plant wax, resin, fat, gum; or choline, etc. The physiological action of opium depends on its content of alkaloids, especially morphine, which is the chief in amount, importance, and narcotic effect. Of the other alkaloids of opium (about 22 are known) codeine most closely resembles morphine in chemical structure, and its physiological effect is similar but much weaker.

Most of the other opium alkaloids are present in insignificant proportions. The other principal alkaloids are narcotine, narceine, thebaine, and papaverine. None of these is used as such by drug addicts. Narcotine has comparatively little physiological effect, and that mainly stimulative rather than narcotic. Narceine is almost inert. Thebaine is probably the most poisonous opium alkaloid. Although chemically related to morphine it has a very different effect, more like that of strychnine. It is of no use to addicts as such, although it can be converted by chemical industry into habit-forming derivatives.

The plants, if there are any such, that may belong under the Opium Poppy Control Act along with *Papaver somniferum*, are considered to £all in the following groups:

(a) Plants producing "opium":

Any plant, if any other than *Papaver somniferum* should be found, having a narcotic juice of use to opiate addicts, and containing compounds chemically identical with some of the compounds essential or peculiar to opium.

At the present time no plant other than *Papaver somniferum* is known to yield a latex actually used by any opiate addicts. Hence this group is only a speculative possibility except as chemical analysis for opium products may reveal some plant as a potential source of a product sufficiently similar to true opium.

(b) Plants producing "opium products":

I. Any plant found to be a source, actual or potential, of morphine.

II. Any plant which could constitute a real source of codeine even if it produces no morphine.

III. Any plant which may hereafter be found of actual use to addicts, by reason of the extraction or production therefrom of a compound of narcotic action which otherwise is obtainable from opium.

Groups II and III are listed chiefly for completeness. No plant is known that produces codeine without morphine, but it is conceivable that this might be the case with some close relative of *Papaver somniferum*, unanalyzed as yet—or, that some strain or hybrid of *P. somniferum* might be developed which would do this. No plant other than *Papaver somniferum* is known that has been actually used to produce any narcotic opium product for drug addicts.

This leaves Group 1. The determination of opium poppies, under the law, is primarily chemical, and in practice resolves itself into proof of the presence or absence of morphine. If morphine is extracted from the plant, or from its latex, and identified with certainty, the plant is proved to be an "opium poppy" under the Act.

The closest relatives of *Papaver somniferum* have been discussed in Chapter X. None of the doubtful ones is cultivated in this country.

The question now to be considered is whether any of the quite distinct poppies, so frequently grown for their flowers, such as the California Poppy, the Mexican Poppy, the Oriental Poppy, the Shirley Poppies, and others, may be found to come under the Act. The genera and then the cultivated species of poppies will be given in the next two chapters. In Chapter XV the question of morphine in other plants than *Papaver somniferum* is discussed at length. Chapter XVI tells what is known about the occurrence of certain secondary opium alkaloids and characteristic but nonnarcotic opium products in some other plants. In Chapter XVII the alkaloidal components of "Other Poppies" are given, so far as known.

XII. REFERENCE

1. Bureau of Narcotics Regulations No. 7. Washington, 1943. (This publication includes the text of the "Opium Poppy Control Act of 1942.") (XI, 1).

XIII. The genera of the family Papaveraceae

The family of Papaveraceae is given by Fedde in Die Natürliche Pflanzenfamilien as comprising the following genera: (1)

- A. Hypecoideae
    - 1. Pteridophyllum
    - 2. Hypecoum
- B. Papaveroidae
    - a. Platystemoneae
        - 3. Hesperomecon
        - 4. Meconella
        - 5. Platystemon
    - b. Romneyeae
        - 6. Romneya
        - 7. Arctomecon
    - c. Eschscholzieae
        - 8. Dendromecon
        - 9. Hunnemannia
        - 10. Eschscholzia
        - 11. Petromecon
    - d. Chelidonieae
        - 12. Sanguinaria
        - 13. Eomecon
        - 14. Stylophorum
        - 15. Hylomecon
        - 16. Coreanomecon
        - 17. Dicranostigma
        - 18. Chelidonium
        - 19. Macleaya
        - 20. Bocconia
    - e. Papavereae
        - 21. Glaucium
        - 22. Roemeria
        - 23. Cathcartia
        - 24. Meconopsis
        - 25. Argemone
        - 26. Papaver
        - 27. Canbya

C. Fumarioideae.

a. Corydaleae

28. Dactylicapnos
29. Dicentra
30. Corydalis
31. Roborowskia
32. Phacocapnos
33. Cysticapnos
34. Sarcocapnos
35. Adlumia
36. Ceratocapnos

b. Fumarieae

37. Trigonocapnos
38. Rupicapnos
39. Fumaria
40. Fumariola
41. Platycapnos
42. Discocapnos

Not all botanists recognize all these genera, and some use a genus *Platystigma*, the species of which are referred by Fedde to genera given above.

Most American botanists separate the Fumarioideae from the Papaveraceae, distinguishing them as a separate family, the Fumariaceae. The Fumariaceae, while closely related (botanically) to the restricted family of Papaveraceae, are not commonly known as "Poppies". In the following pages chief attention will be given to the restricted family of Papaveraceae.

XIII. REFERENCE

1. Fedde, Friedrich. "Papaveraceae", in Die natürliche Pflanzenfamilien, vol. 17 b. Leipzig, 1336. (VI, 7).

XIV. Principal species of poppies in American Horticulture

The principal species of poppies grown in the United States for their flowers are given in the following list. For the most part the information is taken from the Standard Cyclopedia of Horticulture, by Bailey. (1) This Cyclopedia should be consulted for more complete descriptions, as well as mention of a number of other species which may be occasionally but not commonly cultivated. In regard to illustrations, those in the

Cyclopedia are noted in parentheses, and some references have been added to certain colored plates illustrating poppies, chiefly in books that may be referred to for colored illustrations of the Opium Poppy.

Platystemon californicus Benth. "Cream-Cups." Sometimes called "California Poppy," but this name should be reserved for *Eschscholzia californica*. Annual, native of U. S. west coast, flowers light yellow, cream color, or white. One species, according to Gray and other American authors, but Fedde considered there are about 60.

Romneya coulteri Harv. "Matilija Poppy." A native of California and Mexico, a sub-shrub, perennial, flowers large, white. (Full page illustration.)

Romneya trichocalyx Eastw. Similar. The only other species; also native to California.

Dendromecon rigida Benth. "Tree Poppy." A semi-evergreen shrub, perennial, bright yellow flowers, native of California. This genus originally considered to be a single species, but redefined by Fedde into 20 species.

Hunnemannia fumariaefolia Sweet. "Mexican Tulip Poppy," "Giant Yellow Tulip Poppy." Perennial but usually treated as an annual, bushy habit, yellow flowers, native of Mexico. The only species of this genus.

Eschscholzia californica Cham. "California Poppy." Perennial but treated as an annual. Flowers ordinarily single; yellow, orange, or cream-colored. Cultivated varieties extend the color range to white, rose, and carmine. There are also double forms. There are probably a number of species. Some botanists recognize about 12, others more than 100. Little if anything is known of the correlation of cultivated forms with the botanical species. Generally, in speaking of the California Poppy, all kinds are lumped together as *Eschscholzia californica*. (Illustration.) Another species and some varieties recognized in horticulture are those passing under the names of *Eschscholzia tenuifolia* Hook., and the following varieties of *E. californica* Hort. (not of Greene), *aurantiaca* Hort., *alba* Hort., *thornburnii* Hort., and *crocea* (Benth) Jepson. Seed catalogs sometimes give colored illustrations of California Poppy. Colored plate, (2).

Sanguinaria canadensis L. "Bloodroot." A low spring-blooming perennial, flowers white; common in the woods of eastern North America. The latex is red; when the plant is pulled up the broken root bleeds. Not called a "poppy," but it is a member of the restricted family of the *Papaveraceae*. (Illustration.) Pictures can be found In numerous books on wild flowers.

Eomecon chionantha Hance, "Cyclamen Poppy." White Bower, native of eastern China; perennial. The generic name signifies "eastern poppy."

Stylophorum diphyllum (Michx.) Nutt. "Celandine Poppy." Hardy perennial; yellow flowers in clusters of 3 to 5. Western Pennsylvania to Wisconsin and Arkansas. In horticulture sometimes called "Papaver stylophorum." (Illustration.)

Chelidonium majus L. "Celandine." Biennial or perennial; small yellow flowers in umbel-like clusters. A European plant. Colored picture, (3).

The genus Macleya is united to Bocconia by Bailey.

Bocconia cordata Willd. "Plume Poppy," "Tree Celandine." Flowers pinkish. Native of China and Japan. (Illustration.) The common names also apply to the two following species:

Bocconia microcarpa Maxim. Flowers golden-brown or bronzy.

Bocconia frutescens L. Flowers greenish. Native of Mexico and Peru 2, colored, petals wanting. The flowers are very unlike our common poppies, being small and without petals, but borne in large feathery or plumy masses, in terminal panicles rising high above the foliage.

Glaucium flavum Crantz, "Horn Poppy," "Sea Poppy," "Yellow Horned Poppy." Perennial or biennial, sometimes grown as an annual; flowers yellow or orange. A native of Europe. *Glaucium luteum* Scop. is a synonym. (Illustration.) Colored illustrations, (3) (4).

The two following species are also known as "Horned Poppies":

Glaucium corniculatum (L.) Curt. Flowers red or purplish with black spot. Colored plate, (4); uncolored illustration, (3).

Glaucium leiocarpum Boiss. Flowers yellow, not showy.

Meconopsis cambrica (L.) Vig. "Welsh Poppy." Perennial; flowers rather large, pale yellow. *Papaver cambricum* L., is a synonym. Native of Western Europe. Colored plate, (4).

Meconopsis wallichii Hook. "Satin Poppy." Flowers pale blue. Native of central Asia to West China.

Meconopsis integrifolia (Maxim.) French. "Yellow Chinese Poppy." Biennial; flowers bright sulfur yellow or primrose yellow. Native of Western China and Thibet.

There are a number of other species of *Meconopsis* which may be occasionally cultivated. The *Meconopsis heterophylla* given by Bailey, a red poppy native to California, is now classified in the genus *Papaver* by California botanists.

Argemone mexicana L. "Mexican Poppy," "Prickly Poppy." Flowers orange or lemon colored. Native of Mexico, Tropical America. Cultivated as an annual. Also known as *A. speciosa* Hort. ex L. H. Bailey. (Illustration). Variety *ochroleuca* (Sweet) Lindl. has the petals yellowish white, is a native of Texas.

Argemone alba Lestib. Sometimes considered a variety of the preceding, *A. mexicana* var. *albiflora* (Hornem.) DC.

Argemone grandiflora Sweet. Flowers white. (Illustration). Colored plate, (2).

Argemone platyceras Link & Otto. Typically, the flowers are white, or rarely purple. Includes varieties *hispida* (A. Gray) Prain, *hispido-rosca* Fedde (flowers rose or rosy white), *hunnemannii* (Otto & Dietr.) Fedde (flowers white). The last named variety affords a chance of confusion with *Hunnemannia fumariaefolia*.

The genus *Argemone* must not be confused with *Papaver argemone*. Numerous species of the genus *Papaver* are cultivated, at least occasionally. For others besides those listed here consult the reference (Bailey, Standard Cyclopedia of Horticulture).

Papaver argemone L. Flowers red. A European plant. Not to be confused with the genus *Argemone*. Not given by Bailey. Colored illustrations, (3) (4).

Papaver dubium L. Annual; flowers rose, vermillion, occasionally white. Native of Europe, North Africa. Uncolored illustration, (3).

Papaver rhoeas L. "Corn Poppy," "Field Poppy," "Common Red Poppy," "Shirley Poppies," etc. Annual, very commonly grown. Flowers cinnabar-red, deep purple to scarlet,; white, and variously marginate. Native of Europe and Asia. Called "corn poppy" because it commonly grows wild in the grain fields in Europe. The wild flowers are commonly red, most often with black spots at the base of the petals. The Shirley Poppies, the most popular poppies in American flower gardens, are color varieties of this species, developed at Shirley, England. (Illustration). Colored pictures of these poppies are frequent in seed catalogs. Colored illustrations, (3) (4).

Papaver pavoninum Fisch. & Mey. "Peacock Poppy." Annual, flowers scarlet, dark spotted. Native of Turkestan and Afghanistan. Also known as *P. pavonium* Stschegl.

Papaver floribundum Desf. Biennial, flowers vermillion. Native of the Cucasus region.

Papaver somniferum L. "Opium Poppy," "Garden Poppy." (Illustrations of some floral forms). Colored plates, references (2) (3) (4). See Part I for descriptions of varieties, etc. Floral varieties discussed in Chapter VI, b, with references to colored plates.

Papaver glaucum Boiss. & Hausskn. "Tulip Poppy." Annual; flowers red, tulip-like. Has been considered by botanists one of the closest relatives of *P. somniferum*. See Chapter X (Part I).

Papaver orientale L. "Oriental Poppy." Perennial; flowers generally flaming orange-scarlet with large black spots at the base of the petals. Native of eastern Mediterranean region to Persia and Caucasus; introduced from Armenia. The most commonly grown perennial poppy in the United States. (Illustrations; the one on p. 2459 is much the better). Colored plate, (5); but this shows a pure red rather than the commoner orange, *Papaver bracteatum* and its hybrids with *P. orientale* are also known as "Oriental Poppies."

Papaver bracteatum Lindl. Perennial, flowers blood-red, not spotted or claw dark violet. A close relative of the preceding species, also known as *Papaver orientale* var. bracteatum (Lindl.) Ledeb. Colored plate, (2) Hybrids with *P. orientale* have been obtained in color varieties, as white, salmon, pink, pure red, etc. These are all known as "Oriental Poppies." Colored plates, (6) .

Papaver alpinum L. "Alpine Poppy." Flowers white, fragrant. Native of the Alps, Apennines. Cultivated in rock gardens. Sometimes considered a sub-species of the following:

Papaver nudicaule L. "Iceland Poppy." Perennial, often grown as an annual or biennial. Flowers commonly yellow; in cultivated varieties the range extends from white to orange-red or even scarlet. Plant small. Native of the Arctic regions. One of the poppies most commonly cultivated in the United States. (Illustration.)

Papaver heterophyllum (Benth.) Greene, "Wind Poppy," "Flaming Poppy." Annual, flowers red. California, Nevada, Oregon. *Meconopsis heterophylla* Benth. is a synonym. (Illustration.)

P. heterophyllum var. *crassifolium* (Benth.) Jepson, "Blood Drops." Flowers red. California. *Meconopsis crassifolia* Benth. is a synonym.

Less than half Of the above-named poppies are discussed in the later chapter, XVII, with respect to their alkaloidal constituents. This is because less than half of them have been chemically investigated. On the other hand, Chapter XVII includes mention of the alkaloidal constituents of a few poppies that are scarcely, if at all, known in American flower gardens.

FUMARIACEAE

As previously stated, American botanists generally consider the *Fumariaceae* a separate family. In any case they are not commonly known as "poppies"; hut a few of the species may be mentioned:

Dicentra spectabilis (L.) Lem. "Bleeding Heart"
Dicentra canadensis (Goldie) Walp. "Squirrel Corn"
Dicentra cucullaria (L.) Bernh. "Dutchman's Breeches"
Dicentra chrysantha (H. & A.) Walp. "Golden Eardrops"
Corydalis nobilis (Jacq.) Pers. "Corydalis"
Adlumia fungosa (Ait.) Greene, "Climbing Fumitory"
Fumaria officinalis L. "Common Fumitory"

XIV. REFERENCES

1. Bailey, L. H. The Standard Cyclopedia of Horticulture. New York, 1936. (I, 2).

2. Bois, D. Atlas des Plantes de Jardins. Paris, 1896. (VI, 6). (Colored plates of *Papaver somniferum*, red double fringed variety; *Papaver bracteatum*; *Eschscholzia californica*; and *Argemone grandiflora*.)

3. Hegi, Gustav. Illustrierte Flora von Mittel-Europa. IV Band, 1 Hälfte. München, 1913. (II, 1). (Two colored plates, 122 and 123, facing pages 4 and 26, show *Chelidonium majus, Glaucium flavum, Papaver rhoeas, P. pyrenaicum, P. argemone, P. hybridum, and P. somniferum.* Also uncolored illustrations of *Glaucium corniculatum* and *Papaver dubium*.)

4. Syme, John T. Boswell, editor. English Botany. Figures by James Sowerby, 3rd edition, Vol. I. 1873. (Colored plates of *Papaver somniferum* as *P. hortense*; *Papaver rhoeas, P. lamottei, P. lecoqii, P. argemone, P. hybridum*; *Meconopsis cambrica*; *Roemeria hybrida*; *Glaucium corniculatum* and *G. flavum* as *G. luteum*.)

5. Garden, 42, 684 (1892).

6. Garden, 70,174 (1906); 72, 374 (1908).

XV. The question of morphine (and narcotine) in other plants than Papaver somniferum

(a) The uniqueness of opium

Opium is remarkable for the large number of different kinds of alkaloids that it contains. Moreover morphine, its chief alkaloid, has a very complex chemical constitution, so much so that a laboratory synthesis from simpler materials has never been attained. These complexities doubtless partially account for the fact that, so far at least as has been definitely found, morphine and true opium are peculiar to one plant, *Papaver somniferum* the Opium Poppy.

At most, two or three very close relatives of *P. somniferum* (in the section Mecones of genus *Papaver*) possibly also produce morphine, but as they have not been analyzed even this extension is in doubt; and it is really probable only for *Papaver setigerum*. (Chapter X).

Frank O. Taylor, writing on the Opium Alkaloids in Allen's Commercial Organic Analysis (5th edition, 1929), stated:

"With one or two exceptions, the alkaloids of opium are strictly peculiar to *Papaver somniferum*; whilst, on the other hand, the poisonous alkaloid Sanguinarine, which is present in all other papaveraceous plants, does not appear to exist in Papaver. Indeed, with the exception of Protopine, which has been found in numerous other plants, and is also known as Macleyine and Fumarine, none of the nitrogenized substances found in opium appear to be identical with any of those extracted from other plants of the family." (1)

This statement of the case requires several amendments, chiefly from additional knowledge gained since 1929. It is, however, true in spirit, so far as opium is concerned.

Sanguinarine is generally accompanied by chelerythrine, a related alkaloid, and in fact both names seem to have been originally applied to a mixture of the two. Formerly, even when the distinction was made, sanguinarine was poorly defined, or some confusion existed, and it was probably reported present in some cases on inadequate evidence. Sanguinarine has been reported from certain plants that have been investigated, belonging to the following genera: *Eschscholzia, Sanguinaria, Stylophorum, Chelidonium*, *Bocconia, Glaucium* and *Dicentra*, but not be correct to say that it occurs in every species of these genera. In fact, Dr. R. H. Manske, referring to the alkaloid now strictly defined as sanguinarine, writes: "Sanguinarine has been reported from a variety of plants but it is positively present only in genera Sanguinaria, Chelidonium and Bocconia (Macleya); not in Eschscholtzia, Stylophorum, Glaucium or Dicentra. You will notice that its occurrence is restricted to the tribe Chelidonieae." (2) The present writer assumes that by "positively present" Dr. Manske means, "known with certainty to be present."

Even including chelerythrine with "sanguinarine," the statement that it "is present in all other papaveraceous plants" is far too broad. However, these are alkaloids characteristic of certain Papaveraceae which, as yet, have never been reported found in any species of the genus *Papaver*; nor, for that matter, in *Argemone* or *Roemeria*.

Protopine or fumarine occurs in insignificant proportion in opium, but is of interest because it is found in so many other plants. Within recent years cryptopine, another minor alkaloid of opium, closely related to protopine, has also been found in several species of *Dicentra* and *Corydalis*. The only other exception that need be made with respect to the natural occurrence of alkaloids, so far as our present knowledge goes, is for thebaine, reported as occurring in *Papaver orientale*. Taylor, however, used the term "nitrogenized substances." This would certainly include choline, which occurs in a host of other plants. (3)

We may say, at least, that the alkaloids of opium are highly characteristic of one plant. With three exceptions these alkaloids, numbering more than 20, are strictly particular to *Papaver somniferum*, so far as we yet know. Morphine in particular has not been proved to occur in any other plant.

The United States Dispensatory (23rd edition) in its useful but occasionally inaccurate article on Opium, contains at the outset a careless misstatement, as follows:

"Opium is generally believed to be derived exclusively from *Papaver somniferum* and its variety *album* - although every species of poppy is capable of yielding it to a greater or less degree." (4)

No evidence or authority is given for this statement. Of course almost any poppy has a milky juice, or latex, which will doubtless dry up into something superficially resembling opium; but produced from other species it would be entirely devoid of the morphine content and other properties that distinguish real opium.

Occasionally one meets with statements that "all kinds of poppies" produce opium, when what is meant is, all varieties of *Papaver somniferum*. Such statements either have that meaning, or they are entirely incorrect.

As recently as the 20th edition of the United States Dispensatory the above-quoted sentence appeared as follows:

"Opium is generally believed to be derived exclusively from *Papaver somniferum*, though every species of poppy is capable of yielding it to a greater or less extent, and some authors assert that *Papaver orientale,* is its real source." (5) This combined two misstatements into one. The second part, regarding *Papaver orientale*, can hardly have anything more substantial for its basis them confusion of the Opium Poppy with the Oriental Poppy, and of the Far Eastern with the Near Eastern "Orient," along with the delusion that the Opium Poppy is a native of the Far East. This second part of the statement was dropped in the 21st edition of the Dispensatory, and it will be a great improvement when the rest of the statement is also dropped.

(b) Reports of Morphine in Other Plants

In the very early days of alkaloidal chemistry morphine was reported on insufficient evidence as occurring in 3 or 4 species of poppies other than *Papaver somniferum*. Later investigators were unable to confirm any such finds. It is also the common belief, enshrined, too, in a number of reference books, that morphine has been found or at least reported as occurring in hops.

The following table shows the plants other than *Papaver somniferum* in which it has been claimed that morphine is present, together with the names and dates of investigators who made such claims, and of the other investigators, most of them of later date, who reported that these plants contain no morphine whatever. This table was originally compiled from references given by Small and Lutz (6) and Wehmer (3), but has been corrected, so far as mistakes were discovered, from some of the original references, and also brought up to date; and Filhol, who is cited by the U. S. Dispensatory for morphine in *Papaver rhoeas*, added to it.

MORPHINE REPORTED

In	By	Denied by
Humulus lupulus (Hops).		Chapman (1914) (7)
Papaver rhoeas (Corn poppy, Field poppy),	Filhol (1842) (8) Dieterich -(?)-Pharm. Zeitschrift Russland 27,269 (1888)	Riffard (1830). Meylink & Stratnik (1831). Hesse (1865-69, 1877 and again in 1890). Selmi (1876). Awe (1941).
Papaver orientale (Oriental poppy),	Petit (1827) (9)	Klee & Gadamer (1914). Konovalova, Yunusov, and Orekhov (1935).
Eschscholzia californica. (California poppy).	Bardet & Adrian (1888) (10)	Reuter (1889). Danekwortt (1890). Wintgen (1898). Schmidt (1901), Fischer (1901). Fischer & Tweeden (1902).
Argemone mexicana (Mexican poppy).	Charbonnier (1868) (11)	Schmidt (1901). Schlotterbeck (1902). Bloemendahl (1906); Le Prince (1909). Santos & Adkilen (1932). Almeida Costa (1935).

As this table was first made up, the central column contained nearly twice as many names of investigators who had supposedly reported the presence of morphine in other plants. On looking up the references about this, as given in several books, it was found that three of these investigators had made no such claims. Consequently the table has been freed of some erroneous entries commonly found in reference books. It has not been feasible at the present time to check the reference to Dietrich's article, given by Wehmer, Small & Lutz, etc., so it can only be hoped that this one is correct. The probability is not too high, since three of seven such references were incorrect, and another not what it claimed to be. A few of the old references in the right hand column have not been checked, but since they accord with modern results this probably does not matter much.

Tilloy (1827) and Selmi (1876) are supposed to have reported finding morphine in *Papaver rhoeas*. (3) (6) (12) As a matter of fact Tilloy's procedure for extracting morphine from poppy capsules referred to the "indigenous poppy", which was none other than *Papaver somniferum*, cultivated in France for its seeds from the earliest times. (13) The reference given for Selmi is not to his original article, which was in Italian, but to the German abstract— which, however, makes it quite clear that Selmi made no claim to the extraction of morphine from *Papaver rhoeas*. He said, according to this summary, that he had extracted an alkaloid from the green capsules of the corn poppy, which showed certain similarities to morphine, but which he specifically denied was morphine. (14) It is practically certain now that what he really referred to was choline with an associated impurity, very likely gallic acid. (See chapter XVII.) Selmi was one of the first to use micro-crystal tests for the identification of alkaloids (probably the first discoverer of the valuable iodine-iodide test for morphine). He and Tilloy deserve honor for their work rather than the doubtful treatment they have had at the hands of later commentators.

The space in the table for the name of claimants to the discovery of morphine in hops has been left blank for the sufficient reason that no investigator made any such claim. The two references given in regard to the claim of morphine in hops are to articles by Williamson and Ladenburg, or sometimes Ladenburg alone; never any others. Williamson claimed to have isolated from hops a new alkaloid which lie called "hopeine"; he did not say that this was morphine but denied that it was. Ladenburg had nothing whatever to do with hops, but was one of those who proved that the "hopeine," then being sold throughout Europe, actually consisted chiefly of morphine. The story of "hopeine" is a very strange one, which will be related here because nearly all reference books that mention the subject at all have it exactly wrong.

(c) The story of "Hopeine"

"Hopeine," as it appears from contemporary accounts, never was anything but a blatant fraud; an attempt to pass off a mixture of morphine and cocaine as a new alkaloid from hops. In this case fraud and fiction have shown immensely more vitality than the truth, and the current reference books cite Williamson and Ladenburg as proving the presence of morphine in hops, or at least as having extracted an alkaloid, similar to morphine, from hops. (3) (6) (12) (15) (16).

The discovery of hopeine, claimed to be a natural alkaloid obtained from hops, was announced in 1885, and it was soon put on sale by the (Concentrated Produce Company of London (and Brooklyn). Some other drug companies sold it, but obtained their supplies from the Concentrated Produce Co.

(Apparently the asserted discovery was first published by Williamson in the Pharmazeutische Zeitschrift für Russland, in the latter part of 1885, and was also given in the Pharmazeutische Zeitung of 1885. It has not been feasible to check these articles, but the French and English accounts in 1885 (17a) (18a) show that they contained about the same statements as Williamson's first article in the Chemiker- Zeitung, which is the source usually cited. This does not affect the later developments, anyway.)

On January 6,1886, an article by Williamson was published in the Chemiker-Zeitung, in which he announced himself as the discoverer of hopeine, claiming he had extracted it from "wild American hops." European hops, he said, contain so little hopeine that it was not worth while to try to extract it from that source. (19a) This article, though published in a (German magazine and in the German language, was from London, under date of November 1885; in fact Williamson had some sort of connection with the Concentrated Produce Co.

A scientific controversy broke out almost at once. In France, Bardet and Petit had each found that "hopeine" from the drug companies gave all the reactions of morphine. On January 27th Dr. Dujardin-Beaumetz, to whom they had communicated their results, at a meeting of the French Academy of Medicine stated that "hopeine" presented all the characteristics of morphine, except for an odor of hops, and he did not hesitate to indicate his own opinion that it was a fraud. (18b, c) Later the French made some severe comments about English drug companies sending such a product to France and selling it at a higher price than was commanded by morphine.

Petit in the meantime had prepared his observations for publication in the Journal de Pharmacie et de Chimie, and he added a footnote (as another article by Williamson had just appeared) to the effect that no matter what Williamson might say, the “hopeine” he had examined was unquestionably morphine; and had even been tested by conversion to apomorphine. (20a) Bardet also published his results. (Referred to in (18c).)

Williamson in another article in the Chemiker-Zeitung said that he himself had noticed the similarity between morphine and hopeine, but the elementary analysis had shown that hopeine was different; and he described some other differences. (19b) Petit tried the tests claimed to distinguish hopeine, and reported that there was not the least difference between the “hopeine” that he had, and morphine. He remarked that the asserted mode of preparation was bizarre—a fair statement. (20b) In Germany, Ladenburg analyzed some of the “hopeine” that was being sold or offered for sale, and recrystallizing it from alcohol, showed that it consisted mainly of morphine. (21a) Paschkis in Austria came to the same result. (Referred to in (22a).)

Williamson now claimed that the drug companies were not offering the pure alkaloid, the one he had extracted. They precipitated out all the alkaloids from hops, he said—probably one of them was identical with morphine, but his hopeine was not. (19d) (From this doubtful bean, as planted—according to commentators—by Ladenburg, has grown the enormous bean-stalk of the tradition of morphine in hops.) Petit remarked, that if these were now the claims made, it was for Williamson to prove, first, that American hops contain morphine “or an identical substance,” and secondly, that another alkaloid has the formula assigned by Williamson to hopeine. He repeated that the compound he had analyzed contained morphine and no considerable amount of impurities. (20b)

Ladenburg tested a small sample submitted by Williamson. It weighed 0.47 gram; by recrystallization from amyl alcohol he obtained 0.1 gram alkaloid which he showed to be morphine. The remainder he showed consisted of a different alkaloid, which he did not identify. (21 b or c). Ladenburg's article in Berichte der Deutschen Chemischen Gesellschaft is sometimes the only source cited for the evidence of morphine in hops. To be sure, he stated at its face value Williamson's claim that the material had been extracted from hops, but this is hardly sufficient reason to make him responsible for the story of its origin.

Williamson conceded, in his final article, that the hopeine of "wild American hops" (from Arizona!) was divisible into two parts by means of amyl alcohol; one, however, he would designate "isomorphine," the other was pure hopeine. (19e) He even submitted some further samples for examination.

In the meantime, however, Paul in England had shown the second alkaloid in "hopeine" was cocaine. (23) (In various examinations there were also indications of the presence of a little atropine or hyoscine, as well as odorous substances, usually smelling of hops, sometimes of wintergreen. Moreover, the material was not always the same.) (22a) (23) (17b) In Germany, Leuken examined a sample submitted by Williamson, and found it to consist essentially of morphine and cocaine. Leuken concluded his article—in the same journal usually cited for the "evidence" of morphine in hops as follows:

"We are faced with the alternatives, either in some of the Urticaceae we find the active constituents of two absolutely different plants united, or we must accept that the manufacture of 'Hopeine'—has been made with very impure materials." (24)

Paul, after some cautious provisos (after all, a number of reputable drug companies were involved), had remarked that "the attempt to introduce upon a pseudo-scientific basis an article that is only a mixture of two well-known substances, is, I may say, a piece of foolish impudence that almost passes belief." (23)

Messrs. Christy, a reputable English drug firm, had been involved in the sale of "hopeine," and when it was first publicly questioned had obtained a "guarantee" from the Concentrated Produce Company that the hopeine supplied them was prepared exclusively from hops. (18c) But after writing Professor Gray in the United States, and receiving a reply from him in regard to wild American hops, particularly of the Arizona variety, Mr. Thomas Christy was about ready to concede that he and his customers had been victimized. (18d)

July 17, 1886, the Austrian minister of commerce and the interior issued a decree forbidding the carrying of hopeine in the drug stores, likewise the sale of hopeine and all preparations containing it, including "hopeine-beer." (22c) (18e) The editor of the Deutsche Chemiker-Zeitung expressed the wish that Germany would take similar action. (22c) However, in 1887 he had occasion to write of "The Hopeine Swindle in a New Edition"—the Concentrated Produce Company of London had sent out a "Prize Announcement," inviting research on the physiological effect of the narcotic principle of hops! The editor appealed to German physicians and professors, and warned them to have nothing to do with this brazen attempt to revive the Hopeine sensation. (22d)

No doubt numerous other references to the great "Hopeine Swindle" could be found in the European journals of 1885 to 1887, but time considerations have prevented an exhaustive study. A definite conclusion to the story in England, France, and Germany has not been found as yet in the journals. Perhaps "hopeine" died a natural death after such numerous exposures. The laws in those days did not restrict morphine a great deal, and the price at which "hopeine" had been offered was much above that of morphine.

The foregoing will probably suffice as a sufficiently complete account of the true story of "Hopeine," but what the reference books have done to it "almost passes belief." In them, Ladenburg, who was one of the exposers of the fraud, appears as one who found, or claimed to have found, morphine in hops! (16) (12) (15) (3) (6) Williamson appears in the same light (15) (3), or even as a more conservative scientist who had extracted something from hops, but was not quite satisfied that it was morphine! (6)

(In 1887 the editor of the Deutsche Chemiker-Zeitung inquired in a footnote, when the Concentrated Produce Company cited Williamson as an authority, "Was für ein Williamson 9' (22d) What, indeed, when the scientific reference books treat the story in this fashion!)

The current Allen's Commercial Organic Analysis actually includes under "Constituents of the Hop" the following (references and all):

"In addition to carbohydrates and fibrous matter (6.11%), moisture, and traces of diastase, there is also evidence of the presence of morphine and choline. Certain American wild hops certainly do contain morphine and another substance of alkaloidal character to the extent of 0.15% but not more than infinitesimal traces of these substances have been found in cultivated hops (Williamson, Chem. Zeit. 1886,*10*, 20, 38,147, and Ladenburg, Berichte, 1886,*19*,783)." (15)

Strangely enough, the 4th edition of Allen's (1912, vol. VI), in the article on Cocaine (by a different author, Sadtler) contained a footnote referring to Paul's exposure of the fraud. (25) This was an unusual exception. Apparently, as soon as "hopeine" died, the myth of morphine in hops sprang up to take its place. Peculiarly enough, there is no traditional belief that cocaine also occurs in hops!

(d) Wild lettuce

There seems to be a popular folk-belief that wild lettuce (*Lactuca virosa* L.) contains morphine; and some people even assign the notion to ordinary lettuce. The plants of the genus *Lactuca* (family Compositae) have a milky juice, to which they owe their name. This juice of the strong-scented wild lettuce dries up into a product somewhat resembling, or thought to resemble, opium, in odor and appearance. The ancients believed that lettuce has soporific properties, and the belief survives to modern times. In fact, Lactucarium, the dried milky juice, was an official drug as recently as the U. S. P. IX. (1916) (26), but has now been dropped from official medicine. It contains some bitter principles and possibly a small amount of alkaloid, but certainly not an alkaloid of opium. Merck's Index credits it with containing hyoscyamine. (27) This statement seems to be due to the work of T. S. Dymond (1891), though it does not correspond with his findings. Dymond was interested in the extract of lettuce, then in official medicine, obtained by pressing the juice from the whole plant when in flower, coagulating the proteid, and evaporating to dryness at 60°. He examined both *Lactuca virosa* and *Lactuca sativa* L. (ordinary lettuce) and in both found small quantities of a mydriatic alkaloid which he identified as hyoscyamine, not exceeding 0.02% in the extract of common lettuce, or not more than .001 percent in the plant itself. In Lactucarium, however (the dried milky latex of *Lactuca vitrosa*, corresponding to opium), he could find no alkaloid at all. (28) The presence of a mydriatic alkaloid in *Lactuca virosa* was denied for a time (29), but was confirmed by Farr and Wright (1904), (30). Hyoscyamine, if it is the alkaloid present, is in exceedingly small amount; and in any case this is a far cry from morphine. Apparently the attribution of morphine to this plant has never received any support from chemists. Modern medicine considers its sleep-producing qualities a superstition, its therapeutic action doubtful or nil. (4)

(e) Narcotine

Narcotine will be summarily dealt with here, as it would not make so much difference if it were found in some other plant. Before disposing of it, a vague report of narceine may be mentioned. In 1912 Dawson reported on an examination of the fruit of the bush honey suckle. (31) An alkaloid found was tentatively identified as narceine, but on such inadequate grounds as not to merit consideration until we have something further.

In 1863 T. and H. Smith separated an alkaloid from *Aconitum napellus* (aconite), which they distinguished from "aconitina." They called it "aconella," but thought it was the same as narcotine. (32) Subsequent investigators have found no narcotine in this species of aconite, nor in any of its relatives.

In a remarkably recent case a group of writers reported narcotine as found in green oranges, lemons, potatoes, and cabbages. (33) (34) They claimed that it was the precursor of vitamin C, which, they said, was methyl-nor-narcotine. As their claimed results were soon disproved by others (30) (36); and vitamin C, now known as ascorbic acid, soon shown to be entirely unrelated to narcotine or methyl-nor-narcotine, the whole affair seems to have been something of a brainstorm.

Since narcotine is truly related, quite closely, to hydrastine, found in *Hydrastis canadensis* L., family Ranunculaceae, there is a good possibility that it may be found sometime in some other plant, not even a member of the Poppy family. If we enter the field of pure conjecture, it is even possible that morphine may be found in some plant unrelated or hardly related to the opium poppy; but at present we have no evidence at all of such a contingency.

REFERENCES

1. Taylor, Frank O. "Opium Alkaloids" in Allen's Commercial Organic Analysis, Vol. VII, 5th edition, 1929 (IV, B.)

2. Manske, Richard H. F. Letter of comment on the first draft of this treatise, to Col. C. H. L. Sharman, Chief, Narcotic Division, Department of Pensions and National Health, Ottawa, Canada.

3. Wehmer, E. Die Pflanzenstoffe, Verlag von Gustav Fischer. 2d edition, Jena 1931. Choline—see Index. Papaveraceae, pp. 376-391, Volume I.

4. The Dispensatory of the United States of America, 23d edition, 1943. (II, 7.)

5. The Dispensatory of the United States of America. 20th Edition. By Joseph P. Remington, Horatio C. Wood, Samuel P. Sadtler, Charles H. LaWall, Henry Kraemer, and John F. Anderson. J. B. Lippincott Company. Philadelphia and London, 1918.

6. Small, Lyndon F., and Lutz, Robert E. Chemistry of the Opium Alkaloids. Washington, 1932. (IV, 12.) (Except for the matter of hops, the references found erroneous are cited from Starkenstein, #12. These were included in an Appendix of material that had not been thoroughly checked.)

7. Chapman, Alfred Chaston. "The Nitrogenous Constituents of Hops," Journal of the Chemical Society, 105, 1895 (1914).

8. Filhol. "Analyse des Capsules du *Papaver rhoeas*." Journal de Pharmacie et de Chimie (series 3) 2, 510-513 (1842).

9. Petit, P. H. "Memoire, Sur le Pavot d'Orient ou de Tournefort, et Analyse Chimique de Cette Plant." Journal de Pharmacie, series II, 13, 170-184 (1827).

10. Bardet and Adrian. "Sur l'*Eschscholtzia california*." Journal de Pharmacie et de Chimie, series V, 18, 625 (1888). (This was a note, rather than an article.)

11. Charbonnier, M. "Recherches pour servir à l'histoire botanique, chimique et physiologique de l'Argémone du Mexique." Journal de Pharmacie et de Chimie series IV, 7, 348 (1868).

12. Starkenstein, E. "Die Papaveraceenalkaloide" (pp. 817-1085) in Handbuch der Experimentellen Pharmakologie, 2 Band, 2 Hälfte. Herausgegeben von A. Heffter. Berlin. Verlag von Julius Springer, 1924. ("Morphin-Vorkommen," (pp. 821-823). This section in

its citation of references and statements as to what the articles contain is full of errors.)

13. Journal de Pharmacie, series II, 13, 31 (1827). Note from Robiquet, enclosing a method by Tilloy (pp. 31-32). See also the note by Pelletier on p. 184.

14. Berichte der Deutschen Chemischen Gesellschaft, 9, 195 (1876). This is not the original article but a communication from H. Schiff, aus Florenz. The original is given as "Nuove ricerche tossicologiche per riconoscere gli alcaloidi venefici," by F. Selmi. (Akten der Akad. zu Bologna Ser III, vol. VI.)

15. Grant, Julius. "Non-Glucosidal Bitter Principles," "Constituents of the Hop," in Allen's Commercial Organic Analysis, 5th edition, vol. VIII, p. 117. P. Blakiston's Son & Co., 1930.

16. Pictet, Amé. The Vegetable Alkaloids. Rendered into English, Revised and Enlarged by H. C. Biddle. 1st edition. John Wiley & Sons. New York, 1904.

17. Journal de Pharmacie et de Chimie.

(a). "Hopéine, alcaloïde narcotique du houblon, *Humulus lupulus* L." Vol. 12 (5th series) 460-462 (1885).

(b). Vol. 13 (5th series), p. 513 (1886).

18. The Pharmaceutical Journal and Transactions

(a). 16, 185 (1885). "The Month."

(b). 16, 669, Feb. 6, 1886.

(c). 16, 687, Feb. 13, 1886. "Hopeine."

(d). 16, 916 (1886) Letter from Thomas Christy on Hopeine.

(e). Issue of August 7, 1886.

19. Williamson, W. In Chemiker-Zeitung, vol. 10 (1886).

(a). "Hopeïn, das Alkaloid des Hopfens." p. 20 (first part), p. 38 (second part)

(b). "Hopeïn und Morphin." p. 147.

(c). p. 228 (letter).

(d). "Hopeïn und Morphin." p. 238.

(e). "Ueber Hopeïn." p. 491.

20. Petit, M. A. In Journal de Pharmacie et de Chimie, vol. 13 (5th series), (1886).

(a). "Note sur une substance vendue sous le nom d'Hopéine crystallisée." p.177

(b). "Hopéine et Morphine," p. 317.

21. Ladenburg, A.

(a). "Ueber die Identität des Hopeïns mit dem Morphin." Chemiker-Zeitung 10, 207 (1886). (Editorial note follows, asking Williamson to provide a sample of his own hopeine for examination.)

(b). "Ueber das Hopeïn." Chemiker-Zeitung 10, 319 (1886).

(c). "Ueber das Hopeïn." Berichte der Deutschen Chemischen Gesellschaft 19, 785 (1886).

22. Deutsche Chemiker-Zeitung.

(a). Vol. 1, #22, p. 200. (1886).

(b). Vol. 1, #28, p. 250. (1886).

(c). Vol. 1, #38, p. 334. (1886).

(d). Vol. 2, pp. 93, 94. (1887).

23. Paul, B. H. "Note on a sample of 'Hopeine'. " The Pharmaceutical Journal and Transactions, 16, pages 877-78 and 885 (1886).

24. Leuken, C. "Ueber Hopeïn." Chemiker-Zeitung 10, 553 (1888).

26. Sadtler, Samuel P. "Cocaine" in Vol. VI, Allen's Commercial Organic Analysis, 4th edition. P. Blakiston's Son & Co. Philadelphia, 1912.

26. The Pharmacopoeia of the United States of America, Ninth Decennial Revision. By authority of the United States Pharmacopoeial Convention. Official from September 1, 1916. Philadelphia. P. Blakiston's Son & Co.

27. The Merck Index. 5th Edition. Rahway, N. J., 1940 (V, 4).

28. Dymond, T. S. "The Existence of Hyoscyamine in Lettuce." Journal of the Chemical Society 61, 90 (1892). (Also in shorter form in The Pharmaceutical Journal 51, 449 (Dec. 5, 1891).)

29. Braithwaite, J. O., and Stevenson, H. E. "The Non-existence of Mydriatic Alkaloid in Lactuca virosa." The Pharmaceutical Journal 71, 148 (1903).

30. Farr, E. H., and Wright, R. "The Disputed Presence of a Mydriatic Alkaloid in *Lactuca virosa*." The Pharmaceutical Journal 72, 186 & 195 (1904).

(a) Regarding another species of *Lactuca*: Wright, R. "Note on the Occurrence and Distribution of Mydriatic Alkaloid in *Lactuca muralis*." The Pharmaceutical Journal, 74, 548 (1905).

31. Dawson, Lowell E. "The Fruit of *Diervilla florida*." The Chemical News 106, 18-20 (1912). Small & Lutz, in citing this report, add a note:

"The fruit which Dawson describes is not that of *Diervilla*, but rather of the family *Lonicera*." (Reference #6, page 81.)

32. Smith, T. and Smith, H. "A New Alkaloid Found in *Aconitum napellus*. Description and Mode of Preparation." Pharmaceutical Journal and Transactions, (2nd series) 5, 317-320 (1863-64).

33. (a) Rygh, Ottar, "Chemical investigations concerning the anti-scorbutic vitamin." Norske Videnskaps-Akad. Oslo, Avhandl. I Mat. Naturv. Klasse No. 8, 1-23 (1931). Chemical Abstracts 26, 5994.

(b) Rygh, Ottar; Rygh, Aagot; and Laland, Per. "Chemical investigations on the anti-scorbutic vitamin. I." Z. physiol. Chem. 204, 105-11, (1932). Chem. Abs. 26, 3005.

(c) Laland, Per. "Attempts at isolation of narcotine from various vegetables." Z. physiol. Chem. 204, 112-114 (1932). Chemical Abstracts 26, 2799.

(d) Rygh, O. "Narcotine and vitamin C." Z. Vitaminforsch. 1, 134 8 (1932). Chemical Abstracts 27, 2177.

34. Ott, Erwin; and Packendorff, Kurt. "Critical review of recent papers on vitamin C." Z. physiol. Chem. 210, 94 6 (1932). Chemical Abstracts 26, 5611.

35. Dalmer, O., and Moll, Th. "Narcotine and vitamin C. " Z. physiol. Chem. 209, 211-230 (1932). Chemical Abstracts 26, 5611.

36. Grant, Reginald L.; Smith, Sydney; and Zilva, Sylvester S. "Narcotine as the alleged Precursor of Vitamine C." Biochemical Journal 26, 1628-32 (1932).

XVI. Opium alkaloids and characteristic opium products which occur in other plants

(a) Protopine or fumarine

One alkaloid which occurs in opium is known to occur in a great many other plants. This is protopine or fumarine. In opium it occurs in insignificant proportion, said to be about .003 per cent, but in numerous other plants it is one of the chief alkaloids. It occurs in the great majority of papaveraceous and fumariaceous plants that have been investigated.

This alkaloid was originally named fumarine, as the principal alkaloid of *Fumaria officinalis* L. Hesse did not recognize it as an alkaloid already known when he found it in opium and called it protopine in 1871. (1) It seems, indeed, to have been very inadequately characterized prior to Hesse's work. References to the alkaloid of *Fumaria officinalis* go back to 1829: Peschier, Trommsd. N. J. Pharm. 17, 280 (1829); Dana, Mag. Pharm. 23, 125 (1829); later, Hannon, J. chim. méd. (3) 8, 705 (1852). It was probably Hannon who gave the name "fumarine." It has not been feasible to check the original articles, but it is probable that these early accounts contained nothing that could have enabled another investigator to recognize the same base in another plant; if they did, the Jahres-Bericht summaries of Peschier's and Hannon's work do not indicate it. (2) (3) Even in 1866 the report of the work of Preuss contained, at least in summary, little enough to characterize the alkaloid, merely the rather striking sulfuric acid reaction, and mention of some solubilities, and the crystalline form of some salts. (4) Battandier, in 1892, apparently before the identity of fumarine with protopine was recognized, considered that the sulfuric acid reaction, the chloroplatinate crystallizing in octahedra (mentioned by Preuss), and solubilities, proved the identity of fumarine from *Fumaria officinalis* with that from *Glaucium corniculatum* L. Very likely he was right thus far, with direct laboratory comparisons; but he seemed to think the sulfuric acid reaction by itself sufficient to show the presence of fumarine in the alkaloidal mixtures from a large number of plants, and so he has been considered a rather unsafe guide. Although his evidence was inadequate, fumarine or protopine probably is present in all the species and genera he named. (5)

Hesse characterized protopine so that other investigators were able to recognize it, and did recognize it when they found it in other plants than the Opium Poppy. By the time the identity of protopine and fumarine was established, the name protopine had more recognition in scientific articles, and prevailed.

The question of which name should be used is perhaps not very important, unless too much stress is laid, legally or in interpretation of the law, on protopine as an "opium alkaloid". However, the double nomenclature has somewhat confused the history. A number of reference books state that Hesse discovered protopine in 1871. It may be possible to argue that fumarine was so poorly described, and perhaps so contaminated with impurities as obtained, that it was not really "discovered" prior to Hesse's work. Probably Schmidt in 1901 thought so, for when he mentioned that Trowbridge had proved its identity with protopine, he only referred to "Fumarin" in quotation marks. He mentioned the names of earlier investigators but did not give their dates nor citations to their articles. (6) *Fumaria officinalis* contains no less than six other alkaloids besides protopine, but in much smaller amount. (7).

It is difficult to see, however, how Hesse could have discovered an alkaloid already known, merely by giving it a new name and describing it better; and the statements that he was the discoverer seem to be usually due to a misunderstanding of the dates. For this Danckwortt seems to be chiefly to blame. In a long article on protopine and cryptopine in 1912 he proclaimed Hesse the discoverer of protopine, saying that while Hesse did not specifically designate it as a newly discovered opium alkaloid, no previous mention of it was detectable in the literature. He gave a list of plants in which the presence of protopine had been proved, with a bibliography for each, but simply omitted *Fumaria officinalis* and its investigators, and mentioned this plant and its alkaloid only to say that fumarine was "soon" found identical with protopine. (8) Really this took place some 70 years after the earliest reports. Schlotterbeck in 1900 had already said, "Since fumarine was discovered and named long before its discovery in opium by Hesse, it is but proper that the name protopine be dropped"; but he did not follow his own recommendation. (9)

The name protopine is now the accepted one, perhaps with sufficient reason. This name, moreover, indicates its close chemical relationship to cryptopine, which really was first discovered in opium. On the other hand, the name fumarine better indicates that it is the characteristic alkaloid of the Fumariaceae and Papaveraceae, was first discovered in *Fumaria officinalis*, and is only incidentally found in opium. There is a scanty commercial supply, not obtained from opium, but from plants of the Fumariaceae. *Dicentra spectabilis* is said to be a good source.

It seems to be used only experimentally, and probably only as a control alkaloid for chemical-botanical researches. A too rigid or too extensive interpretation of the Opium Poppy Control Act would bring under it not only virtually all poppies, but even many plants which are not known as poppies, but which contain protopine.

Protopine has been reported in the following genera: (10) (11) (12)

Papaveraceae (restricted family):
- Hypecoum
- Hunnemannia
- Eschscholzia
- Sanguinaria
- Stylophorum
- Dicranostigma
- Chelidonium
- Macleaya
- Bocconia
- Glaucium
- Argemone
- Papaver

Fumariaceae:
- Dactylicapnos
- Dicentra
- Corydalis
- Adlumia
- Fumaria
- Platycapnos

There is also Battandier's rather vague report of its presence in the following genera of the Fumariaceae: (5)

Sarcocapnos
Ceratocapnos
Petrocapnos (?—not a generic name now used)

Following are species in which protopine has been found, accompanied by other alkaloids but not by any other opium alkaloids: (11) (12) (13) (14) (15)

Papaveraceae (restricted family):
- *Argemone mexicana*
- *Bocconia arborea*
- *Bocconia cordata (Macleya cordata)*
- *Bocconia frutescens*

Chelidonium majus
Eschscholzia californica
Dicranostigma franchetianum
Glaucium corniculatum
Glaucium fimbrilligerum
Glaucium flavum (G. luteum)—(also *G. flavum* var. *serpieri)*
Hunnemannia fumariaefolia
Hypecoum procumbens
Sanguinaria canadensis
Stylophorum diphyllum

Fumariaceae:

Adlumia fungosa (A. cirrhosa)
Corydalis ambigua
Corydalis aurea
Corydalis caseana
Corydalis cheilantheifolia
Corydalis claviculata
Corydalis crystallina
Corydalis decumbens
Corydalis lutea
Corydalis micrantha
Corydalis montana
Corydalis ochotensis
Corydalis ochroleuca
Corydalis ophiocarpa
Corydalis pallida
Corydalis platycarpa
Corydalis solida
Corydalis ternata
Corydalis thalictrifolia
Corydalis tuberosa (C. cava)
Dactylicapnos macrocapnos
Dicentra canadensis
Dicentra eximia
Dicentra formosa
Dicentra oregana
Dicentra pusilla
Dicentra spectabilis
(Diclytra and *Dielytra*—erroneous names for *Dicentra)*
Fumaria officinalis
Platycapnos spicatus

This list is believed to cover practically all the definite information. So far this alkaloid has been found only in the two related families, Papaveraceae and Fumariaceae. Numerous species of *Corydalis* and

Dicentra have been examined by Manske in recent years, hence the preponderance of these genera in the table.

(b) Cryptopine

Some plants of the Fumariaceae contain other alkaloids chemically related to protopine, and in recent years this has been found to include cryptopine, another opium alkaloid. Cryptopine is also a minor alkaloid in opium, but by no means so negligible as protopine. In some samples of opium it may come to at least 0.3 percent. It has been found in the following species: (10) (11b).

Corydalis nobilis
Corydalis scouleri
Corydalis sempervirens
Corydalis sibirica
Dicentra chrysantha
Dicentra cucullaria
Dicentra ochroleuca

These plants contain both protopine and cryptopine, and also other alkaloids, but no other opium alkaloids.

(c) Thebaine, opianic acid, hydrastinine, meconin, and meconic acid

Completion of the list of protopine-bearing plants requires the following:

Papaver orientale
Papaver somniferum

Thebaine, as well as protopine, has been reported found in *Papaver orientale*. An alkaloid related to thebaine, named sinomenine, is found in *Sinomenium acutum* (Thunb.) Rehd. & Wils., of the Family Menispermaceae. (10)

The alkaloid hydrastine, found in *Hydrastis canadensis* (family Ranunculaceae) is very closely related to narcotine. Narcotine by hydrolytic oxidation yields opianic acid and cotarnine. Hydrastine in the same way yields opianic acid and hydrastinine, and the latter is allied to cotarnine and can be prepared from it. Thus two substances which could be called "opium products," namely opianic-acid and hydrastinine, can be obtained from an entirely different plant (*Hydrastis canadensis*, "Golden Seal"), which does not even belong to the same family as the Opium Poppy. Meconin, a neutral substance found in opium, has also been found in *Hydrastis canadensis*. (10)

Meconic acid is often said to be "peculiar" to opium—presumably in comparison with other drugs, since scarcely any attempts have been made to find out what other plants may contain it. It is nonnarcotic, anyway. The fact to be borne in mind until we learn more is that the presence of meconic acid in a poppy, even if proved conclusively and not just by the ferric chloride reaction, does not prove that the plant in question produces any real opium, morphine, or other narcotic principle. Meconic acid has been reported in *Papaver rhoeas* and *Papaver orientale*. The evidence seems inadequate, but it may be present in them, and perhaps in many other species.

XVI. REFERENCES

1. Hesse, O. "Chemische Studien über die Alkaloide des Opiums." Berichte der Deutschen Chemischen Gesellschaft 4, 693-697 (1871).

2. Jahres-Bericht über die Fortschritte der physischen Wissenschaften. Tübigen, 1832. Peschier, page 245.

3. Jahres-Bericht über die Fortschritte der Chemie, 1852, p. 550. Hannon: "Fumarin."

4. Preuss, Gustav. "Ueber das Fumarin." Zeitschrift für Chemie 9, 414 (1866). From Gesellschaft der Wissenschaften in Göttingen, 1866, 206.

5. Battandier, J. A. "Présence de la fumarine dans une Papavéracée." Comptes Rendus Hebdomaires des Séances de L'Académie des Sciences 114, 1122 (1892).

6. Schmidt, Ernst. "Ueber Papaveraceen Alkaloide." Archiv der Pharmazie 239, 395-408 (1901).

7. Manske, Richard H. F. "The Alkaloids of Fumariaceous Plants. XVIII. Fumaria officinalis L." Canadian Journal of Research 16 B, 438-444 (1938).

8. Danckwortt, P. W. "Zur kenntnis des Protopins und Kryptopins." Archiv der Pharmazie 250, 590-646 (1912).

9. Schlotterbeck, J. O. "*Adlumia Cirrhosa*—A New Protopine-Bearing Plant." American Chemical Journal 24, 249-263 (1900).

10. Henry, Thomas Anderson. The Plant Alkaloids, 3rd edition. Philadelphia, 1939. (IV, 13).

11. Manske, Richard H. F. "The Alkaloids of Fumariaceous Plants." (XXIII, XXXII, XXXIV, and XXXVIII, "of Papaveraceous Plants.") (Starting at XVII; previous articles in the series are covered by Henry.) Canadian Journal of Research: 16 B, 153 and 438 (1938); 17 B, 51, 57, 89, 95, and 399 (1939); 18 B, 75, 80, 97, and 288, (1940); 20 B, 49, 53, and 57 (1942); 21 B, 13, 111, 117, and 140 (1943). XXVII, XXIX, and XXX are omitted from these citations as not directly concerned with the plants. XXXIV, reference 12.

(a) With Miller, M. R. "XVII Corydalis caseana A. Gray." C. J. R. 16 B, 153-157 (1938).

(b) "XXVIII. *Corydalis nobilis* Pers." C. J. R. 18 8, 288 292 (1940).

(c) For Manske's method of separation see Canadian Journal of Research 8, 210 (1933).

12. Manske, Richard H.F.: Marion, Léo; and Ledingham, Archie E. "The Alkaloids of Papaveraceous Plants. XXIV. *Hunnemannia fumariaefolia* Sweet and the Constitution of a New Alkaloid, Hunnemannine." Journal of the American Chemical Society, 64, 1659-1661 (1942).

13. Manske, Richard H. F. "The Alkaloids of Papaveraceous Plants." (Same series with Fumariaceous Plants.) Canadian Journal of Research.

(a) "XXIII. *Glaucium flavum* Crantz." C.J.R. 17B, 399-403 (1939). (Cf. XXXV, C. J. R. 21 B, 13 (1943).)

(b) "XXXII. *Stylophorum diphyllum* (Michx.) Nutt.) *Dicranostigma franchetianum* (Plain) Fedde, and *Glaucium serpieri* Heldr." C. J. R. 20 B, 53-56 (1942). (Cf. XXXV, C. J. R. 21 B, 13 (1943).)

(c) "XXXVIII. *Bocconia arborea* Wats." C. J. R. 21 B, 140-143 (1943).

14. Small, Lyndon F., and Lutz, Robert 10. Chemistry of the Opium Alkaloids. Washington, 1932. (IV, 12).

15. Konovalova, R. A., Yunusov, S., and Orekhov, A. P. "Alkaloids of the family Papaverae. VI. Alkaloids of *Glaucium fimbrilligerum.*" J. Gen. Chem. (U. S. S. R.) 9, 1939-46 (1939). Chemical Abstracts 34, 4072.

XVII. The alkaloidal constituents of some poppies.

Following is some account of what is known at the present time of alkaloids present in poppies other than *Papaver somniferum*. Henry in "The Plant Alkaloids," third edition, summarizes in excellent fashion the constituents found in species examined up to that time, 1939. (1) Wehmer may also be consulted. (2) The attempt has been made to bring this information up to date.

Hypecoum procumbens L.

Contains protopine; very likely other alkaloids as well; has not been investigated since 1901. (1)

Hunnemannia frumariaefolia

Sweet Mexican Tulip Poppy, Giant Yellow Tulip Poppy, etc.

This plant was recently, and apparently for the first time, examined by Manske, Marion, and Ledingham, 1942. (8) It was found to contain 0.14 percent protopine, 0.03 percent allocryptopine, traces of a nonphenolic alkaloid not fully characterized, and 0.18 percent of a new alkaloid, hunnemanine (9-desmethylallocryptopine), the first known example of a phenolic base of the cryptopine type. Analysts who may possibly be called on to test this plant under the Opium Poppy Control Act, and who are merely looking for morphine, must take care not to confuse hunnemanine with morphine.

Eschscholzia californica Cham. California Poppy

Most of our knowledge of the alkaloidal constituents of this popular poppy comes from Fischer and Tweeden (Fischer 1901, with Tweeden 1902). (4) They found in it protopine, α and β allocryptopines (β and γ homochelidonines) sanguinarine, and chelerythrine. It has been examined several other times. (Henry's references, by insertion of a wrong number, are somewhat confused with those for *Dicentra spectabilis*.) (1) A reference to an investigation apparently hitherto unnoticed by compilers was noted in the Deutsche Chemiker-Zeitung for 1889 (vol. 4): L. Reuter (Heidelberg), Pharm. Ztg. 1889, S. 635. The original reference could not be checked. Apparently he found, but did not identify, two alkaloids (one surely protopine) and traces of others; he did show that none of them was morphine (see table in Chapter XVI, b). Brindejonc (1911) reported finding in the roots of the variety grown in Brittany only one alkaloid, which he named ionidine. (5) The constitutional formula was not determined. The uncertainty as to species of *Eschscholzia* is so great that analyses may not all relate to the same species, nor to the true species *californica*. If there are a number of distinct species of *Eschscholzia* in cultivation, commonly lumped together as *Eschscholzia californica*, it is quite likely that they do not all have the same alkaloidal constituents; but there is no likelihood that any of them contains morphine. None of the alkaloids mentioned above as being present, except protopine, corresponds to any alkaloid of opium.

Sanguinaria canadensis L. Bloodroot

This flower is not commonly called a poppy, but it is a member of the restricted family of Papaveraceae. The alkaloidal constituents of the plant have been investigated a number of times. It contains sanguinarine, chelerythrine, protopine, and α and β homochelidonines. (1) Protopine is the only opium alkaloid present.

Stylophorum diphyllum (Michx.) Nutt. Celandine Poppy

Recently investigated by Manske (1942), this plant was found to contain protopine, 1-stylopine, and chelidonine. (6) Schlotterbeck and Watkins (1902) reported also diphylline and sanguinarine. Diphylline is probably dl-stylopine, but neither it nor sanguinarine was found by Manske. (1) (2) (6) None of these is an opium alkaloid except, of course, protopine.

Dicranostigma franchetianum (Prain) Fedde

This plant was also investigated by Manske (1942) and reported on along with the preceding one. It was found to contain protopine, dl-stylopine, and chelidonine. (6)

Chelidonium majus L. Celandine

This contains numerous alkaloids and has been investigated a number of times. As summarized by Henry, it contains α homochelidonine, hydroxychelidonine, methoxychelidonine, sanguinarine and chelerythrine as one group of related alkaloids; protopine and α and β allocryptopines as another; and perhaps berberine, sparteine, and another base. (1) None of these except protopine is an opium alkaloid.

Bocconia arborea Wats.

This plant, the only real tree of the Poppy family, has been first reported on just last year, 1943, by Manske. (7) It contains chelerythrine as the principal alkaloid (0.86%), and very much smaller amounts of protopine and allocryptopine. Another alkaloid, related to chelerythrine but not fully identified, was also found.

Bocconia cordata Willd.
Plume Poppy, Tree Celandine

This has been investigated a number of times. The alkaloidal constituents as given by Henry are protopine, α allocryptopine, chelerythrine, and perhaps sanguinarine and another base. (1) Protopine is the only opium alkaloid.

Bocconia frutescens L.

The alkaloidal constituents are given as protopine, α and β allocryptopines, and perhaps chelerythrine. (1)

Glaucium flavum Crantz (*G. luteum* Scop.)
Horn Poppy, Sea Poppy, Yellow Horned Poppy

This has been investigated by Manske, both the typical plant (1989) and variety *serpieri* (1942).(8) The alkaloids are protopine, glaucine, isocorydine, aurotensine, and another in quantity too small for complete characterization. (Protopine is the only opium alkaloid.)

Glaucium corniculatum (L.) Curt.

Contains protopine; probably other alkaloids but has not been investigated since 1901. (1)

Glaucium fimbrilligerum Boiss.

Investigated by Konovalova, Yunusov, and Orekhov (1940); found to contain protopine, corydine, allocryptopine, chelerythrine, and bsanguinarine. (9) (Protopine is the only opium alkaloid.)

Roemeria refracta DC.

Konovalova, Yunusov, and Orekhov report remerine, d-pseudoephedrine, and l-ephedrine in this plant. The last mentioned is widely distributed but this is the first report of its occurrence in a member of the Papaveraceae. (10) None of those mentioned is an opium alkaloid.

Argemone mexicana L.
Mexican Poppy, Prickly Poppy

This was investigated by Almeida Costa (1935). (11) He reported that it contains protopine and berberine, but no morphine, confirming earlier results of Santos and Adkilen (1932), and the still earlier researches of Schlotterbeck (1902). (12) (13) Morphine had at first been reported, back in 1868 (probably protopine was mistaken for it), but Schmidt, Bloemendahl, and Le Prince also reported it is not present. (1) Berberine is not an opium alkaloid, but is very widespread in numerous families of plants.

There have been reports of Mexicans obtaining "opium" from this plant. However, it appears that any attempts in that direction, which really had illicit purpose, were due to the belief (unfounded) that the plant produces morphine. Descriptions of symptoms of those who were supposed to have used it indicated that they had poisoned themselves to a degree, rather than obtaining the effects of real opium. (14)

In this connection, however, it should be noted that in Mexico, Brazil, and other Latin-American countries, *Argemone mexicana* is considered a valuable medicinal plant. Cases of the use of it, even to incising the green capsules and using the spurious "opium" obtained, may be solely for medicinal purposes, and have no relation to drug addiction.

Argemone alba Lestib. White Mexican Poppy

Sometimes considered a subspecies of *A. mexicana,* has also been shown to contain berberine. (1)

Papaver dubium L.

This poppy was investigated by Pavesi, first in 1905, and again in 1907, and was found to contain an alkaloid, aporeine, and another alkaloid, aporeidine, which is apparently formed from aporeine. Aporeine has not been found in opium, and no opium alkaloid is known to exist in this plant. (1) (15)

Papaver glaucum Boiss. & Hausskn. The Tulip Poppy, Red Tulip Poppy

In the summer of 1943 the writer examined this species, as known in floriculture, to determine if it should be considered an opium poppy. Not much material was available, as it is not commonly grown. Several plants were kindly furnished the Bureau of Narcotics by the Waller-Franklin Seed Company of Guadalupe, California. An extraction of some mixed parts of the plants was first made. No morphine was found, and it was discovered that the chief alkaloid is not one of the familiar opium alkaloids. An extraction of the capsules alone was then undertaken, using 18 grams dry weight, almost the entire amount available at the time. While not very large, this amount of material is at least 50 or 100 times as great as needed for the identification of morphine in the true Opium Poppy by the procedure used. As a result of extractions which would have separated morphine, if any were present, a residue of alkaloidal material weighing 7 mg. was obtained. Whatever this may have been, it certainly was not morphine. It yielded no striking reactions, so far as examined. No indication of the presence of any other opium alkaloid was observed.

The chief alkaloid, present to the extent of about 0.45 percent in the capsules, is a weak base. It can be extracted by ether or carbon tetrachloride from weak acetic acid solution, and by chloroform even from 1 n sulfuric acid. It is also soluble in petroleum ether. It is precipitated from acid solution by the addition of ammonia or alkali, in which it is insoluble. In dilute sulfuric acid (0.5 normal) this alkaloid gradually develops a purplish-pink or deeper color, exactly as does rhoeadine, the alkaloid of *Papaver rhoeas*. A thin film of the dry alkaloid on white porcelain yields the following characteristic color reactions:

Concentrated Sulfuric acid—strikes red, at once changing to intense brown-yellow, gradually to intense green,

Fuming Sulfuric acid (15 percent free SO3)—a strong dull purplish red color.

Marquis' reagent (Formaldehyde in Sulfuric acid)—strikes orange-red, at once changing to intense green,

Rhoeadine gives somewhat similar color reactions, but can be distinguished. It is less soluble in organic solvents than the alkaloid of *Papaver glaucum*, but was extracted by the same procedures. Also, the rhoeadine at once crystallized when precipitated by ammonia, whereas the alkaloid from *P. glaucum* yielded only minute spheres or droplets, which probably were not crystals. Rhoeadine from the capsules of Shirley Poppies was used for direct comparisons.

There is also present in the capsules of *Papaver glaucum* a fairly large proportion of choline. This was identified by microcrystals with KI_3 (Wagner's No. 1), Reinecke's salt, brom-auric acid in concentrated HCl or in (2+3) H_2SO_4, platinic iodide, and Mayer's reagent, these various reagents being added to an aqueous acidified solution of the base. (16) KI_3 reagent gave the most sensitive and characteristic test. Reinecke's salt was equally sensitive, but the crystals were very distorted until with much difficulty a purer solution was obtained. The identification has been kindly confirmed by Mr. Keenan of the U. S. Food and Drug Administration, using the optical properties of the crystals with Reinecke's salt. The same base was found in similar amount in the capsules of *Papaver rhoeas*, and in very minute amount in the capsules of *Papaver somniferum*. Choline is very widespread in the vegetable kingdom, but seems not to have been previously reported from the Papaveraceae. (2)

The chemical affinities of this plant are obviously with *Papaver rhoeas* rather than *Papaver somniferum*.

Papaver rhoeas L.
Corn Poppy, Field Poppy, Common Red Poppy, Shirley Poppies, etc.

This poppy has been investigated a number of times. The most recently published article was by Awe, 1941. He reported that rhoeadine appears to be the only alkaloid. (17) Rhoeadine was discovered by Hesse in this poppy in 1865. In his method of obtaining rhoeadine (1866), Hesse mentioned the separation from it of a very slight amount of another base, which he thought was thebaine. (18b) Besides being somewhat uncertain in the first place, thebaine is unconfirmed by any subsequent investigator, and apparently was not mentioned again by Hesse himself. (18) Pavesi (1906) has also investigated *Papaver rhoeas*, finding rhoeadine. (15) Rhoeadine yields rhoeagenine by treatment with acids.

In 1943 the writer found that in addition to rhoeadine the capsules contain a substantial proportion of choline. This without doubt is the "alkaloid" showing certain similarities to morphine which Selmi found in the green capsules in 1876. (Chapter XV.) Apparently, it has usually been overlooked. Selmi noted that iodine in hydriodic acid yielded crystals which, as distinguished from those of morphine, formed immediately but soon redissolved. (19) (This is due to evaporation of iodine, and the crystals are more permanent if a cover glass is applied.) Such slight resemblance as choline shows to morphine would not be considered worth mentioning today. Some associated gallic or tannic acid probably was responsible for reduction of iodic acid and a blue color with ferric chloride in Selmi's experiments, thereby adding to the resemblance.

This poppy probably contains no opium alkaloid. A color reaction, like the purplish red developed by rhoeadine with dilute mineral acids, has been observed with alkaloidal extracts from some kinds of opium, according to various authors. This probably is not due to rhoeadine but to meconidine or porphyroxine.

Papaver orientale L. The Oriental Poppy

The most thorough examination of this species thus far was made by Gadamer and Klee. The investigation was begun by Gadamer and extended over several years. Klee in 1914 published his results on the presence of the two principal alkaloids at different stages of growth, as well as his researches on the constitution of isothebaine. Professor Gadamer at the same time contributed a short article on the associated alkaloids. (1) (20) The principal alkaloids were found to be thebaine and isothebaine, the former an alkaloid found also in opium, the latter a previously unknown phenolic alkaloid. Protopine was present, a phenolic alkaloid named glaucidine from its resemblance to glaucine, and several other alkaloids which were not fully characterized nor identified.

This plant was more recently investigated by Konovalova, Yunusov, and Orekhov (1935). (21) They reported that it contained only 0.16% total alkaloids, and that the chief alkaloids are thebaine and a new phenolic base which they named oripavine. They were unable to find the isothebaine previously reported. However, Klee had shown that thebaine and isothebaine replace one another at different stages of growth. At the period of most vigorous growth thebaine was present almost exclusively, both in the leaves and the roots, while in the late fall and earliest spring, and also in the semidormant stage in midsummer, the total of these two alkaloids was chiefly isothebaine. Klee's analyses of the dormant stage were chiefly made on the roots of late autumn, but the predominance of isothebaine extended also to the old leaves.

The writer recently made an examination of 20 grams of the dried mature capsules. About 0.59 percent total crude alkaloids was obtained, but this probably includes a little non-alkaloidal material. Choline was present, and an indication of meconic acid was obtained (ferric chloride test), but the latter was not positively identified. The principal alkaloid was isothebaine, 0.22 percent of the capsules, while no thebaine at all could be found. Klee did not give an analysis of the capsules when fully mature and dry, but showed for the withered vegetation at the end of July 0.052 percent isothebaine (no thebaine), the roots at this stage containing 0.599 percent isothebaine and 0.031 percent thebaine, and young leaves of the second vegetative period 0.122 percent isothebaine and 0.116 percent thebaine. On the other hand he reported capsules sampled 10 days after the blossoms as containing 0.057 percent isothebaine and 0.342 percent thebaine. Presumably this would be the ratio of these alkaloids in "opium" from *Papaver orientale*.

The writer's isothebaine gave the following characteristic reactions

> Concentrated Nitric acid—intense purple.
> Marquis' reagent—almost negative; with addition of nitric
> acid oxidizing solution (22) a strong beautiful purplish red color.
> Fuming Fröhde's reagent (23)—strikes green and blue, dissolves blue.
> Buckingham's reagent—strikes intense blue-green, dissolves green.
> Gold cyanide reagent (16a)—the precipitate from aqueous solution of the
> alkaloidal salt crystallizes readily and completely in rosettes of threads.

The reaction with nitric acid, as mentioned by Klee, is very striking and unlike that given by other natural papaveraceous alkaloids. Apomorphine, a laboratory derivative of morphine, gives a similar but less persistent color.

Isothebaine, although a phenol, is not extracted by alkali from chloroform-isopropanol; in fact even ether will extract it from alkaline solution. It therefore would not accompany morphine in the usual extraction. Petroleum ether extracts it readily from ammoniacal solution.

The writer obtained another alkaloid which is readily characterized and constituted 0.035 percent of the capsules. It is a phenol which is extracted by alkali from chloroform-isopropanol; and by carbon tetrachloride from ammoniacal solution.

Concentrated Nitric acid—strong brown.

Fröhde's reagent—strong gray-blue-green gradually changing to intense violet.

Mecke's reagent—bright blue-green gradually changing to intense violet.

Sulfuric acid containing a little ferric salt—bright blue-green, gradually greenish blue slowly dark violet.

Fuming Fröhde's reagent strikes greenish at once changing to intense maroon red (slowly dark violet).

Iodine reagent C-1 (24)—crystallization in dark needles, similar to those given by morphothebaine, which is undoubtedly related.

Apparently this is the alkaloid named glaucidine by Gladamer. The writer found several other alkaloids present, but not so readily characterized.

Thebaine is an opium alkaloid related to morphine, but its physiological action is altogether different from morphine. It is extremely poisonous, and its action is similar to strychnine. Isothebaine, oripavine, and glaucidine are not known to occur in opium or *Papaver somniferum*, and apparently nothing is known of their physiological properties. Isothebaine is related to thebaine, or more closely to morphothebaine, a laboratory derivative of thebaine. (20) It may also be described as an isoquinoline derivative of the apomorphine type. (15)

Papaver armeniacum Lam.

This poppy is probably not cultivated in the United States. It was another investigated by Konovalova, Yunusov, and Orekhov, (1935). They reported that it contains 0.65 percent total alkaloids, chiefly armepavine (not an opium alkaloid). Other alkaloids were present, but not enough of them could be obtained for complete identification. (21)

Papaver floribundum Desf.

This plant was also investigated by Konovalova, Yunusov, and Orekhov (1935) and was found to contain 0.36 per cent total alkaloids. They isolated from it armepavine, floripavine, floribundine, floripavidine, oripavine, and another base probably related to protopine. Most of these were newly discovered alkaloids. Protopine itself was absent, and so were all the other opium alkaloids. (25)

XVII. REFERENCES

1. Henry, Thomas Anderson. The Plant Alkaloids, 3rd edition. Philadelphia, 1939. (IV, 13).

2. Wehmer, E. Die Pflanzenstoffe Jena, 1929. (XV, 3).

3. Manske, Richard H. F.; Marion, Léo; and Ledingham, Archie E. "Alkaloids of Papaveraceous Plants. XXIV. *Hunnemannia fumariaefolia*." Journal of the American Chemical Society, 64, 1659-61 (1942). (XVI, 12).

4. (a). Fischer, R., and Tweeden, M. E. "The Alkaloids of *Eschscholtzia californica*." Pharmaceutical Archives (Milwaukee), vol. 5, no. 7, p. 117 (1902). (Summarized without details, Pharm. Jour. 70, 61 (1903).).

(b) Fischer, R. "The Alkaloids of *Eschscholtzia californica*." Proceedings of American Pharmaceutical Association, 49, 438 (1901).

5. Brindejonc, Georges. "Sur un alcaloïde de l'*Eschscholtzia californica*." Bulletin Société Chimique de France 9 (4), 97 (1911).

6. Manske, Richard H. F. "The Alkaloids of Papaveraceous Plants. XXXII. *Stylophorum diphyllum* (Michx) Nutt., D*icranostigma franchetianum* (Prain) Fedde, and *Glaucium serpie*ri Heldr." Canadian Journal of Research 20, B, 53-6 (1942). (XVI, 13b).

7. Manske, Richard H. F. "The Alkaloids of Papaveraceous Plants. XXXVIII. *Bocconia arborea* Wats." Canadian Journal of Research 21 B, 140-143 (1943). (X V I , 13c).

8. Manske, Richard H. F.

(a) "The Alkaloids of Papaveraceous Plants. XXIII. *Glaucium flavum* Crantz." Canadian Journal of Research 17, B, 399-403 (1939) (XVI, 13a)

(b) G*laucium serpieri*, reference #6.

(c) Correction, luteanine=isocorydine, C. J. R. 21, B, 13-16 (1943).

9. Konovalova; R. A., Yunusov, S., and Orekhov, A. P. "Alkaloids of the family Papaverae. VI. Alkaloids of *Glaucium fimbrilligerum*." J. Gen. Chem. (U. S. S. R.) 9, 1939-46 (1939). Chemical Abstracts 34, 4072. (XVI, 15).

10. Konovalova, R. A., Yunusov, S., and Orekhov, A. P. "Alkaloids of papaveraceous plants. IV. Alkaloids of Roemeria refracta DC. Constitution of remerine and synthesis of 2,3-methylenedioxyphenanthrene." Bull. soc. chim. 6, 1479-85; J. Gen. Chem. (U. S. S. R.) 9, 1507-11 (1939). Chemical Abstracts 34, 2852.

11. Almeida Costa, Oswaldo de. "Mexican Poppy, *Argemone mexicana* L." Rev. flora med. 1, 271-82 (1935). Chemical Abstracts 29, 4901.

12. Santos, Alfredo C., and Adkilen, Pacifica. "The Alkaloids of *Argemone mexicana*." Journal of the American Chemical Society 54, 2923 (1932).

13. Schlotterbeck, J. O. "Does '*Argemone Mexicana*' Contain Morphine?". Journal of the American Chemical Society 24, 238 (1902).

14. Files of the Bureau of Customs, U. S. Treasury Department.

15. Small, Lyndon F., and Lutz, Robert E. Chemistry of the Opium Alkaloids. Washington, 1932. (IV, 12).

16. Fulton, Charles C.,

(a) "The Precipitating Agents for Alkaloids." American Journal of Pharmacy 104, 244-271 (1932).

(b) "New Precipitating Agents for Alkaloids and Amines." American Journal of Pharmacy 112, 51-64 and 134-154 (1940).

17. Awe, Walther. In Archiv der Pharmazie und Berichte der Deutschen Pharmazeutischen Gesellschaft:

(a) "Uber das Rhoeadin." 279, 116-34 (1941).
(b) "Uber die Inhaltstoffe des Klatschmohn (*Papaver Rhoeas*)." 274, 439-45 (1936).
18. Hesse, O. In Annalen der Chemie und Pharmacie.
(a) "Vorläufige Notiz über Rhoeadin." Supplementband IV.50 (1865-66).
(b) "Ueber Rhoeadin." 140, 145 (1866).
(c) "Ueber Rhoeadin und Rhoeagenin." 149, 35 (1869).
(d) "Ueber den Milksaft der Fruchtkapseln von *Papaver Rhöas*." 185, 329 (1877).
19. Berichte der Deutschen Chemischen Gesellschaft, 9, 195-199 (1876), (Selmi, F.) (XV, 14).
20. (a) Klee, Walter. "Ueber die Alkaloide von *Papaver orientale*." Archiv der Pharmazie 252, 211-273 (1914).
(b) Gadamer, J. "Ueber die Nebenalkaloide von *Papaver orient*ale." Archiv der Pharmazie 252, 274-280 (1914).
21. Konovalova, R. A., Yunusov, S., and Orekhov, A. P. "Alkaloids of the Papaver Genus. I. Alkaloids of Papaver armeniacum and Papaver orientale." Berichte der Deutschen Chemischen Gesellschaft 68 B, 2158-63 (1935).
22. Fulton, Charles C. "Aldehyde-Oxidation Reactions for Phenols, Particularly the Opium Alkaloids." Journal of the Association of Official Agricultural Chemists, 12, 434-441 (1929).
23. Fulton, Charles C. "Fröhde's Reagent—A Reagent for Morphine and for Other Phenolic Compounds." Journal of Laboratory and Clinical Medicine, 23, 625-630 (1938).
24. Fulton, Charles C. "Iodosulfate Microchemical Identification Tests for Cinchona Alkaloids." Industrial and Engineering Chemistry, Analytical Edition, 13, 848-850 (1941).
25. Konovalova, R. A., Yunusov, S., and Orekhov, A. P. "Alkaloids of the Papaver Genus. II. Alkaloids of *Papaver floribundum*." Berichte der Deutschen Chemischen Gesellschaft, 68 B, 2277-82 (1935). Chemical Abstracts 30, 2571.

XVIII. Edible poppy seeds

There is a considerable interest in the question, whether any poppy not subject to the Opium Poppy Control Act can be found or developed to replace *Papaver somniferum* in the culture for edible seeds. The possibilities would seem to be three:

1. Development by selective plant breeding of an alkaloid-free variety of *Papaver somniferum*, or at least one not producing morphine or codeine.

2. Development of a hybrid of *Papaver somniferum* with some other poppy, the hybrid to produce seed comparable to that of *Papaver somniferum* but lack its capacity to produce narcotic alkaloids.

3. Use of some other poppy.

1.

This possibility was mentioned in Chapter VIII, but, as there pointed out, we have strong reasons to doubt if it is very practicable. We have no knowledge of any present variety that fails to produce morphine, and we do not know whether such a variety could be obtained merely by selection. If obtained, we do not know whether it would continue to breed true. If selection were based solely on low morphine it is likely enough that plants would be obtained which would elaborate primarily codeine instead of morphine.

2.

Papaver somniferum can be hybridized with some very different poppies. Unfortunately, we know nothing at all about the inheritance of the capacity to produce morphine in these hybrids. If the attempt is made to develop some poppy not producing narcotics from *Papaver somniferum*, it would seem that hybridization together with selection would be logical, and the most hopeful procedure.

3.

The chief trouble with using some other kind of poppy is that none other has been cultivated for 4000 years or more. If the other poppies available to us had to stand comparison only with the miserable wild specimens of *Papaver somniferum*, the task would seem far from hopeless. When we look at the finest specimens of the "garden poppy," with their huge indehiscent capsules, we realize that the gap is one that cannot be overcome in just a year or two.

The other common annual poppy, *Papaver rhoeas*, is a much smaller plant. The seeds are probably edible, but they are quite minute. The seeds of *Papaver somniferum* are small enough; with *Papaver rhoeas* they are almost dust-like.

The writer has, in former years, eaten the seeds of the Oriental Poppy, *Papaver orientale*, though only in small amount. They have a sweet, nutty flavor, somewhat like that of hazelnuts, and probably indistinguishable from that of the opium poppy seeds. They are somewhat smaller, but not too small. *Papaver orientale* is a perennial, and it may be questioned whether it could be made so prolific of seeds as an annual plant. The capsules are large, but probably do not average even half, perhaps not a third, the size of the highly cultivated varieties of opium poppy. A great deal might be done here by selective breeding, if the attempt were made. It is just possible that *Papaver orientale* even as it is at present might not be altogether unsatisfactory for home gardens. It would probably require about four times as much space, but perhaps less labor than *P. somniferum* for the same amount of seed. Naturally its seed production could not compete commercially with the importation of seed from the opium and garden poppies grown in other countries.

The seeds of *Glaucium flavum* (*G. luteum*), the Yellow Horned Poppy, are said to yield an oil with properties similar to that from the seeds of the opium poppy. (1) It seems impossible to learn much about this oil, and probably it has not been an article of commerce. However, Hegi states that it is edible. (2)

The seeds of *Argemone mexicana* are not edible, for they have a purgative action. This is also true of the oil from the seeds; and the cake left from pressing out the oil is useless for cattle feeding. (3)

On the whole the best chance would seem to be *Papaver orientale* some similar poppy, or the development of a suitable hybrid of *Papaver somniferum*, in which the morphine-forming quality would not be inherited, or from which it could be bred away.

XVIII. REFERENCES

1. Encyclopaedia Britannica 14th edition 1929, article "Poppy Oil."

2. Hegi, Gustav. Illustrierte Flora von Mittel-Europa. IV Band 1 Hälfte. München 1913. (*Glaucium flavum*). (II, 1).

3. Elsdon, G. D. Edible Fats and Oils. Ernest Benn Ltd. London, 1926.

PART III XIX. SUMMARY

[With regard to the poppy covered by the Opium Poppy Control Act]

1. The Opium Poppy is *Papaver somniferum* L., an annual, which is also cultivated for seeds, flowers, capsules, and alkaloids, as well as opium. It can be recognized by the large size of the plant and flowers and its smooth glaucous foliage. (Ia, III).

2. *Papaver somniferum* is a native of the Mediterranean region (southern Europe, Asia Minor), and was first reduced to cultivation, probably for its seeds, in the northeastern corner of the Mediterranean lands (Greece, Anatolia). It has been cultivated in Europe for at least some 4000 years. (II).

3. The "Garden Poppy" of Central Europe is a variety, or an ecological group of varieties, of *Papaver somniferum*, cultivated for the edible and oil-producing seed. It is not essentially different from the varieties actually used for opium production. It produces the opium

alkaloids and if incised will yield opium. (III, a, d).

4. The Opium Poppy should not be confused with the Oriental Poppy. That name rightfully belongs to *Papaver orientale* L., a perennial poppy grown for its flowers. To the flower-gardener only *Papaver somniferum*, its near-relative *Papaver bracteatum* Lindl., and their hybrids, are "Oriental Poppies." (I b, IX a, XIV).

5. The Opium Poppy should not be confused with the other common annual poppy, *Papaver rhoeas* L, the "corn poppy" or "field poppy" of Europe, grown in this country for its flowers. *Papaver rhoeas* is a smaller plant, more hairy, and the foliage is a strong green. (I b, XIV).

6. The Opium Poppy is cultivated in many floral forms and varieties. The flowers may be single, double plain, or double fringed; white, pink, red, mauve, purple, violet, and combinations; the single kinds generally with either a white or a violet spot at the base of each petal. American seedsmen generally listed them as "Tall Annual Poppies:" single, "paeony-flowered," "carnation-flowered," and various named varieties. These different forms are still the same poppy. (III b, VI b, IXc).

7. The variations of the Opium Poppy with respect to seed colors, capsule shapes, floral varieties, and agricultural varieties have no significance with regard to its capacity to produce morphine ana opium. The seeds may be white, yellow, pink, red, blue, gray, brown, or black. The so-called "Blue Poppy" of Europe is so named from the color of its seeds. There is no basis for the idea that only the white-seeded kind produces opium and that the blue-seeded or some other kind does not. (VI, VII).

8. There is only the one poppy cultivated now for opium or commercially cultivated for edible seed, although it has sometimes gone under a variety of names. That is *Papaver somniferum*, the Opium Poppy. (IX, Xa, XVa, XVIII).

9. The determination of opium poppies will be chemical. Positive proof of the presence of morphine will show that a poppy is an opium poppy within the meaning of the Opium Poppy Control Act. It need not be proved to belong to the species *Papaver somniferum* (XI, XII).

O

Opium Poppy Cultivation and Heroin Processing in Southeast Asia

Drug Enforcement Administration
Intelligence Division
Strategic Intelligence Section
September 1993

Executive Summary

The opium poppy has been cultivated in China and mainland Southeast Asia for more than two centuries. The mature plant produces a highly addictive latex which may be refined to produce opium for smoking, or treated with certain chemicals to produce morphine or heroin. This report focuses on the necessary steps in this process—taking a mature but raw opium poppy plant and synthesizing it's contents into finished heroin.

This report gives a brief history of the opium poppy plant and analyzes the plant in botanical detail. Cultivation methods are described, to include field selection, land clearing and soil preparation. It further explains the method of extracting morphine from opium, as the operation typically occurs in clandestine jungle laboratories in Southeast Asia. Finally, the intricate procedures used by heroin chemists to convert morphine to heroin are depicted step by-step.

A glossary of terms related to opium poppy cultivation and heroin processing in Southeast Asia is included for reference.

ORIGIN AND HISTORY OF THE OPIUM POPPY

The sole source of opium is the opium poppy. The plant is believed to have evolved from a wild strain, *Papaver setigerum*, which grows in coastal areas of the Mediterranean Sea. Through centuries of cultivation and breeding for its opium, a species of the plant evolved that is now known as somniferum. Today, *Papaver somniferum* is the only species of Papaver which produces opium. The genus, Papaver, is the Greek word for "poppy." The species, somniferum, is Latin for "sleep inducing."

The psychological effects of opium may have been known to the ancient Sumerians (circa 4000 B.C.) whose symbol for the poppy was hul ("joy") and gil ("plant"). The plant was known in Europe at least 4,000 years ago as evidenced by fossil remains of poppy seed cake and poppy pods found in the Swiss Lake Dwellings of the Neolithic Age. Opium was probably consumed by the ancient Egyptians and was known to the Greeks as well. The poppy is also referred to in Homer's works The Iliad and The Odyssey. In addition, Hippocrates (460-357 B.C.), the father of medicine, recommended drinking the juice of the white poppy mixed with the seed of nettle.

The opium poppy probably reached China about the 7th century A.D. through the efforts of Arab traders who advocated its use for medicinal purposes. In Chinese literature, however, there are earlier references to its use. The noted Chinese surgeon Hua To of the Three Kingdoms (220-264 A.D.) used opium preparations and *Cannabis indica* for his patients to swallow before undergoing major surgery.

The beginning of widespread opium use in China has been associated by some historians with the introduction of tobacco into that country by the Dutch from Java in the 17th century. The Chinese were reported to mix opium with tobacco. The practice was adopted throughout the area and eventually resulted in increased opium smoking, both with and without tobacco.

Flowering poppy plant with two younger flower buds.

In 1803, the German pharmacist Serturner isolated and described the principal alkaloid in opium, which he named morphium after Morpheus, the Greek god of dreams. The invention of the syringe and the discovery of other alkaloids of opium soon followed: codeine in 1832 and papaverine in 1848. By the 1850's, the medical use of pure alkaloids rather than crude opium preparations was common.

In the United States, opium preparations became widely available in the 19th century and morphine was used extensively as a painkiller for wounded soldiers during the Civil War. The inevitable result was opium addiction, contemporarily called "the army disease" or "soldier's disease." These opium and morphine abuse problems prompted a scientific search for potent but nonaddictive painkillers. In the 1870's, chemists developed an opium-based and supposedly non-addictive substitute for morphine. The Bayer pharmaceutical company of Germany was the first to produce the new drug in large quantities under the brand name *Heroin*. This product was obtained by the acetylation of morphine. Soon thereafter studies showed heroin to have narcotic and addictive properties far exceeding those of morphine.

Although heroin has been used in the United Kingdom in the

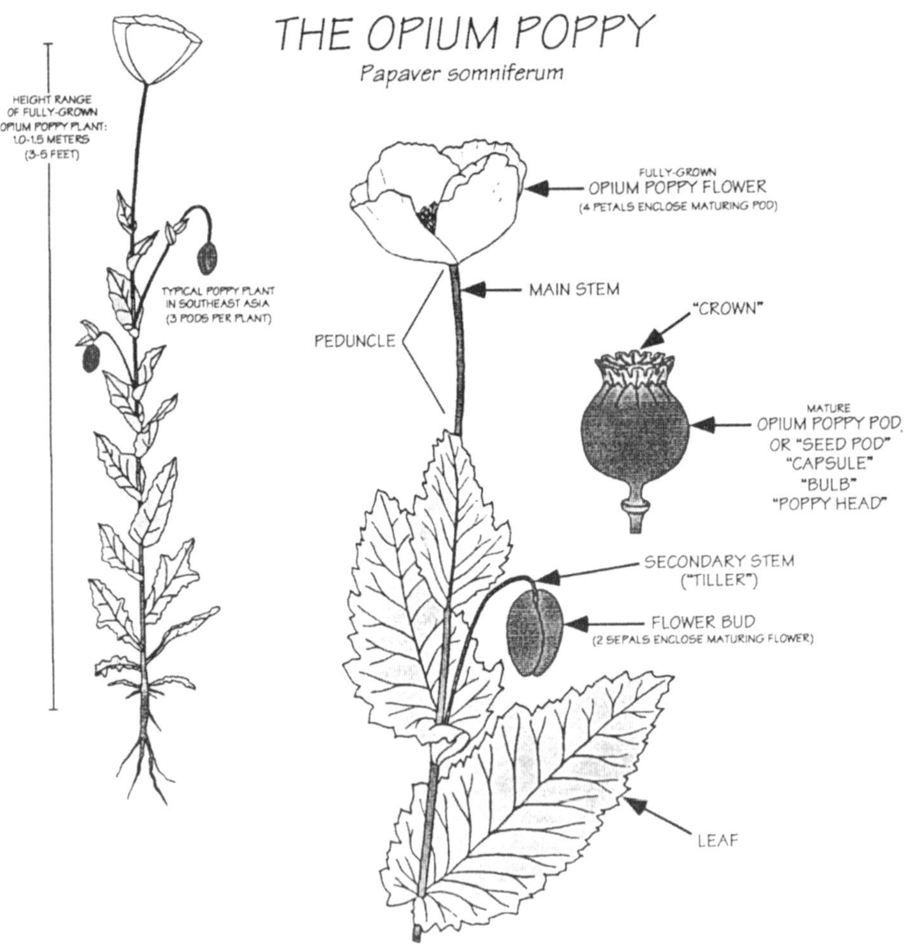

Figure No. 1. Basic Parts of the Opium Poppy Plant.

treatment of the terminally ill, its "medical value" is a subject of intense controversy.

THE OPIUM POPPY PLANT

The opium poppy, *Papaver somniferum*, is an annual plant. From a small seed, it grows, flowers, and bears fruit (a "pod") only once. The entire growth cycle for most varieties of this plant takes about 120 days. The tiny seeds, like the seeds on a poppy seed roll, germinate quickly in warmth and sufficient moisture. In less than six weeks, the young plant emerges from the soil, grows a set of four leaves, and resembles a small cabbage in appearance. The lobed, dentate leaves are glaucous green with a dull gray or blue tint.

Within two months, the plant will grow from one to two feet in height, with one primary, long, smooth stem. The upper portion of this stem is without leaves and is called the "peduncle" (see Figure 1). One or more secondary stems, called "tillers," may grow from the main stem of the plant. Single poppy plants in Southeast Asia often have one or more tillers.

The main stem of a fully-matured *Papaver somniferum* ranges between two and five feet in height. The green leaves are oblong, toothed and lobed and vary between four to fifteen inches in diameter at maturity. The matured leaves have no commercial value except for use as animal fodder.

As the plant grows tall, the main stem and every tiller terminates in a flower bud. During the development of the bud, the peduncle portion of the stem elongates and forms a distinctive "hook" which causes the bud to be turned upside down. As the flower develops, the peduncle straightens and the buds point upward. A day or two after the buds first point upward, the two outer segments of the bud, called "sepals," fall away, exposing the flower petals. The exposed flower blossom is at first crushed and crinkled, but the petals soon expand and become smooth in the sun. Poppy flowers have four petals. The petals may be single or double and are either white, pink, reddish purple, crimson red, or variegated.

Opium poppies generally flower after about 90 days of growth and continue to flower for two to three weeks. The petals last for two to four days and then drop to reveal a small, round, green fruit which continues to develop. These fruits or pods (also called "seedpods," "capsules," "bulbs," or "poppy heads") are either oblate, elongated, or globular and mature to about the size of a chicken egg. The oblate shaped pods are more common in Southeast Asia.

Only the pod portion of the plant can produce opium alkaloids. The skin of the poppy pod encloses the wall of the pod ovary. The ovary wall consists of three layers: the outer, middle and inner layers. The plant's latex (opium) is produced within the ovary wall and drains into the middle layer through a system of vessels and tubes within the pod. The cells of the middle layer secrete more than 95 percent of the opium when the pod is scored and harvested.

Cultivators tap the opium from each pod while it remains on the plant. After the opium is scraped, the pods are cut from the stem and allowed to dry. Once dry, the pods are cut open and the seeds are removed and dried in the sun before storing for the following year's planting. An alternative method of collecting planting seeds is to collect them from intentionally unscored pods, because scoring may diminish the quality of the seeds. Aside from being used as planting seed, the poppy seeds may also be used in cooking and in the manufacture of paints and perfumes. Poppy seed oil is straw-yellow in color, odorless, and has a pleasant, almond-like taste.

OPIUM POPPY GROWING AREAS

The opium poppy does best in temperate, warm climates with low humidity and requires only a moderate amount of water before and during the early stages of growth. In addition, the opium poppy is a "long day" photo-responsive plant. As such, poppies require long days and short nights before they will develop flowers.

The opium poppy plant can be grown in a variety of soils—clay, sandy loam, sandy, and sandy day—but it grows best in a sandy loam soil. This type of soil has good moisture-retentive and nutrient-retentive properties, is easily cultivated and has a favorable structure for root development. Clay soil types are hard and difficult to pulverize into a good soil texture. The roots of a young poppy plant cannot readily penetrate clay soils, and growth is inhibited. Sandy soil, by contrast, does not retain sufficient water or nutrients for proper growth of the plant.

Excessive moisture or extremely arid conditions will adversely affect the poppy plant's growth, thus reducing the alkaloid content. Poppy plants can become waterlogged and die after a heavy rainfall in poorly drained soil. Heavy rainfall in the second and third months of growth can leach alkaloids from the plant and spoil the harvest. Dull, rainy, or cloudy weather during this growth stage may reduce both the quantity and the quality of the alkaloid content.

The major legal opium poppy growing areas in the world today are in government-regulated opium farms in India, Turkey and Tasmania, Australia. The major illegal growing areas are in the highlands of mainland Southeast Asia, specifically Burma, Laos and Thailand (the Golden Triangle), as well as adjacent areas of southern China and northwestern Vietnam (see Figure 2 and Map 1); in Southwest Asia, specifically Pakistan, Iran, Afghanistan and in Mexico. Opium poppy is also grown in Lebanon, Guatemala, and Colombia.

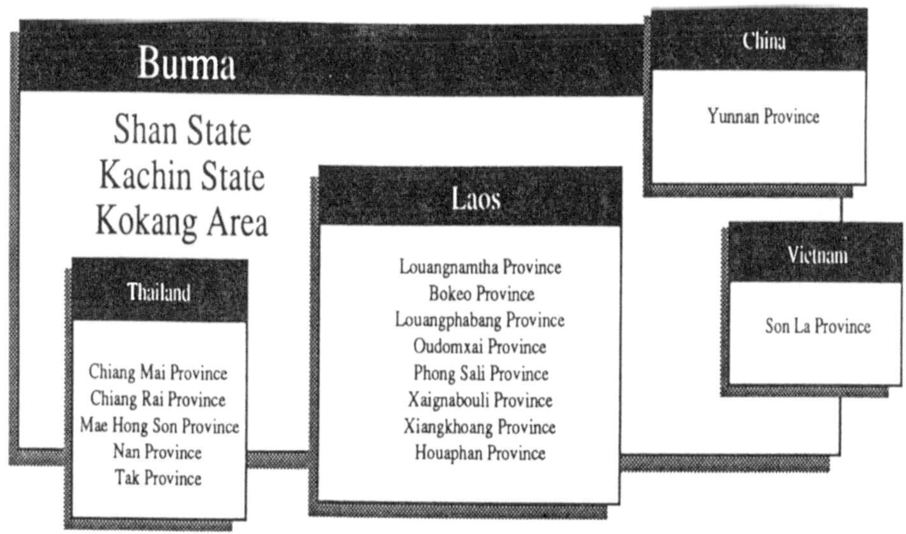

Figure No. 2. Major Opium Poppy Growing Areas in Southeast Asia.

Opium poppies were widely grown as an ornamental plant and for seeds in the United States until the possession of this plant was declared illegal in the Opium Poppy Control Act of 1942.

The highlands of mainland Southeast Asia, at elevations of 800 meters or more above sea level, are prime poppy growing areas. Generally speaking, these poppy-farming areas do not require irrigation, fertilizer, or insecticides for successful opium yields. Most of the opium poppies of Southeast Asia are grown in Burma (Myanmar), specifically in the Wa and Kokang areas which are in the northeastern quadrant of the Shan State of Burma Laos is the second-largest illicit opium-producing country in Southeast Asia and third-largest in the world. In this country, poppy is cultivated extensively in Houaphan and Xiangkhoang Provinces, in addition to the six northern provinces of

Bokeo, Louangnamtha, Louangphabang, Oudomxai, Phongsali and Xaignabouli. Poppy is also grown in many of the remote, mountainous areas of northern Thailand, particularly in Chiang Mai, Chiang Rai, Mae Hong Son, Nan and Tak Provinces.

In China, opium poppies are cultivated by ethnic minority groups in the mountainous frontier regions of Yunnan Province, particularly along the border area with Burma's Kachin and Shan States. Son La Province, situated between China and Laos, is a major opium poppy cultivation area in Vietnam.

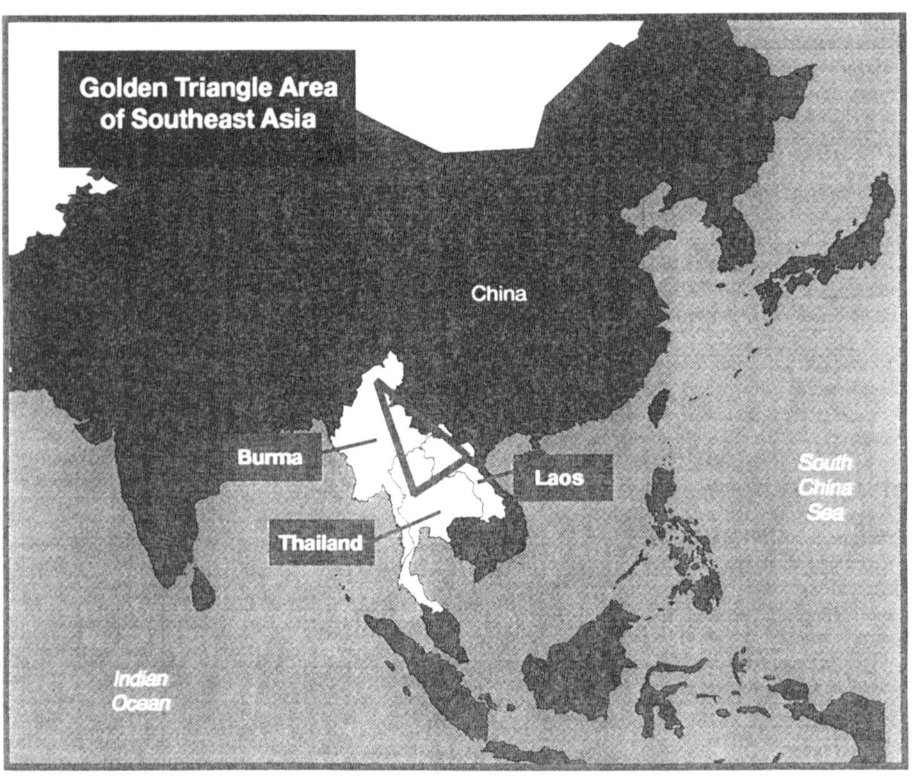

It is noteworthy that the dominant ethnic groups of mainland Southeast Asia are not poppy cultivators. The Burmans and Shan of Burma, the Lao of Laos, the Thai of Thailand, the Han Chinese of Yunnan, China, and the Vietnamese of Vietnam are low landers and do not traditionally cultivate opium poppies.

Rather, it is the ethnic minority highlander groups, such as the Wa, Pa-O, Palaung, Lahu, Lisu, Hmong, and Akha who grow poppies in the highlands of the countries of Southeast Asia. (See Figure 3.)

Opium Poppy Growers & Smokers

Kachin; Palaung; Wa;
Lahu (Musser, Musoe);
Lisu (Lisor, Lisaw);
Akha (I-kor, I-kaw);
Hmong (Meo, Miao);
Mien (Iu Mien. Yao); *et al.*

Opium Traders & Middlemen

Kachin; Palaung; Wa;
Shan (Tai Yai);
Yunnanese Chinese (Haw);
Guokang Chinese (Kokang);
Lahu (Musser, Musoe); Lisu (Lisor, Lisaw);
Akha (I-kor, I-kaw);
Hmong (Meo, Miao); Mien (Iu Mien. Yao);
Lao; Thai; *et al.*

A typical nuclear family of Southeast Asian highlanders ranges between five and ten persons, including two to five adults. An average household of poppy farmers can cultivate and harvest about one acre of opium poppy per year. Most of the better fields can support opium poppy cultivation for ten years or more without fertilization, irrigation, or insecticides, before the soil is depleted and new fields must be cleared.

FIELD SELECTION AND LAND CLEARING

In choosing a field to grow opium poppy, soil quality and acidity are critical factors and experienced poppy farmers choose their fields carefully. In Southeast Asia, westerly orientations are typically preferred to optimize sun exposure. Most fields are on mountain slopes at elevations of 1,000 meters (3,000 feet) or more above sea level. Slope gradients of 20 degrees to 40 degrees are considered best for drainage of rain water.

In Mainland Southeast Asia, virgin land is prepared by cutting and piling all brush, vines and small trees in the field during March, at the end of the dry season. After allowing the brush to dry in the hot sun for several days, the field is set afire. This method, called "slash-and burn" or "swidden" agriculture, is commonly practiced by dry field farmers—both highland and lowland—throughout Mainland Southeast Asia in order to ready the land for a variety of field crops.

The slash and-burn method is also used to clear fields for poppy cultivation. Before the rainy season in April, fields by the hundreds of thousands all over the region are set ablaze. A fog-like yellow haze hangs over the area for weeks, reducing visibility for hundreds of miles. In the mountains, the density of haze blocks out the sun and stings the eyes.

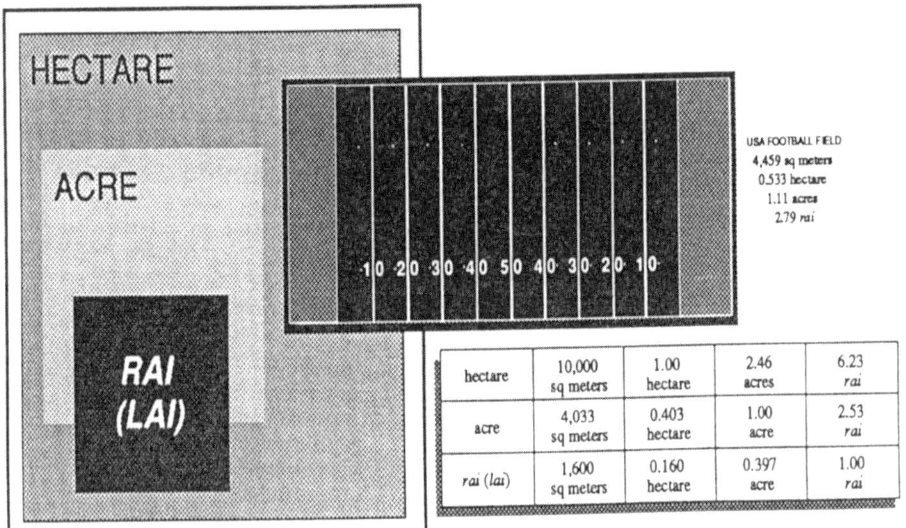

hectare	10,000 sq meters	1.00 hectare	2.46 acres	6.23 *rai*
acre	4,033 sq meters	0.403 hectare	1.00 acre	2.53 *rai*
rai (*lai*)	1,600 sq meters	0.160 hectare	0.397 acre	1.00 *rai*

A typical highlander family will plant an area of two or three rai in opium poppy (2.53 rai is equivalent to one acre). (See Figure 4.)

LAND PREPARATION AND CULTIVATION METHODS

In August or September, toward the end of the rainy season, highland farmers in Southeast Asia prepare fields selected for opium poppy planting. By this time, the ash resulting from the bum-off of the previous dry season has settled into the soil, providing additional nutrients, especially potash. The soil is turned with long-handled hoes after it is softened by the rains. The farmers then break up the large clumps of soil. Weeds and stones are tossed aside and the ground is leveled off.

Traditionally, most highland and upland farmers in Southeast Asia do not use fertilizer for any of their crops, including the opium poppy, but in recent years opium poppy farmers have started using both natural and chemical fertilizers to increase opium poppy yields. Chicken manure, human feces or the regions's abundant bat droppings are often mixed into the planting soil before the opium poppy seed is planted. The planting must be completed by the end of October in order to take advantage of the region's "long days" in November and December. (See Figure 5.)

Opium poppy field cleared by "slash-and-burn" method.

The opium poppy seed can be sown several ways: broadcast or tossed by hand; or fix-dropped by hand into shallow holes dug with a metal-tipped dibble stick. About one pound of opium poppy seed is needed to sow one acre of land. The seeds may be white, yellow, coffee-color, gray, black, or blue. Seed color is not related to the color of the flower petals. Beans, cabbages, cotton, parsley, spinach, squash or tobacco are usually planted with opium poppy. These crops neither help nor hinder the cultivation of the opium poppy, but instead are planted solely for personal consumption or as a cash crop.

In the highlands of Southeast Asia, it is also common practice to plant maize and opium poppies in the same fields each year. The maize keeps down excessive weeds and provides feed for the farmer's pigs and ponies. It is grown from April to August. After harvesting the maize, and with the stalks still standing in the fields, the ground is weeded and pulverized. Just before the end of the rainy season, in successive sowings throughout September and October, the poppy seed is broadcast among the maize stalks. These stalks can protect young opium poppy plants from heavy rains.

Figure 5. Opium poppy cultivation in Southeast Asia.

The opium poppy plants form leaves in the first growth stage, called the "cabbage" or "lettuce" stage. After a month of growth, when the opium poppy is about a foot high, some of the plants are removed (called "thinning") to allow the others more room to grow. The ideal spacing between plants is believed to be 20 to 40 centimeters, or about eight to twelve plants per square meter, although some researchers in northern Thailand have reported as many as 18 plants per square meter.

During the first two months, the opium poppies may be damaged or stunted by nature through the lack of adequate sunshine, excessive rainfall, insects, worms, hail storms, early frost, or trampling by animals. The third month of growth does not require as much care as the first two months.

Three to four months after planting, from late December to early February, the opium poppies are in full bloom. Mature plants range between three to five feet in height. Most opium poppy varieties in Southeast Asia produce three to five mature pods per plant.

A typical opium poppy field has 60,000 to 120,000 poppy plants per hectare, with a range of 120,000 to 275,000 opium-producing pods. The actual opium yield will depend largely on weather conditions and the precautions taken by individual farmers to safeguard the crop. The farmer and his family generally move into the field for the final two weeks, setting up a small field hut on the edge of the opium poppy field.

Opium poppy field showing flowers, pods and leaves.

OPIUM HARVESTING METHODS

The scoring of the pods (also called "lancing," "incising," or "tapping") begins about two weeks after the flower petals fall from the pods. The farmer examines the pod and the tiny crown (see figure 1) portion on the top of the pod very carefully before scoring. The grayish-green pod will become a dark green color as it matures and it will swell in size. If the points of the pod's crown are standing straight out or are curved upward, the pod is ready to be scored. If the crown's points turn downward, the pod is not yet fully matured. Not all the plants in a field will be ready for scoring at the same time and each pod can be tapped more than once.

A set of three or four small blades of iron, glass, or glass splinters bound tightly together on a wooden handle is used to score two or three sides of the pod in a vertical direction. If the blades cut too deep into the wall of the pod, the opium will flow too quickly and will drip to the ground. If the incisions are too shallow, the flow will be too slow and the opium will harden in the pods. A depth of about one millimeter is desired for the incision. Using a Wade-tool designed to cut to that depth, scoring ideally starts in late afternoon so the white latex-like raw opium can ooze out and slowly coagulate on the surface of the pod overnight. If the scoring begins too early in the afternoon, the sun will cause the opium to coagulate over the incision and block the flow. The opium oxidizes, darkens and thickens in the cool night air. Early the next morning, the opium gum is scraped from the surface of the pods with a short-handled flat, iron blade three to four inches wide.

Opium harvesters work their way backwards across the field scoring lower, mature pods before the taller pods, so as not to inadvertently spill the sticky ooze. The pods will continue to secrete opium for several days. Farmers will return to these plants—sometimes up to five or six times-to gather additional opium until the pod is totally depleted. The opium is collected in a container which hangs from the farmer's neck or waist.

The opium yield from a single pod varies greatly, ranging from 10 to 100 milligrams of opium per pod. The average yield is about 80 milligrams. The dried opium weight yield per hectare of opium poppies ranges between eight and fifteen kilograms of opium.

As the farmers gather the opium, the larger or more productive pods are tagged with colored string or yarn. These pods will later be cut from their stems, cut open, dried in the sun and their seeds will be used for the following year's planting.

The wet opium gum collected from the pods contains a relatively high amount of water and needs to be dried for several days. High-quality raw opium will be brown (rather than black) in color and will retain its sticky texture. Experienced opium traders can quickly determine if the opium has been mixed with tree sap, sand or other such material.

Standard Units of Weight used in Opium Trafficking in Southeast Asia

pong (Thai-Shan-Lao)		375.0 gms.	13.23 ozs.
pound	lb.	453.592 gms.	16.0 ozs.
jin/chin (Chinese)		500.0 gms.	1.1023 lbs.
kilogram	kg.	1,000.0 gms.	2.2046 lbs.
choi/joi (Thai-Shan-Lao)		1.6 kgs.	3.528 lbs.
viss (Tamil-Burmese)		1.657 kgs.	3.652 lbs.
ton	T	907.184 kgs.	2,000.0 lbs.
metric ton	MT	1,000.0 kgs.	2,204.6 lbs.

Raw opium in Burma, Laos and Thailand is usually sun-dried, weighed in a standard 1.6 kilogram quantity (called a *"viss"* in Burma; a *"choi"* in Laos and Thailand), wrapped in banana leaf or plastic and then stored until ready to sell, trade, or smoke. Opium smoking is common among most adult opium poppy farmers, whereas heavy addiction is generally limited to older, male farmers. The average yearly consumption of cooked opium per smoker is estimated to be 1.6 kilograms.

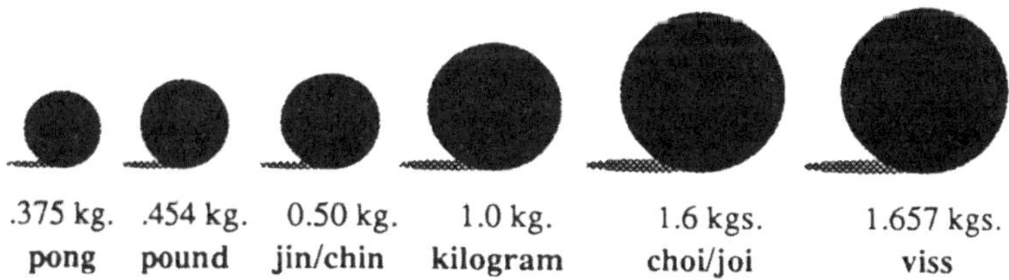

Figure 6. Units of opium weight in Southeast Asia.

A typical opium poppy farmer household in Southeast Asia will collect 2 to 5 choi or viss (3 to 9 kilograms) of opium from a year's harvest of a one acre field. That opium will be dried, wrapped and stacked on a shelf by February or March. If the opium has been properly dried, it can be stored indefinitely. Excessive moisture and heat can cause the opium to deteriorate but, once dried, opium is relatively stable. In fact, as opium dries and becomes less pliable, its value increases due to the decrease in water weight per kilogram.

COOKING OPIUM

Before opium is smoked, it is usually cooked. Uncooked opium contains moisture, vegetable matter and other impurities which detract from a smooth-smoking product. The raw opium which is collected from the opium poppy pod is placed in an open cooking pot of boiling water where the sticky glob of opium alkaloids quickly dissolve. The soil, twigs, plant scrapings, etc. remain undissolved. The solution is strained through cheesecloth to remove these impurities. The clear brown liquid, sometimes called "liquid opium," is actually opium in solution. This liquid is then re-heated over a low flame until the water turns to steam and is driven off into the air. When the water has evaporated, a thick paste remains. This paste is called "prepared opium," "cooked opium," or "smoking opium" and it is dried in the sun until it has a putty-like consistency. The net weight of the cooked opium is generally about twenty percent lighter than the original raw opium. Likewise, cooked opium is also more pure than in its original, raw form.

Heroin (trafficking level)

gram (gm.)	0.001 kg.	.0022 oz.
unit	0.700 kgs.	1.54 lbs.
kilogram (kg.)	1,000.0 gms.	2.2046 lbs.
ounce (oz.)	28.35 gms.	0.0625 lb.
pound (lb.)	453.59 gms.	16.0 ozs.

Figure 7. Units of heroin weight in Southeast Asia.

Cooked opium is suitable for smoking or eating by opium users. Traditionally there is only one group of opium poppy farmers, the Hmong, who prefer to not cook their opium before smoking. Most other ethnic groups, including Chinese opium addicts, prefer smoking cooked opium.

If the opium is to be sold to traders for use in morphine or heroin laboratories, it is not necessary to cook it first. The laboratory operators generally use 55-gallon oil drums or huge cooking vats to cook the raw opium before beginning the morphine extraction process (described in the next chapter).

EXTRACTION OF MORPHINE FROM OPIUM

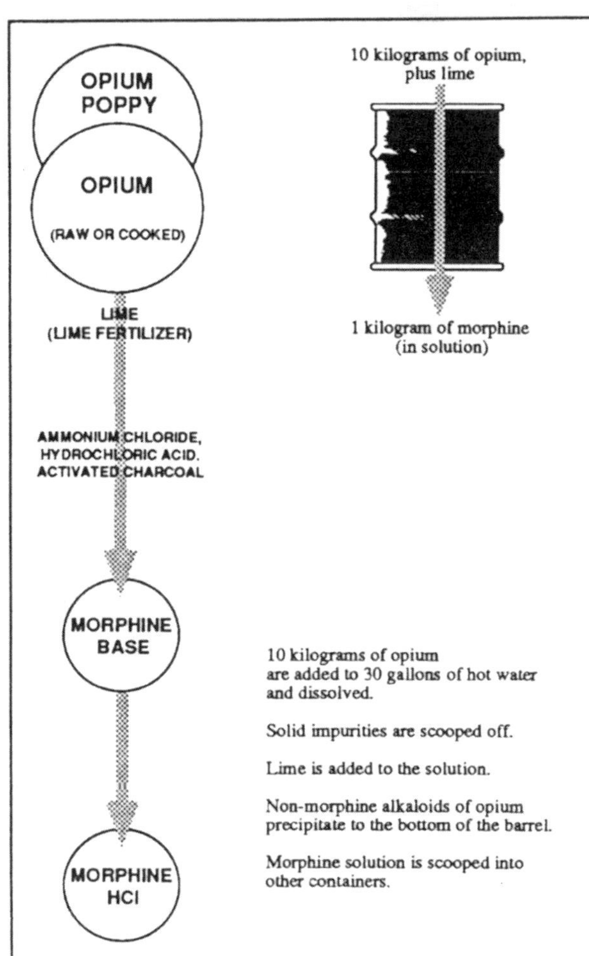

Figure 8. Morphine extraction process.

Raw or cooked opium contains more than 35 different alkaloids, including morphine, which accounts for approximately ten percent of the total raw opium weight. Heroin manufacturers must first extract the morphine from the opium, before converting the morphine to heroin. The extraction is a simple process, requiring only a few chemicals and a supply of water. Morphine is usually extracted from opium in small clandestine "laboratories" which are typically set up near the opium poppy fields. Since the morphine base is about one-tenth the weight and volume of raw opium, it is desirable to reduce the opium to morphine before transporting the product from the field to a heroin laboratory.

The process of extracting morphine from opium involves dissolving opium in hot water, adding lime to precipitate non-morphine alkaloids and then adding ammonium chloride to precipitate morphine from the solution. An empty oil drum and some cooking pots are needed. Following is a step-by-step description of morphine extraction in a typical Southeast Asian laboratory:

1. An empty 55-gallon oil drum is placed on bricks about a foot above the ground and a fire is built under the drum. Thirty gallons of water are added to the drum and brought to a boil. Ten to fifteen kilograms of raw opium are added to the boiling water.

2. With stirring, the raw opium eventually dissolves in the boiling water, while soil, leaves, twigs, and other non-soluble materials float in the solution. Most of these materials are scooped out of the clear brown "liquid opium" solution.

3. Slaked lime (calcium hydroxide) or more often a readily available chemical fertilizer with a high content of lime is added to the solution. The lime will convert the water insoluble morphine into the water soluble calcium morphenate. The other opium alkaloids do not react with the lime to form calcium salts. Codeine is an opium alkaloid which is slightly water soluble and which will be carried over with the calcium morphenate in the liquid. For the most part, the other alkaloids will become a part of the "sluge."

4. As the solution cools, the morphine solution is scooped from the drum and poured through a filter of some kind. Burlap rice sacks are often used as filters and can then be squeezed in a press to remove most of the solution from the wet sacks. The solution is then poured into large cooking pots and re-heated, but not boiled.

5. Ammonium chloride is added to the heated calcium morphenate solution to adjust the alkalinity to a pH of 8 to 9, and the solution is then allowed to cool. Within one or two hours, the morphine base and the unreacted codeine base precipitate out of the solution and settle to the bottom of the cooking pot.

6. The solution is then poured off through cloth filters. Any solid morphine base chunks in the solution will remain on the cloth. The morphine base is removed from both the cooking pot and from the filter cloths, wrapped and squeezed in cloth, and then dried in the sun. When dry, the crude morphine base is a coffee colored powder.

7. This "crude" morphine base, commonly known by the Chinese term *pi-tzu* in Southeast Asia, may be further purified by its dissolution in hydrochloric acid, adding activated charcoal, re-heating and filtering. The solution is filtered several times, and the morphine (morphine hydrochloride) is then dried in the sun. (See Figure 8.)

8. Morphine hydrochloride (tainted with codeine hydrochloride) is usually pressed into small brick-sized blocks in a press and wrapped in paper or cloth. The most common block size is 2 inches by 4 inches by 5 inches weighing about 1.3 kilograms. The bricks are dried for transport to heroin processing laboratories.

Approximately 13 kilograms of opium, from one hectare of opium poppies, are needed to produce each morphine block of this size. The morphine blocks are then bundled and packed for transport to heroin laboratories by human couriers or by pack animals. Pack mules are able to carry 100 kilogram payloads over 200 miles of rugged mountain trails in less than three weeks.

CONVERSION OF MORPHINE TO HEROIN BASE

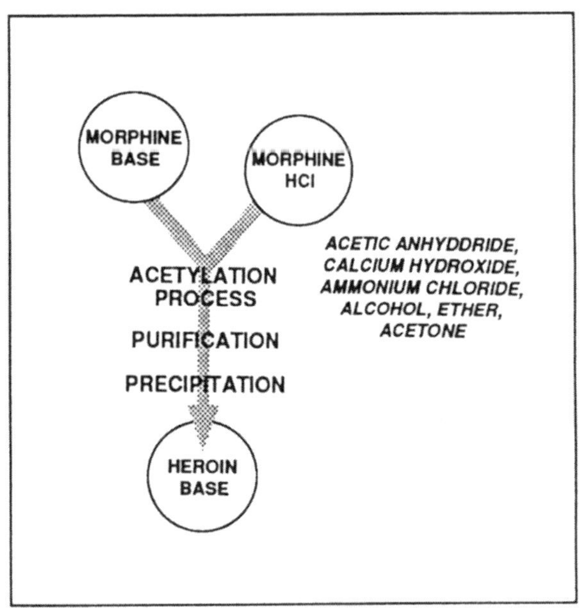

Figure 9. Process of Acetylation of Morphine.

The conversion of morphine to heroin base is a relatively simple and inexpensive procedure. The necessary chemicals for conversion to heroin are commonly available industrial chemicals. (See Fig. 10.) The equipment is very basic and quite portable. Heroin conversion laboratories are generally located in isolated, rural areas due to the telltale odors of the lab's chemicals. Acetic anhydride, in particular, is a key chemical with a very pungent odor resembling pickles.

Chemicals used to isolate the morphine from the opium include ammonium chloride, calcium carbonate (limestone) and calcium hydroxide (slaked lime). The preferred chemical normally used in the conversion of morphine to heroin is acetic anhydride. Chemical reagents used in the conversion process include sodium carbonate and activated charcoal. Chemical solvents needed are chloroform, ethyl alcohol (ethanol), ethyl, ether and acetone. Other chemicals may be substituted for these preferred chemicals, but most or all of these preferred chemicals are readily available through smugglers and suppliers.

Laboratory equipment includes measuring cups, funnels, filter paper, litmus paper and a stainless steel pot. Only the most sophisticated heroin labs use glass flasks, propane gas ovens, Bunsen burners, vacuum pumps, autoclaves, electric blenders, venting hoods, centrifuges, reflux condensers, electric drying ovens and elaborate exhaust systems. It is also possible to find portable, gasoline-powered generators at clandestine heroin conversion laboratories used to power various electrical devices.

Heroin synthesis from morphine is a two-step process which requires twelve to fourteen hours to complete. Heroin base is the intermediate product. Typically, morphine hydrochloride bricks are pulverized and the dried powder is then placed in an enamel or stainless steel rice cook pot. Acetic anhydride is then added. The acetic anhydride reacts with the morphine to form diacetylmorphine (heroin).

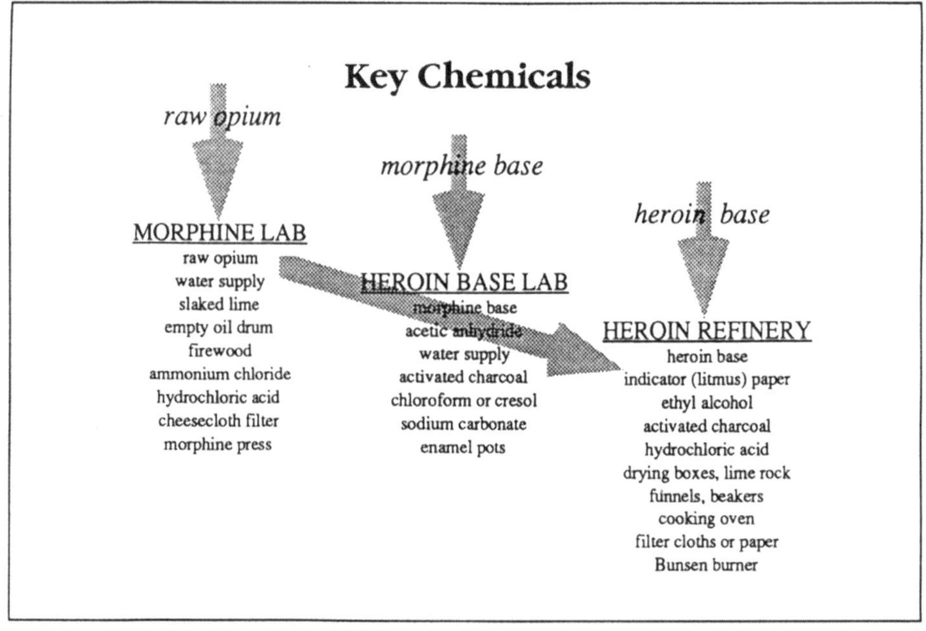

Figure 10. Key chemicals used in heroin processing.

This acetylation process will work either with morphine hydrochloride or morphine base. The pot lid is tied or clamped on, with a damp towel for a gasket. The pot is carefully heated for about two hours, below boiling, at a constant temperature of 185 Fahrenheit. It is never allowed to boil or to become so hot as to vent fumes into the room. It is agitated by tilting and rotation until all of the morphine has dissolved.

When cooking is completed, the pot is cooled and opened. During this step, morphine and the anhydride become chemically bonded, creating an impure form of diacetylmorphine (heroin). (See Figure 9.)

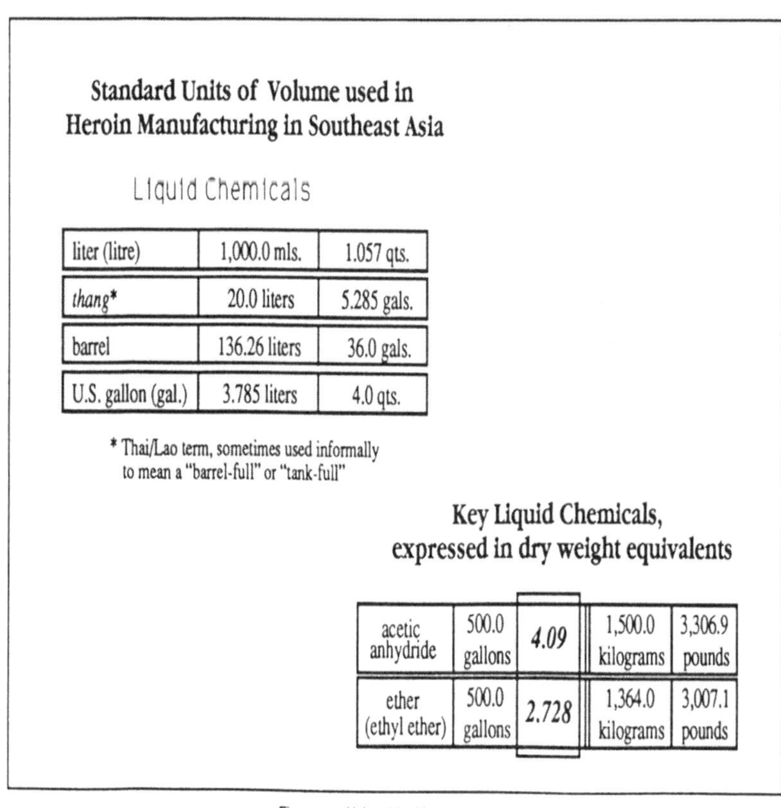

Standard Units of Volume used in Heroin Manufacturing in Southeast Asia

Liquid Chemicals

liter (litre)	1,000.0 mls.	1.057 qts.
*thang**	20.0 liters	5.285 gals.
barrel	136.26 liters	36.0 gals.
U.S. gallon (gal.)	3.785 liters	4.0 qts.

* Thai/Lao term, sometimes used informally to mean a "barrel-full" or "tank-full"

Key Liquid Chemicals, expressed in dry weight equivalents

acetic anhydride	500.0 gallons	*4.09*	1,500.0 kilograms	3,306.9 pounds
ether (ethyl ether)	500.0 gallons	*2.728*	1,364.0 kilograms	3,007.1 pounds

Figure 11. Units of liquid measurement.

Water is added at three times the volume of acetic anhydride and the mixture is stirred. Activated charcoal is added and mixed by stirring and the mixture is then filtered to remove colored impurities. Solids remaining on the filter are discarded. Sodium carbonate at 2.5 pounds per pound of morphine is dissolved in hot water and added slowly to the liquid until effervescence stops. This precipitates the heroin base which is then filtered and dried by heating in a steam bath for an hour. For each pound of morphine, about 11 ounces of crude heroin base is formed.

The heroin base may be dried, packed and transported to a heroin refining laboratory or it may be purified further and/or converted to heroin hydrochloride, a water-soluble salt form of heroin, at the same site.

Southeast Asian heroin base is an intermediate product which can be further converted to either smoking heroin ("heroin no. 3") or injectable heroin ("heroin no. 4").

CONVERSION OF HEROIN BASE TO HEROIN

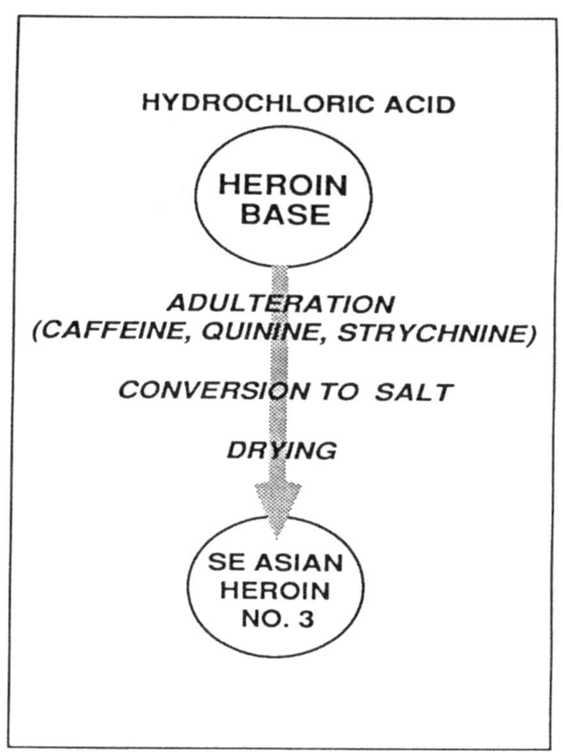

Figure 12. Conversion Process to Southeast Asian Heroin No. 3.

Heroin No. 3
(Smoking Heroin)
(Heroin hydrochloride)

To make heroin no. 3, the crude base is mixed with hydrochloric acid resulting in heroin hydrochloride. Adulterants including caffeine are added after this conversion. For each kilogram of crude heroin base about one kilogram of caffeine is used. Various "flavorings" such as quinine hydrochloride or strychnine hydrochloride may be added in 7 gram or 14 gram increments. Next, the wet paste mix is stirred to dryness over the steam bath.

The resulting dry heroin no. 3 will be in the form of coarse lumps. These are crushed and passed through a no. 8 to no. 10 mesh sieve, and the grains (pieces) are then packaged for sale.

The entire process takes about eight hours and requires only minimal skill. While extra attention to stirring is required to assure dryness, one man can prepare a one-kilogram block of heroin no. 3 during this time.

Heroin No.4 (Injectable Heroin)

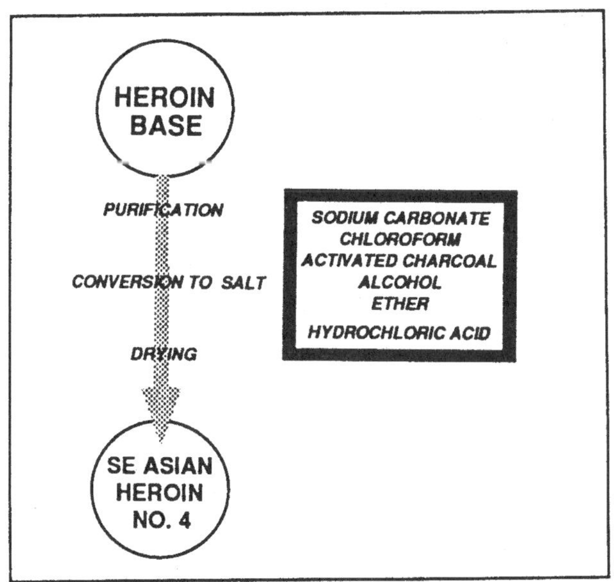

Figure 13. Conversion process to Southeast Asian heroin no. 4.

To the heroin base mixture in the pot, water is added at three times the volume of acetic anhydride and mixed by stirring. A small amount of chloroform is added. The mixture is stirred and then allowed to stand for twenty minutes. Doing so precipitates highly-colored impurities and a red, greasy liquid. The water layer is carefully poured off and saved in a clean pot, leaving the red grease in the pot.

In a clean pot, activated charcoal is stirred into the aqueous solution and is filtered to remove solid impurities. The decolorizing effects of the charcoal, combined with the chloroform treatment, will leave a light yellow solution. The use of charcoal is repeated one or more times, until the solution is colorless.

Approximately 1.1 kilograms of sodium carbonate per 0.5 kilograms of morphine is dissolved in hot water and added slowly to the mixture until the effervescence stops. This precipitates the heroin base which is then filtered and dried by heating on a steam bath. The heroin base is heated until dryness is complete, an imperative for the preparation of heroin no. 4. The powder should be very white at this stage. If not white, the base is redissolved in diluted acid, treated repeatedly with activated charcoal, reprecipitated and dried. The ultimate purity and color of the resulting heroin hydrochloride depends largely on the quality of the heroin base.

An optional step taken by skilled heroin chemists to increase the quality of the heroin follows:

Steel press used to compact heroin into blocks. Note the dry chemical containers in foreground.

For each pound of heroin base, 1,100 milliliters of ethyl alcohol is heated to boiling. The heroin base is added and stirred until completely dissolved. The heated solution is then quickly filtered through a Büchner funnel that has been preheated and poured into a heated flask. This hot filtration removes the traces of sodium carbonate that remained in the base. The solution is quickly cooled in an ice bath, where it becomes very thick like ice cream. The substance is put into a pan and set in a large refrigerator. A fan is set to blow across the pan to cause slow evaporation of the alcohol while the paste crystallizes. After several hours, it is vacuum-filtered. The filtrate, pure ethyl alcohol, is reused. The solid material, "alcohol morphine base," is actually re-crystallized heroin base.

The heroin product, either heroin base or re-crystallized heroin base, is weighed. For each pound of solid product, 3,000 milliliters of ethyl alcohol, 3,000 milliliters of ether, and 102 milliliters of concentrated hydrochloric acid are measured out. The solid is dissolved by heating with one-third of the alcohol and one-half of the acid. Another one-third of the acid is added and mixed by stirring. Next, acid is added slowly, drop by drop, until the product is completely converted to the hydrochloride. Two methods of testing this end product may be used. Either a drop of solution evaporates on a clean glass plate, leaving no trace of cloudiness in the residue, or a drop of the solution placed on Congo red paper causes the paper to turn blue.

Once the acid is added, the remaining alcohol is stirred in. Then, half of the ether is added with stirring and the mixture is allowed to stand for fifteen minutes. It must be examined with great care since it is extremely volatile and flammable. Once the first small crystals are detected, the remaining ether is added at once. The vessel is stirred, covered and allowed to stand for twenty minutes to one hour.

No. 4 heroin in cardboard drying box.

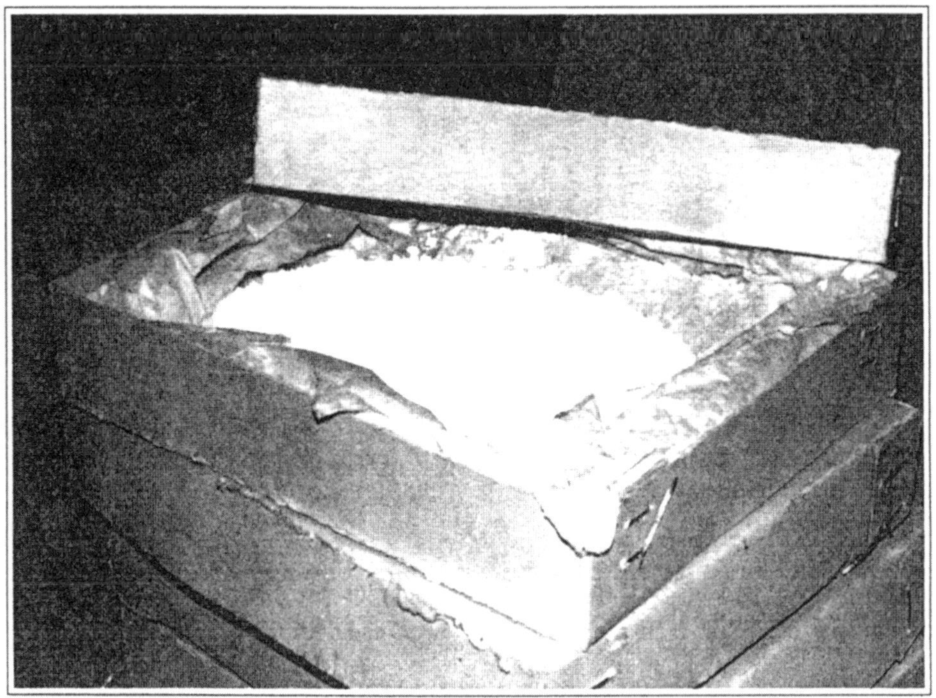

The mixture becomes nearly solid after an hour. At this point, it is filtered and the solids are collected on clean filter paper. The paper is wrapped around the crystals and placed on wooden trays, usually over lime rock, to dry. When the crystals of pure heroin hydrochloride are dry, they are packaged. Batches of 5 to 10 kilograms are commonly made at one time, the largest batch being an estimated 20 kilograms.

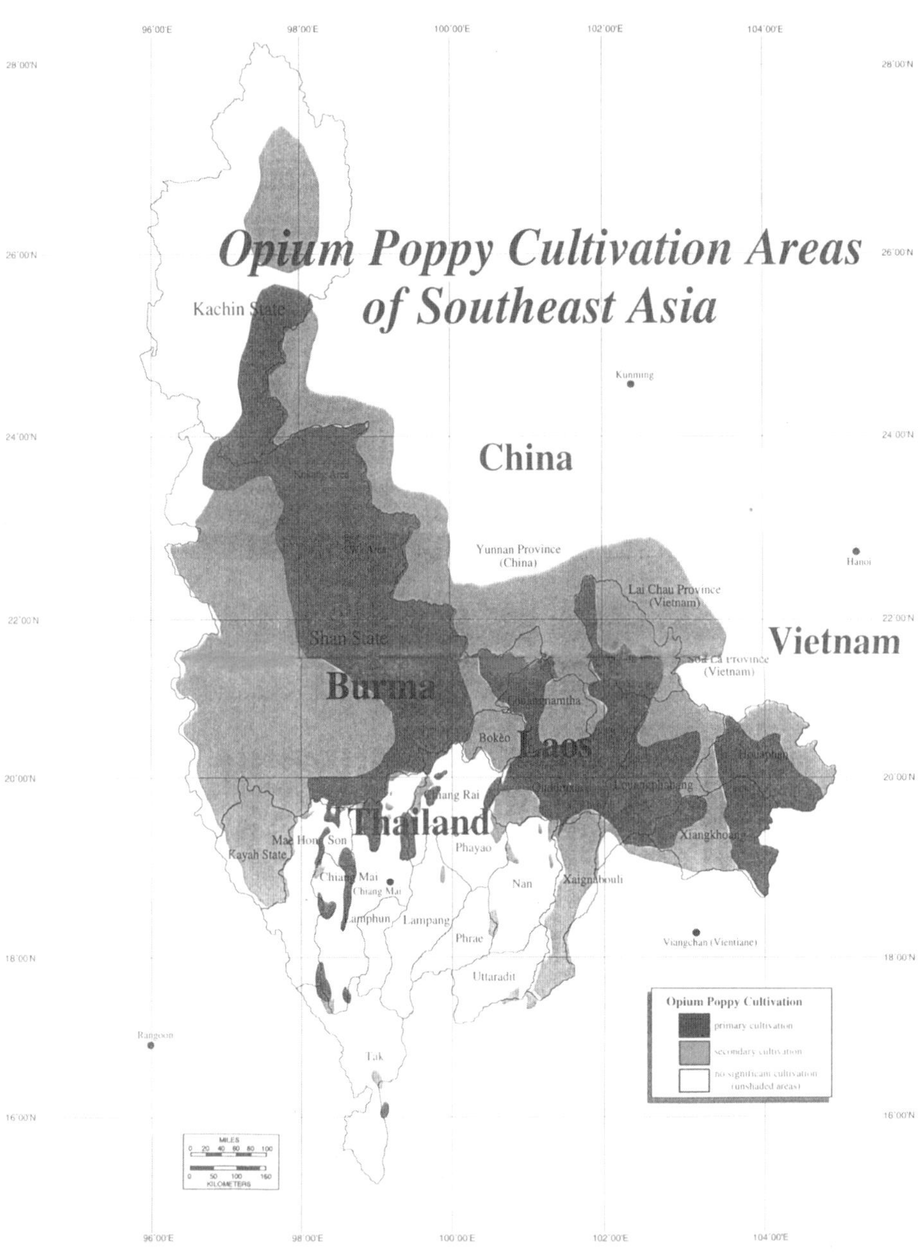
Opium Poppy Cultivation Areas
of Southeast Asia
Kachin State
Kunming
China
Yunnan Province
(China)
Hanoi
Lai Chau Province
(Vietnam)
Shan State
Vietnam
(Vietnam)
Burma
Bokèo
Laos
Thailand
Phayao
Kayah State
Nan
Xiangkhoang
Chiang Mai
Lampang
Phrae
Uttaradit
Tak
Rangoon
Opium Poppy Cultivation
MILES
KILOMETERS

Figure 15. Double U-O Globe trademark of Southeast Asian heroin.

CONCLUSION

Southeast Asia, especially the Golden Triangle area, is ideally suited for the propagation and synthesis of the opium poppy—geographically, topologically and culturally.

Although the opium poppy plant will grow remarkably well with little tending, farmers in recent years have introduced the use of fertilizers that have produced bumper crop yields. In addition, the chemicals used in the synthesis of heroin are inexpensive and readily available. At the same, the time laboratory equipment needed to synthesize heroin is very basic and easily obtainable.

GLOSSARY OF TERMS

acetic acid, glacial

Also known as ethanoic acid or vinegar acid. Glacial acetic acid is the pure compound, as distinguished from the usual water solutions known as acetic acid. A clear, colorless liquid with a pungent odor. Miscible with water, alcohol, glycerin, and ether. Highly-concentrated, produces burns on the skin. Chronic exposure may cause erosion of dental enamel, bronchitis, eye irritation. Excellent solvent for many organic compounds. Widely used in commercial organic synthesis. Normally contained in 5-lb bottles (corrosive liquid). Can be used in place of ammonium chloride or ammonia solutions as a reagent to adjust alkalinity in the precipitation of morphine (as crude morphine base) from an opium solution.

acetic anhydride

Also known as acetic oxide; acetyl oxide. A colorless liquid with a strong, pickle-like odor. Fumes in moist air, and its vapor is extremely irritating to eyes, nose, and throat. Not readily miscible with water, forming a separate layer on the bottom, but will eventually form acetic acid. Soluble in chloroform or ether. Readily combustible (fire hazard). Normally contained in various sizes of glass or plastic bottles, 5-gallon glass carboys, and 55-gallon metal drums lined with stainless steel or polyethylene. Used in the textile, leather tanning, pharmaceutical (particularly aspirin), and photography industries. Under strict government regulation in some countries. Manufactured in United States, Western Europe, and Japan. Acetic anhydride is also the most commonly used acetylating agent in the acetylation of morphine. A key precursor chemical and reagent in heroin synthesis.

acetone

Also known as 2-propanone or dimethyl ketone; pyroacetic ether. A volatile, highly flammable liquid with a mildly pungent and somewhat aromatic odor. Acetone vapor is irritating to the eyes and nose in high concentrations. Miscible with water, alcohol, chloroform, ether, etc. Must be stored in closed containers and kept away from fire. Industrial uses as a solvent include manufacture of rayon, photographic films, paint and varnish removers. Shipped in cans, steel drums, barrels, and tank cars. Can be used as a solvent in processing opium and in the purification of morphine base, but is not commonly used in Southeast Asia.

acetyl chloride

Also known as ethanoyl chloride. A flammable, fuming, colorless liquid with a pungent odor. Soluble in ether, acetone, acetic acid. Highly toxic and corrosive. Extremely irritating to the eyes. Dangerous fire risk. Reacts violently with water and alcohol. Used as an acetylating agent; in testing for cholesterol, determination of water in organic liquids. Shipped in polyurethane-lined iron drums and 110 lb glass carboys in cool, dry area with adequate ventilation. Protect from moisture. Controlled or regulated in Hong Kong and Thailand. Can be used in place of acetic anhydride as an acetylating agent in the acetylation of morphine, although it is more hazardous to use.

acetylation

The key chemical process in converting morphine base to heroin. Can be accomplished using either acetyl chloride or acetic anhydride. Acetyl chloride is flammable, irritating to the eyes, reacts violently with water or alcohol, and requires careful handling in laboratory processes. For these reasons, acetylation using acetyl chloride is not favored by processors of heroin. Although acetic anhydride is corrosive and requires care in handling, it is less hazardous to the user than acetyl chloride and hence is the key chemical used in processing of heroin.

adulterant

Substance added to heroin after the heroin conversion process is completed. Adulterants are pharmacologically active. Quinine and procaine are typical adulterants added to heroin.

alcohol (ethyl alcohol)

An anhydrous alcohol, also known as ethanol, grain alcohol, fermentation alcohol, "drinking alcohol," anhydrous alcohol, ethyl hydroxide, and methyl carbinol. A clear, colorless, volatile, flammable liquid with a pleasant, sweet odor. Absorbs water rapidly from air. Miscible with water. Must be stored in tightly closed container, cool, and away from flame. Most ethyl alcohol is used in alcoholic beverages in suitable dilutions. Shipped in metal or plastic containers, such as 55-gallon drums, gerry cans, etc. Some drums may be lined with phenolic resin. Used as a solvent during purification of heroin base and in conversion of heroin base to heroin hydrochloride.

alkaloid

Any of various physiologically active, nitrogen containing organic bases derived from plants. Common alkaloids include atropine, caffeine, cocaine, codeine, mescaline, morphine, narcotine, nicotine, noscapine, papaverine, quinine, strychnine, and thebaine.

ammonium chloride

Also known as ammonium muriate, sal ammoniac, salmiac. Colorless, odorless crystals or crystalline chunks; may also be a white, granular powder. Tendency to cake. Soluble in ethanol; near-insoluble in acetone or ether. Cooling, saline taste. Major industrial uses are in manufacture of dry cell batteries; dyes; fertilizers; washing powders; etc. Medical use as an expectorant. Normally packaged in barrels or multiwall paper or polyethylene sacks. Ammonium chloride can be used as a reagent to adjust alkalinity in the precipitation of morphine (as crude morphine base) from an opium solution.

benzene

Also known as benzol. A colorless to light-yellow liquid with an aromatic odor. Its vapors bum with a smoky flame. Highly flammable; dangerous fire risk. Toxic by ingestion, inhalation, and skin absorption. A carcinogen. Commonly used in petroleum industry for use in anti-knock gasoline. Shipped in drums, tanks, and on barges with adequate ventilation. Can be used to initially extract morphine alkaloid from opium, but its high flammability and acute toxic properties make it a poor choice for this process.

brown sugar heroin

A common name for heroin (any source) which has the appearance of light brown, granulated sugar. Used in contrast with the white, fluffy powder or crystals form of heroin, such as Southeast Asian "China White" heroin. Injected, snorted, or smoked.

caffeine

White, fleecy masses of long, flexible, silky crystals. A bitter, white alkaloid found in coffee, tea, and cola nuts. Caffeine is generally used in combined forms, as a monohydrate, acetate, or other compounds. In addition to its use as a stimulant and diuretic, crystalline caffeine is commonly used as an adulterant in heroin hydrochloride, or as a necessary ingredient in "smoking heroin" (e.g., Southeast Asian heroin no. 3).

calcium hydroxide. See "lime, slaked."

carbon, activated. See "charcoal, activated."

chandu

A Hindi-Bengali term for cooked opium ("smoking opium"). Term used in India and some parts of Burma. Term is used in some reports on Southeast Asian opium.

charcoal, activated

A fine black carbonaceous powder prepared commercially from wood and vegetables. Also known as "activated carbon" or "animal black." Highly adsorptive. Used in medicine as an antidote and in treatment of diarrhea. Used in laboratories for clarifying, deodorizing, decolorizing, and filtering various chemicals. Marketed under trade names as Norit, Carborafffin, Ultracarbon, Opocarbyl, etc. Used as a reagent in the purification of heroin.

China White

Southeast Asian heroin no. 4, in white powder form. Term is used by English-speaking westeners to contrast the white powder form with the light brown, granular form of heroin (see "brown sugar heroin," above). May be injected, snorted, or smoked. The term "China White" has also been used in recent years as an alternate name for fentanyl, a synthetically-produced compound with heroin-like properties.

chloroform

Also known as trichloromethane. A clear, colorless, heavy, and very volatile liquid with a characteristic sweet odor. It is an irritant to the skin and eyes and may also be carcinogenic. Not miscible with water, forming a separate layer on the bottom. Miscible with alcohol. Shipped in bottles, tins, or drums; stainless steel for very high-purity products. Used in industry as a solvent for fats, oils, rubber, alkaloids, waxes, and resins. Used extensively as a solvent in the rubber industry; used to make the refrigerant Fluorocarbon-22. Can be used as a solvent in the synthesis of heroin.

choi

A standard unit of weight used in Southeast Asia for opium (only). Equivalent to 1.60 kilograms (3.528 pounds). See Figure 7.

conversion (heroin conversion)

A chemical conversion process wherein heroin base is converted into a soluble salt form of heroin, generally heroin hydrochloride.

diluent

A chemical diluent is an ingredient used to reduce the concentration of an active material. Another common definition of diluent is a substance added to finished product (e.g., heroin) to increase bulk. In this sense, there is no clear distinction between a diluent and an extender. In heroin manufacture, "diluents" refer to extenders. Typical diluents for heroin are mannitol, sucrose, lactose, and starch.

ether (ethyl ether)

Also known as diethyl ether; ethyl oxide; diethyl oxide; sulfuric ether, anesthetic ether, or simply "ether." A colorless, mobile, very volatile and highly flammable liquid. Characteristic, sweetish, pungent odor, more agreeable than chloroform. Ether vapors are heavier than air; tends to form explosive peroxides under the influence of air and light. When shaken under absolutely dry conditions, ether can generate enough static electricity to start a fire. Shipped in cans, drums, barrels, and tank cars. Not miscible with water, forming a separate layer on the surface. In addition to its well-known use as an anesthetic, ether is used as a solvent in fats, waxes, dyes, perfumes, oils, resins, etc. Ether is also used as a solvent in conversion of heroin base to heroin hydrochloride.

ethyl alcohol. See "alcohol."

ethyl ether. See "ether."

Golden Triangle

Area of mainland Southeast Asia comprising the Shan Plateau and Kachin Hills of northeastern Burma, the highlands of northwestern Laos, and the highlands of northern Thailand. Term was popularized by Western journalists in the 1970's to designate one of the principal source areas in the world for illicit opium and its derivatives, morphine and heroin.

gram

A standard unit of weight in the metric system equal to one-thousandth of a kilogram. 28.350 grams equal one ounce.

hai

Northern Thai-Shan term used with land areas. See *"rai"* and *"lai"* (Lao).

hectare

A metric unit of area equal to 2.471 acres (10,000 square meters). See Figure 4.

heroin

Also known as diacetylmorphine. A highly-addictive synthetic narcotic derived from morphine.

heroin base (Southeast Asia)

Diacetylmorphine. Also known as "crude heroin." Actually, is morphine base that has undergone acetylation. Formed as a precipitate (solid) by adding soda ash (sodium carbonate) to an acetylated morphine solution. Sometimes called Southeast Asian heroin no. 2. Not readily soluble in water, and therefore not injectable in this form. This form of heroin can be smoked. However, heroin base is generally considered an intermediate form of heroin which may be further refined to either no. 3 or no. 4 heroin.

heroin hydrochloride

A chemical salt form of heroin, usually powder or crystal, that is water soluble and therefore suitable for injection. Sometimes called Southeast Asian heroin no. 4. Formed when heroin base is treated with hydrochloric acid. This type of heroin is most commonly used by heroin abusers who inject the drug.

Southeast Asian heroin no. 3

A smokeable form of Southeast Asian heroin. Not as highly refined as no. 4. Color ranges from purple to tan to off-white. Although considered a smoking heroin, it may also be injected intravenously. Caffeine is a necessary component of heroin no. 3. In contrast, strychnine or quinine are adulterants which are sometimes added to heroin no. 3, allegedly to modify the taste of the product.

Southeast Asian heroin no. 4

An injectable form of Southeast Asian heroin. Also known as heroin hydrochloride or "China White." Highly refined heroin produced from

Southeast Asian opium. Usually a fine white powder, flakes, or crystals. May be smoked or snorted, although, from the standpoint of the abuser, these are expensive and wasteful uses of this form of heroin. Diluents, such as lactose, are not normally added until the heroin is diluted, or "cut."

highlander (Southeast Asia)

A hill dweller. Hill tribesmen are a typical example of highlanders in Southeast Asia However, some hill tribesmen have migrated into the lowlands, and are now permanent dwellers in lowland communities. Conversely, some members of ethnic groups which are generally lowland dwellers have permanently settled in highland areas in mainland Southeast Asia

hill tribe (Southeast Asia)

Any one of numerous ethnic groups which share a distinct culture, language, and social structure and who are regarded, as a group, to be hill dwellers or *montagnards* (French). The Hmong (Miao), the Iu Mien (Yao), Lahu (Musoe), *inter alia*, are hill tribe groups in mainland Southeast Asia

hydrochloric acid

A solution of hydrogen chloride gas (HCl) in water. Also known as muriatic acid. Fumes in the air. A colorless liquid (sometimes yellow) with an acrid odor. Acid is poisonous and corrosive. Shipped in glass bottles or glass carboys, or rubber-lined steel drums. Used in petroleum production, as a chemical intermediate, and in ore reduction, food processing, pickling, and metal cleaning. Hydrochloric acid is used to convert morphine base to morphine hydrochloride (e.g., '999' morphine blocks or bricks) or to convert heroin base to heroin hydrochloride.

jin

A metric unit of weight in Chinese system. Equivalent to one-half kilogram (500 grams). Chinese term, romanized: *jin* (Pinyin) or *chin* (Wade-Giles Mandarin). See Figure 7.

joi

Standard unit of weight for opium. See "*choi*."

kilogram

A metric unit of weight equal to 1,000 grams, or 2.2046 pounds.

lactose

Also known as milk sugar, saccharum lactis. Present in milk in mammals. White, hard crystalline mass or white powder, sweet taste, odorless. Stable in air. Soluble in water; insoluble in ether and chloroform; very slightly soluble in alcohol. Used commercially in infant foods, baking and confectionery, margarine and butter manufacture, etc. Shipped in multiwall paper sacks or bulk. Commonly used as a diluent (or "extender") by heroin dealers to increase bulk of "injectable heroin" (e.g., Southeast Asian heroin no. 4).

lai

A standard unit of land area measurement in Laos equivalent to 1,600 square meters. Corresponds to rai measurement used in Thailand (see below). See Figure 4.

lime, slaked

Also known as calcium hydroxide, calcium hydrate, caustic lime, hydrated lime. Crystals or soft, odorless, granules or powder, with a slightly bitter taste. Slightly soluble in water. Readily absorbs CO_2 from air, forming $CaCO_3$. Used in industry to manufacture cement, pesticides, fertilizers, and in water treatment. Normally packaged in tightly closed and dry containers, such as wooden barrels or multiwall paper sacks. Used as a reagent in the extraction of morphine from opium by forming an intermediate calcium salt (calcium morphenate).

liter

A metric unit of volume. Equivalent to 1.056 liquid quarts. See Figure 11.

low lander (Southeast Asia)

A lowland dweller, in either a rural or urban community. The ethnic Lao are a typical example of low landers in Southeast Asia. However, some Lao have migrated into the highlands and are now permanent dwellers in highland communities. Conversely, some members of ethnic groups which are generally highland dwellers (e.g., the Hmong hill tribe) have permanently moved into lowland areas in Laos and Thailand.

mannitol

Also known as mannite, manna sugar. A white, crystalline, sweetish, water-soluble carbohydrate alcohol. Used as a nutrient, a dietary supplement, and as the basis of dietetic sweets. Mannitol is commonly used as a mild laxative for infants. Shipped in multiwall paper sacks or bulk. Commonly used as a diluent (or "extender") by heroin dealers to increase bulk of "injectable heroin" (e.g., Southeast Asian heroin no. 4).

morphine

An organic compound (alkaloid) found in the *Papaver somniferum* (opium poppy). Morphine must first be extracted from opium. The soluble salts of morphine (morphine carbonate, morphine sulfate; morphine hydrochloride, etc.) are used in human and veterinary medicine as a light anesthetic or as a sedative.

morphine base

Morphine base is an intermediate product between morphine alkaloid in opium and a morphine brick (morphine hydrochloride). The base is formed as a precipitate (solid) when ammonium chloride is added to a solution of calcium morphenate. This base is usually quite crude (50% to 70% pure) because of the marginal conditions under which it is prepared. Morphine base is not easily soluble in water, and thus is not readily absorbed by the human body. Morphine base must therefore be converted to a (water-soluble) salt form, viz., morphine hydrochloride or heroin hydrochloride, by treating with hydrochloric acid.

morphine brick

Morphine hydrochloride, compressed (by a morphine press) into a standard-sized brick shape measuring approximately 2 inches by 4 inches by 5 inches and weighing approximately 1.3 kilograms (about 3 pounds). Also known as a morphine block. Properly compressed morphine hydrochloride is very dry and hard.

morphine press

A metal or wood piece of equipment which can squeeze water from morphine hydrochloride, leaving the morphine dry and in uniform, brick sized blocks.

morphine salt

A water-soluble chemical form of morphine. In extracting morphine from opium, slaked lime (calcium hydroxide) powder is added to opium dissolved in water. Lime reacts with morphine in opium (morphine content ranges from 9% to 16% by weight of the opium) to form calcium morphenate in solution. Calcium morphenate is a chemical salt form of morphine. Other morphine salts include morphine sulfate, morphine hydrochloride and morphine acetate—all legitimate compounds used in medicine.

nuai

A general, non-specific term in Thai-Lao-Shan which means "unit." However, has special meaning when used in reference to heroin. A nuai is a standard unit of weight for Southeast Asian heroin, equivalent to 700 grams (.7 kilogram).

opium

A bitter, yellowish-brown, strongly-addictive naturally-occurring narcotic derived from the dried latex juice of the opium poppy, *Papaver somniferum*. Source of morphine and heroin. Opium poppy is cultivated legally in India, Turkey, China, Commonwealth of independent States (formerly the Soviet Union), and Tasmania, Australia; and is cultivated illegally in Afghanistan, Burma, Colombia, Guatemala, Iran, Laos, Lebanon, Mexico, Pakistan and Thailand.

liquid opium

Also known as "opium solution." Refers to opium which has been dissolved in water, either to prepare the opium for smoking, i.e., "cooking" the opium, or as the first step in extracting morphine from the opium. Liquid opium is usually a clear, brown liquid.

prepared opium

Also known as "cooked opium," "processed opium," and "smoking opium." Raw opium is dissolved in hot water in order to remove impurities and vegetable matter. It is heated to reduce its water content. As the solution cools, the opium reverts to a solid. Most opium smokers prefer to smoke prepared opium. By contrast, morphine and heroin laboratory operators can process both cooked and raw opium.

raw opium

Also known as "opium gum," "crude opium," and "opium sap." Opium which has not been "cooked." Often contains plant scraping, leaf pieces, and other impurities. Initially, is soft and pliable due to high moisture content, but may be dried to a hard consistency. Has strong odor. Does not keep as well as prepared opium. Weighs more than prepared opium (contains more water). It is smoked or eaten by addicts.

pitzu

A Chinese term used to refer to impure, or "crude," morphine base. Romanized spellings include *pizi* (Pinyin) and *p'i-tzu* (Wade-Giles Mandarin).

pong

A standard unit of weight used in Southeast Asia for opium only. Equivalent to 0.375 kilogram (13.23 ounces). Thai-Shan-Lao term. See Figure 7.

poppy (opium poppy)

An annual plant, *Papaver somniferum*, originally of Asia Minor, having grayish-green leaves and variously colored flowers. The sole source of opium.

poppy pod

Sometimes called the "seedpod," "capsule," "bulb," or "head." Refers to the egg-sized fruit which enlarges as the flower petals fall from the plant. The poppy pod is the mature ovary of the opium poppy plant. The ovarian wall produces the white latex (opium).

scoring of poppy pod

Cutting into the surface of an opium poppy pod, using a sharp bladed instrument, in order to allow the opium to exude from the pod. Also known as "lancing," "incising," or "tapping."

scraping of poppy pod

Using flat-bladed instrument to collect gummy opium from pod surface.

weeding & thinning of poppies

Removing weeds, grasses, and some poppy plants in order to provide more growing space for remaining poppies.

precipitation (chemical precipitation)

The separation of a solid from a solution. The resulting solid is caused the precipitate.

precursor

A precursor is a chemical that is the raw material for a new product. Morphine is a precursor in the production of heroin.

processing (heroin processing)

A general term which refers to the overall process of manufacturing heroin. Includes the acetylation process, a number of intermediate purification and precipitation processes, and the process of chemically converting heroin base to a soluble salt form of heroin, generally heroin hydrochloride. Heroin processing can also include the extraction of morphine from opium, and may include other operations, such as filtering, drying, pressing, and packaging the finished heroin product.

purification (chemical purification)

The removal of extraneous materials (impurities) from a substance or a mixture by one or more separation techniques. Such techniques include crystallization, precipitation, distillation, adsorption, extraction, etc. For example, heroin base is usually treated with decolorizing charcoal (a purification process) after it is acetylated from morphine base.

rai

A standard unit of land area measurement in Thailand equivalent to 1,600 square meters. Corresponds to *lai* measurement used in Laos (see above). *Rai* is also a general term in Thai-Lao-Shan for cultivated land (except irrigated ricefields). Called *hai* in northern and northeastern Thailand. Called hai in Laos only when used to refer to cultivated fields. See Figure 4.

reagent (chemical reagent)

A reagent is a chemical which reacts with a precursor to form a new compound. For example, acetic anhydride is a reagent used in the manufacture of heroin.

slash-and-burn agriculture

Also known as “swidden” agriculture. Agricultural method of clearing farmland. Involves cutting down all the trees and underbrush on a wooded hillside and, when it is thoroughly dried, burning it off in preparation for planting. This type of shifting cultivation is widely used by highland tribal groups in Southeast Asia.

soda ash

Crude, anhydrous sodium carbonate. Also known as Solvay soda; washing soda; soda. A white or transparent, odorless, crystalline powder with a salty, bitter taste. Shipped in 25-lb, 50-lb, and 100 lb bags; 275-lb and 400-lb drums, or bulk. An industrial chemical used in manufacturing sodium bicarbonate, sodium nitrate, glass; ceramics; water softening agents; detergents; and soaps. An alkaline material commonly used in the production of heroin base.

solvent (chemical solvent)

A solvent does not react chemically with a precursor chemical or reagent and does not become part of the finished product. Solvents are used to dissolve solid precursors or reagents, to dilute reaction mixtures, and to separate and purify other chemicals.

strychnine

Strychnine, or its salts, has been used as an adulterant in the illicit manufacture of "smoking heroin" (e.g., Southeast Asian heroin no. 3). Strychnine salts most commonly used are the nitrate or sulfate.

swidden agriculture

An agricultural method. See "slash-and-burn" agriculture.

tua See "nuai."

unit Special meaning when used in reference to heroin. A "unit" is a standard unit of weight for Southeast Asian heroin. Called *nuai* in Thai and Lao; chien in Chinese. Equivalent to 700 grams (.7 kilogram). Derivation of use not known.

viss

A standard unit of weight used in southern India and Burma Equivalent to 1.657 kilograms (3.652 pounds). Commonly used when weighing meat, flour, rice, and other such bulk items. In Burma, the *viss* is also used in the opium trade. Burmese term: beittha. (The term *viss* is not used in Thailand, Laos, or China.) Derived from Tamil term, *visai*. Also spelled *vise* (Telugu) and *vis*. Often rounded to 3.6 pounds in modem usage. See Figure 7.

DISTRIBUTION

The White House
National Security Council
Office of National Drug Control Policy
Department of Justice
Federal Bureau of Investigation/DIU Federal Bureau of Prisons
Immigration and Naturalization Service
INTERPOL/USNCB
Organized Crime Drug Enforcement Task Forces
U.S. Marshals Service
Department of the Treasury
Bureau of Alcohol, Tobacco and Firearms
Internal Revenue Service
U.S. Customs Service
U.S. Secret Service
Department of Defense
Defense Intelligence Agency
National Security Agency
Central Intelligence Agency/CNC
Department of State
U.S. Coast Guard
DEA Headquarters
DEA held Offices
DEA Laboratories
El Paso Intelligence Center
Financial Crimes Enforcement Network
National Drug Intelligence Center
International Association of Chiefs of Police (Narcotics Committee)
National Alliance of State Drug Enforcement Agencies
National Sheriffs' Association